How to BUY & SELL YOUR HOME in HAWAI'I

Successful Real Estate Strategies for Hawai'i

How to BUY & SELL YOUR HOME in HAWAI'I

Successful Real Estate Strategies for Hawai'i

Frances Lee Britten

MUTUAL PUBLISHING

ISBN 1-56647-732-8

Library of Congress Catalog Card Number: 2005925787

Design by Sachi Kuwahara Goodwin

First Printing, July 2005
Second Printing, November 2005
2 3 4 5 6 7 8 9

Mutual Publishing, LLC
1215 Center Street, Suite 210
Honolulu, Hawai'i 96816
Ph: 808-732-1709 / Fax: 808-734-4094
email: mutual@mutualpublishing.com
www.mutualpublishing.com

Printed in Australia

Dedication

All writers must depend on numerous others if they hope to ever get the job done. Thanks and love to my husband Jim, and my kids, Josh, Angie, and Val, for their support and encouragement, not only with this book, but always. And thanks to my friends and clients, my principal broker Jack Ainlay, and many associates for their advice and assistance over all the years we've worked together. Without them, I'd never have realized my long-held dream of writing a book—or even a pamphlet!

But there is one person without whom I'd never have lasted a year in real estate, to say nothing of gaining enough experience to write a whole book!

Jean Pace Wade was first licensed in Hawai'i real estate in the early 1950s, when she decided to earn the money for a new sewing machine. She was a successful agent, then a successful broker, and finally launched an independent company. Her husband Bob, wisely having great faith in his wife's abilities, lent his expert business mind to the enterprise, keeping an eagle eye on practical matters. Wade Ltd., Realtors came into being in 1970. It soon became the most prestigious and reputable real estate agency in Hawai'i, and it remained so until 1999 when the Wades retired. (Well, yes, that's an opinion, but few who know the Wades would disagree.)

When I entered real estate in 1983, knowledgeable friends and advisors told me if I wanted to be proud of where my brand-new license was hanging, Wade Ltd. was the company to join. They were not wrong. For seventeen years, that license hung proudly alongside those of many others who became not only trusted business associates, but the very best friends a person could ask for.

The Wade Gang—all of us—know our company wouldn't have meant what it did (in fact, none of us would probably even have known each other) if it hadn't been for Jean. She was—and still is—our advisor, mentor, and dear friend. She is the person we went to when we were in trouble, or thought we were about to be, or when someone else was making trouble for us. She is the person whose common sense we trusted and whose integrity we never questioned. She was our champion, our promoter, and our moral support. She was the cool head in the midst of hysteria and chaos. She was also the person who told us when we were off-the-wall, all wet, or out of our minds—and she made us listen.

Jean Wade gave more agents than I can count, much less name, the courage and the stamina to hang in there in one of the toughest, most stressful jobs there is and be happy and grateful for the opportunity.

So this one's for you, Jean.

Thank you for all the years we all looked up to you and were never disappointed, and for all the times we wanted to quit but didn't, because that would have disappointed you! Thank you for being just about the best principal broker ever, making us successful in ourselves, giving us the confidence to help our clients succeed, and, most of all, making us proud to be in real estate.

Table of Contents

Introduction

There are many specialized experts in real estate, from appraisers to contractors, home inspectors to termite inspectors, escrow and loan officers to insurance agents, any or all of whom may be essential to a transaction, but I'm not one of them. Economists and statisticians write volumes on real estate trends and forecasts. I'm not one of them. Attorneys, tax experts, and financial planners all may have valuable knowledge and opinions about real estate, but I'm not one of them.

I'm a real estate agent.

I've been one for a while now, over twenty years as I write this, representing other people when they buy or sell homes. Maybe the reason this business is still so interesting to me is that no two transactions are ever exactly alike; each one teaches me something new.

One thing I've learned is to see things from an average person's point of view and, hopefully, to explain things in a way that will make sense, so that person—you—ends up with the best possible transaction. To serve my clients, I've also had to learn at least a little bit about all the affiliated professions and trades that enter into real estate. I may not have all the answers, but I know where to find them, and I'm also very well acquainted with the right questions to ask!

Part of my job comes under the umbrella of marketing and public relations. If I am a listing agent, I must present a product—a piece of residential real estate—to the public in its most positive light. As a buyer's agent, I must find my clients a property that fills their needs and desires and then help them acquire it. And in both instances, I must establish rapport with my clients— figure out how they think, what they need, how to accomplish their objectives—whether or not I'd choose to do the same in their circumstances.

An even larger part of my job is problem-solving, trouble-shooting, expediting—whatever you'd like to call it. Many agents, myself included, facilitate more transactions in a year than most people do in a lifetime, and we've learned a very important thing: Most problems can be solved—and often never come up at all—if the people involved understand both the situation, and each other's points of view and expectations. One of my goals with this book is to help you do that, too, so you can achieve the very best end result in your individual circumstances.

Besides discussing the basics of how real estate transactions progress from inception to closing, I'll also discuss some common problems and how they may be solved before there is a crisis, or (the worst word in a real estate agent's vocabulary) a surprise. You probably won't get all the answers here, but hopefully you'll learn what questions to ask and where to look for the answers.

Beyond offering instructions, I'll also talk about some of the damaging myths that pervade our industry and how replacing "magical thinking" with practical good sense is the best thing you can do for yourself and your transactions.

To that end, I'm going to deal with the first *MYTH* right now.

"Doing real estate successfully," no matter what you may have been told, is not usually accomplished by beating the other party into submission, or by legally stealing either money or property. And further, the biggest mistake most people make, the single error that leads to failure more than any other, is thinking they don't need to care about the other party's needs, desires, and attitudes. Wrong.

Wrong, wrong, wrong.

Every successful businessperson, in real estate or not, finds out as much as he can about what's going on with the people he's trying to deal with—what they want, what they need, how they think. Why? Because that understanding, that knowledge, is often as valuable as cash. The successful businessperson knows what's a deal-maker, what's a deal-breaker, what's negotiable, what doesn't matter, and should have a pretty good idea about what it'll take to get the job—and the deal—done. Likewise, real estate buyers and sellers, whether they're just starting or highly experienced, need to know what questions to ask and how to interpret the answers to learn those things—to get to the true bottom line.

Here in Hawai'i, many social conventions are different than in other places. It goes way beyond taking off your shoes before entering a house. Formal courtesy and a humble manner, among other things, can make a big difference in how you're treated here—and whether someone wants to do business with you or not. (Dollars matter, but often aren't everything.) It's important for newcomers to understand that the ways they're used to may not send the message they intend—the local point of view may be very different.

We Hawaiians—whether we're born here or not, native or not—prefer our ways and want to keep them. That's why we live here and not someplace else. It's important to us that those who join our communities also join the spirit of our islands. All of us want "Live Aloha" to always be a lot more than just a bumper sticker slogan.

So I also hope to convey those concepts along with practical ideas, to help you succeed each and every time you enter into a real estate transaction—and join our island lifestyle.

Replace the myth with this: **When everyone walks away from a closing smiling, having both given and received what they wanted and needed, that is a successful transaction.**

Welcome to the Joys of Home Ownership

You have decided to buy a home in Hawai'i.

Are you sure about that? Let's take a hard look at just what you're getting into.

Thirty years of payments. Preceded by a lengthy and complicated process that involves salespeople, lawyers, and banks. Borrowing a huge amount of money that may be three times your annual salary or more. Worry about credit ratings and mortgage disapproval. What if there's something wrong with the house or your judgment? What if you end up with a property that requires constant repairs and maintenance you can't afford because the mortgage payment takes every cent you've got? What if you pay more than the property is worth? Good grief, you're taking on an immense responsibility with no guarantee that the value will hold or increase! There's no guarantee that next year you'll still be employed and able to make your payments. What if your spouse or partner dies? What if you get a divorce? What if the market falls and you lose all your equity? What if you get transferred and have to sell just when the market hits bottom?

This is worse than your worst nightmare. Why would anyone consider buying a home in Hawai'i? Why would you? Maybe you should back off now before it's too late. But wait! What about the up-side? What about all the advantages of owning your own home?

Of course, the first consideration is that you'll have a place to live. A home for your family. If you pay rent all your life, you run the risk of eviction and increases in rent. And you have restrictions on your lifestyle when you live in someone else's property. It's the landlord's castle, not yours. They decide whether you can own a pet. Or paint the house blue. Or plant a tree.

And speaking of landlords, all that rent money you're handing over? It's paying somebody else's mortgage, providing someone else's tax shelter, building somebody else's equity.

If your rental property needs repairs, you may not pay for them up front, but you also don't decide how they'll be done or when. And believe me, you'll pay for them anyway, somehow.

Owning your home gives you rights and privileges nothing else does.

And all the while, you have nothing you can call your own and every cent you make is taxed to the max by Uncle Sam. When you die, you'll leave nothing to your children.

If you're the philosophical sort, you've realized that property ownership is one of the few remaining ways Americans have of keeping some control over our highly regulated lives. While owning your home doesn't give you absolute freedom to do exactly as you wish, it does give you rights and privileges nothing else does. Factors such as neighborhood, school district, proximity to your work, community amenities (churches, shopping, beach, whatever), your home's style, décor, landscaping, all are choices you get to make for yourself, governed only by your own ability to pay for them. If the budget won't tolerate buying your dream home today, you can work up to it eventually if you play your cards right. You can make your home a personal expression of your taste and creativity. It can be a statement of pride and success.

Bottom line: In a lot of ways, in this country, your home is still your castle. And those, my friends, among many other good reasons, are why you want to get involved with the joys of home ownership. So should the possible problems be dismissed as unimportant? Absolutely not! The question, however, is not whether you should own your home, but how you go about acquiring it while minimizing the risk of one or more of those nightmare scenarios coming to rest at your doorstep. I wrote this book to answer that question.

2

Why You Need a Personal Real Estate Agent

You may think this chapter is self-interested. And you'd be right—partly. I'm a real estate broker, and I like to have lots of business. But that, as they say, is only the tip of the iceberg. The several thousand real estate agents in Hawai'i wouldn't be able to earn a living doing this job—people simply wouldn't hire us—if we weren't needed.

Even if you think this book will teach you everything you need to know to sell or buy a house, you'll likely be involved with an agent representing the other party to your transaction. And even if you start out thinking you don't need an agent, you may rethink your position once you understand what agents do and how they do it.

Hawaiian real estate is some of the most valuable (and expensive) in the world, and Hawai'i's consumer protection laws are some of the most stringent in the country. Hawai'i's real estate professionals must take continuing education classes every two years to remain current with our industry, partly because the industry is becoming more and more complicated and partly because it is harder and harder to be sure you've done everything possible to assure your transaction has a happy result. You are ultimately responsible for your choices, of course, but most "civilians," those not in the business of real estate, are unaware of the many procedures and resources that exist to protect them against bad decisions—decisions that are uninformed, made with incomplete information, or made as a result of a lie.

Your agent's primary job is usually not, as you may think, to sell you something or to sell something for you. It is to make sure your transaction is managed correctly, for the benefit and protection of all concerned.

In Hawai'i real estate, some potential liabilities to a certain extent can be passed to others, if you do it right. It's important to know which responsibilities you can pass on and which you cannot.

Working with a good agent is your first line of defense against problems during and sometimes after a transaction. *We know how to protect you.* This section will help you understand what you can expect from an agent and how to know if the agent you have selected is up to the task.

A good agent can protect you from problems during and after a transaction.

First, let's get rid of some of the myths about real estate agents that "everybody knows." Everybody knows we get paid huge amounts of money for very little work. Everybody knows it's possible to manage your own transaction from start to finish without anyone else's help. Everybody knows if you buy a home directly from the owner, you'll save tons of money. Everybody knows if you sell your home without an agent, you'll do the same.

If everybody knows all these things, then, why do most people, especially sophisticated buyers and sellers who have bought and sold many properties, work with an agent? Read on, and you'll find out.

Human greed is universal. (Everybody knows that, too, right?) You can state it baldly and tactlessly, as I just did, or you can state it in a politically correct manner: People have the right and obligation to take care of their interests and to do things for their own best interests. Comes down to the same thing.

Why don't you want to work with an agent?

Specifically, one reason you need an agent is that we are highly motivated to arrange transactions so that everyone benefits. Our goal is for everyone to leave the closing table a winner. The two most common replies **buyers** give to the question, "Why don't you want to work with an agent?" are:

> 1) *I can save money if I represent myself;* and

> 2) *I don't want anyone to try to sell me something.*

The two most common replies **sellers** give to the same question "Why don't you want to work with an agent?" are:

1) *I can save money if I represent myself;* and

2) *I know more about my property than any agent, so I can do a better sales job.*

WRONG. Here's why:

Buyer's Reason Number 1

I can save money if I represent myself.

On property that is listed with an agency, the seller has already contracted to pay a commission. It is paid to that agent's company. If there is no buyer's agent, the company receives ALL the commission. If the commission is discounted because there is no buyer's representative—it sometimes happens, saving perhaps one percent of the purchase price—that savings will accrue to the seller, who has no obligation to share.

Do the math and decide if it's worth it to you: Say the real estate commission is six percent of the purchase price. If you, the buyer, are unrepresented, the agent may (but is not required to) discount the commission to five percent. The Seller may (but is not required to) split that one percent savings with the buyer, perhaps take it into consideration on an offer. Total potential net savings to the buyer: one-half of one percent of the sale price. On a sale of, for example, $350,000, that savings amounts to $1,750.00.

As you read on, you'll find out exactly what services you forego in order to save those funds.

Buyer's Reason Number 2

I don't want anyone to try to sell me something.

If you've already decided to buy a home, that's just plain silly. It's also why sellers and sellers' agents see it as the remark of an insincere buyer—one who has not, in fact, made the decision to purchase a home.

What that statement sometimes does mean is: "I don't want to be harassed by agents calling me all the time," or, "I'm afraid I'll be talked into buying the wrong house by a slick sales agent."

The best way to avoid unwanted phone calls is to immediately tell every agent you meet that you are represented, and by whom. Those agents then know who to call (your agent, not you) if they have something of interest.

A good agent will know what you want and need and will find a property that suits you.

And as far as a slick sales agent selling you a house you don't want: It's so much easier to listen to a client's needs and go out and find a property that suits them. To do that, an agent must know you a little—or maybe a lot. And it's important for you to work with somebody you trust. For that, you also need to know someone a little—or maybe a lot. That's why working with one agent rather than several is the best idea.

Communication is the key here. So do two things:

1) Make a list of your requirements in order of priority (a great idea even if you don't work with an agent). Everyone has certain "deal-buster" factors. Decide what those are and write them down, too. Be ready to discuss them with an agent or simply hand over a copy of the list.

2) Secondly, when you meet an agent you might like to work with, take her card, maybe even ask for references. You can then follow through and check them out in whatever manner you feel is necessary and appropriate.

If you're represented, you will find you're treated with much more respect; you're a sincere buyer if you've gone to the trouble of selecting an agent. Even better, if you follow your agent's advice about things like loan preapproval, your offers will be treated with respect as well. And solicitation phone calls will just about stop. Finally, if after all that, you discover you've made a wrong choice, don't like your agent, or don't feel she's doing a good job for you, you are not obligated to keep working with her.

The rule is: **Choice of agent is one hundred percent up to the client.** Insights into how to make that important choice are in the next chapter.

Why Professional Representation is Important

Real Estate Professionals:

- ✔ Protect you from various kinds of liability
- ✔ Have up-to-date real estate education
- ✔ Have expert market knowledge
- ✔ Are experienced in dealing with the public
- ✔ Are experienced negotiators
- ✔ Have an objective viewpoint
- ✔ Understand complex transactions details and know how to manage them
- ✔ Have a fiduciary duty to their clients
- ✔ Must treat everyone fairly and honestly, whether they represent them or not
- ✔ Have a vested interest in being available
- ✔ Cast a wider net to reach a larger pool of potential buyers or sellers

Unrepresented Principals:

- ✔ Are expected to sell for less
- ✔ May not be aware of their rights and obligations
- ✔ May be perceived as potential victims by unscrupulous people
- ✔ May be regarded as potentially unscrupulous
- ✔ May be perceived as being cheap or trying to cut corners (making buyers wonder what other corners have been cut)

Seller's Reason Number 1

I can save money if I represent myself

Take that same $350,000 sale price as above. If you save the six percent commission, that comes to $21,000, a significant piece of change. Even if you pay the typical three percent to a buyer's agent, you'll save $10,500. Still a lot of money. Maybe. Of course, buyers will know you're unrepresented and will undoubtedly expect you to pass the savings on to them by way of a reduced sale price.

Nevertheless, I'm not going to belittle or demean the importance of saving even a few thousand dollars if you can. The real questions are: Will the savings be real in the end? And can you really get the job done alone? Only you can answer those questions. Hopefully, reading the other pertinent chapters in this book will help you find out.

Seller's Reason Number 2

I know more about my property than any agent, so I can do a better sales job.

Knowing all there is to know about your property doesn't mean you know how to communicate its features in the most positive light. It doesn't mean you understand the disclosure laws and all the other legal obligations you may have. It doesn't mean you are willing or even able to take six weeks or more off from your job to manage the marketing and closing process, that you will be home twenty-four–seven to answer phone calls, that you are skilled at dealing with aggressive or even hostile questions, broken or missed appointments and numerous strangers going through your house making tactless remarks—all without losing patience. And it certainly doesn't mean the buying public will trust you to answer questions truthfully and completely. Even if sales is your business, selling your home requires a completely different expertise than any other type of sales work. If I were to sell my own home, I would hire an agent.

Bottom line: Representation by a competent agent can protect both buyers and sellers from some kinds of liability. With expert professionals managing today's increasingly complicated transactions, all concerned have greater assurance that their transaction has been completed according to law and ethical practice. Both buyers and sellers usually have more trust and confidence with a licensed professional by their side—to advise them and to make sure their rights are looked after and their obligations met—than they do when trying to manage alone.

3

How Agents Get Paid, Who Pays Them, and Why You Should Care

Most agents don't discuss pay checks with clients. It's an awkward subject. But there may be a more important reason than simple curiosity as to why you should know.

For the most part, residential real estate agents are independent contractors who receive no salary, no paid holidays or vacations, no paid health insurance, no employee benefits at all. Most companies, but not all, cover the costs of maintaining the office, advertising, and for-sale signs. Everything else, from the car and all its expenses to the soda your agent treats you to while you're on the road to the postage stamp on a thank-you note, is paid for out-of-pocket, up front, in hopes that eventually the investment will result in a commission. In Honolulu at this writing, every agent who belongs to our Board of Realtors—and you may not want one who doesn't— also pays a minimum of $1,200 per year just to maintain his or her state license and to cover required dues and fees, whether or not they receive any pay whatsoever during that year.

Today, with very few exceptions, there is only one occasion when a residential sales agent receives a pay check: when a sale closes or records. Most of the time, all other services, from market analyses to showing property are absolutely free.

When a seller signs a listing (in Hawai'i, almost always a type of agreement called **Exclusive Right to Sell**), it is with the realty company with which his specific agent has an independent contractor agreement. That company almost always agrees to share the commission with a buyer's agency (called a **Cooperating Broker**). The commission money comes from the sales proceeds upon closing and is disbursed by the escrow company. From that money, those companies pay the agents. The "split" between company and agent can range from around 40 percent to the agent with 60 percent remaining with the company to up to 100 percent to the agent—who then pays substantial fees back to the brokerage firm to cover its overhead, profit, and expenses.

Thus, while the seller decides which agency to use and agrees in writing to the commission amount, the money itself comes from the buyer's funds. In the unusual case of the commission not including compensation to a buyer's agent, the seller's commission expense is reduced by at least half, sometimes more.

It's easier for an agent to sell the client a house he wants than one he doesn't.

There are two reasons you should care about this. Many people assume their agent will take home the entire commission upon closing, never considering such things as "splits," overhead, or whether another agency is involved. Thus they have an exaggerated idea of how much money an agent actually makes, and may think they're not receiving good value for the dollar. But most importantly, since this is the only time an agent gets paid, it is critical that we know the difference between a sincere and an insincere client; once we are working with a sincere client, it's Job One to close the transaction.

Does that mean a sales agent will do absolutely anything to get you to sign on the bottom line? Shouldn't you be careful to avoid aggressive agents who'll try to drag you to the closing table?

Somebody's mother (not mine, thank God) once said it's just as easy to fall in love with a rich man as a poor one. Well, maybe you can't control who you fall in love with, but if you rephrase the statement just a little, it holds true for real estate: It's just as easy (easier, if you want the truth) to sell the client a house he wants than one he doesn't. To say the same thing another way, looking at homes is like dating. You won't know if you've found the right partner until you go on at least one date. But most people won't accept a date with just anyone. There are certain minimum standards. When it comes to real estate, you need to communicate those minimum standards to your agent. Your best friend or college roommate wouldn't set you up on a blind date with someone they know you'll hate. If that happens, you haven't successfully communicated your minimum standards. Hopefully, you can do a better and more complete job in telling your agent what is, and is not, acceptable for your new home.

Once you've done that, showing you five homes you like is exactly the same amount of work for your agent as showing you five homes you don't. Why would anyone expend the effort to set up appointments, drive you around for hours, go into house after house, knowing full well the homes are not what you want or can afford? Answer: They wouldn't.

But . . . maybe finding a home you like isn't all that easy. Maybe you're picky. Maybe you have a limited budget. Maybe you have special needs that require a special home. Just about everyone in the universe can make the same statements. If your communications are in order, finding the right home for you is actually the easiest part of the job.

In order to receive our paycheck, we have to successfully complete all the steps from the moment you say, "I love this house!" to the moment we tell you, "The house is yours, here are the keys!" Those steps are detailed in other chapters. The point here is to demonstrate exactly how senseless it is for you to be afraid you're going to be the victim of a shotgun wedding.

There are very real concerns, though, which are entirely justified. Hopefully, those will be dealt with to your satisfaction as we go forward.

Bottom line: While sellers hire agents, the funds to pay them come from buyers. Most agents get paid only when they close a transaction. Thus they are motivated to get the job done, but just simply selling anything to anybody is a losing strategy for agents. It's far easier to find the right home for a client than to persuade them to buy the wrong one. If your agent is showing you homes that don't fit your needs, you are not communicating effectively. That ball is entirely in your court: Clear communication about needs, desires, and budget is the client's job.

Buyer Brokerage

A situation under which a buyer signs a contract with an agent, agreeing to pay that agent himself according to their own mutual agreement. It is lately becoming more common, but is still an unusual practice in Hawai'i. It can make both agent and buyer comfortable and secure. Basically, it says the agent owes a fiduciary duty to the buyer and the buyer will buy only through that agent and pay a commission under whatever conditions are spelled out in the agreement. An agreement like this can be very reassuring for a buyer, especially if your agent is not someone you already know very well.

Specifics of the agreement include a time frame, the type of property, and the amount of compensation. (That may be a dollar amount or a percentage of the sale price, whatever the two parties agree.) If you'd like to review the standard form used by members of the Hawaii Association of Realtors, it is available from HAR as well as most agents and real estate companies.

One misconception that might turn away buyers who would otherwise like this kind of representation is the concern that they could end up paying twice for the same service if they buy property that's listed with an agent—once to the listing agency and again to their own broker. That does NOT happen. If you purchase a property that includes the buyer's agent commission in the terms, it will be either deducted from the commission the seller pays, or you may reduce the purchase price by a like amount and pay your agent directly, depending on circumstances. So if buyer-brokerage is an idea that appeals to you, and you want to know your agent is working for you as a fiduciary, by all means ask for such an agreement.

Important note: There are instances when a project developer or owner states that unless an agent physically accompanies the buyer on his first visit to the property and registers with the developer, the agent will not be paid from the sale proceeds. In these cases, whether the buyer is represented by his own agent or not, the purchase price for the unit in question will not change. To avoid possible confusion and disputes, have your agent accompany you when you go to such properties for the first time.

If You Are Considering a Discount Brokerage or "Menu of Services Brokerage"

Many times, especially in a rising market, the public begins to wonder if paying a commission based on the sale price is excessive and whether they're truly getting good value for their commission dollar. There are real estate companies in Hawai'i that from time to time (usually when there's low inventory and agents need listings) offer home sellers seriously discounted commissions. Sometimes this can result in a win-win situation for both agent and seller. However, the services included in the discounted commission may be limited. Whether a discount brokerage is good value for you is an individual decision, but to make that determination you need all of the facts.

To gain a true picture of what you may actually save, as well as what you may spend in terms of time, effort, and liability, answer the following (and any other questions you think of yourself). Then evaluate the "no's" on the items you feel unable or unwilling to handle for yourself.

YES NO

☐   ☐ Is the cooperating brokerage fee (commission for the buyer's agent) included in the price you pay the discount agency? This is a key component that discount brokerages often don't mention in newspaper ads.

☐   ☐ Does the asking price for your home exceed the maximum price to which an agency's discounted listing fee applies? Look in the fine print for, "Applies to homes up to $500,000" or some similar statement. If your home is more, you need to know what your fee will be.

☐   ☐ Is there an additional charge to you for the Hawai'i General Excise Tax, and if so, how much is it? Some full-service companies charge this to the seller; many do not. It's a negotiable item.

YES NO

☐　☐ Do you plan to provide a "home warranty," a service contract covering many appliances, plumbing and electrical fixtures, for the buyer's benefit? If so, what is its cost to you? (This warranty can be a very valuable tool. Many full-service companies provide it to both sellers and buyers at no additional charge.)

☐　☐ Does the discount brokerage carry errors and omissions insurance, and if so, what is the extent of your protection against mistakes the agent or company may make?

☐　☐ Are the discount listing agent's professional qualifications equal to those of full-service agents you have interviewed?

☐　☐ Have you asked any full-service agents for a commission discount in light of your special circumstances, whatever they may be? (This tells you the full-service agent's true "bottom line." It never hurts to ask.)

☐　☐ Will you have to write and/or pay for your own advertising?

☐　☐ Will the listing agent prepare an objective market study to help you price your property?

☐　☐ Will the listing agent give you knowledgeable advice on improvements prior to sale, on how to make your property show at its best, and/or help you "stage" your home for viewing?

☐　☐ Will your listing appear in the Board of Realtors' Multiple Listings for your island?

☐　☐ Will your listing appear on the internet? If so, where, and is there an additional charge?

☐　☐ Will the listing agent personally attend open houses and/or hold a "broker's open house"?

☐　☐ Will the listing agent prepare fact sheets for the public?

YES NO

☐ ☐ Will those fact sheets contain the listing agent's name and contact numbers?

☐ ☐ Will the listing agent and/or another licensed agent in her office be available during business hours to set up showing appointments and answer questions about the property?

☐ ☐ Will the listing agent help you evaluate offers, point out "red flags" and otherwise assist you in the negotiation process, including the preparation and presentation of counteroffers?

☐ ☐ Will the listing agent act as a "buffer" (negotiator/ peacekeeper/cool head) between you and prospective buyers and/or buyers' agents?

☐ ☐ Will the listing agent facilitate the escrow process?

☐ ☐ Will the listing agent arrange and attend property inspections?

☐ ☐ Will the listing agent obtain all the legally required documentation, such as copies of building permits and condominium documents?

"Menu of services" is a "pay-as-you-go" concept in which actual services on a case-by-case basis are billed and paid for as they occur. It is very unusual in Hawai'i. In fact, I don't know of any company here that has successfully implemented it. Perhaps this is not surprising: As a buyer, do you want to pay an agent by the hour to show you homes, regardless of whether you buy one? And as a seller, do you want agents to show your home only to people who are willing to pay up front to see it?

However, times change, and by the time you read this, the menu of services method of compensating agents may be available. To compare its potential savings in your case, obtain a comprehensive written price list and add up all the various services your transaction may require. To do that, read the questions above and also "Who Does What."

How to Choose a Buyer's Agent

First step: find out if the agent you're interested in is properly licensed.

You're out on a Sunday afternoon. You visit five or six homes, walk through, chat with agents, pick up fact sheets, but while some of the homes are interesting, none is exactly right. By the end of the day, you're confused and frustrated and feel like you've wasted your time. You decide it's time you got some help and find a real estate agent. All those you met were friendly and polite. Several gave you their cards and invited you to call if you had any questions. So do you just call one agent? Or two? Or all? Or do you choose none of those and find somebody else? How do you find a good one?

You need an agent you trust, someone who is intelligent and knowledgeable, someone who has the time and the willingness to work hard for you. What else should you look for?

Personal rapport is critical. That shouldn't surprise you. Whoever represents you needs to understand you, your family, your lifestyle, your expectations, where you've been, where you are, and where you hope to go. It's easiest when you have a lot in common with your agent, and it's absolutely necessary that your personalities mesh nicely. If you already know an agent like this, call him or her immediately. Explain your need for assistance and ask him or her to represent you. Period.

But what if you don't? You're new in town or don't know any agents.

Specifically, before going any further, you need to know if an agent is properly licensed. You may call the **State Department of Commerce & Consumer Affairs** to check on an agent's license status. They will also tell you how to find out if there are any disciplinary actions against an agent or agency that are a matter of record. You may also call the **Board of Realtors®** on your island or in your area. They will tell you if the agent is a member; however, not all licensed agents are members. If you find out an agent is properly licensed, there are no disciplinary actions against her or her company, and she is a member of the **Board of Realtors**, that's a good start. You may ask the agent for references. You may also ask what the letters after her name mean. Some of those are indicative of greater experience or specialized knowledge.

Important note: It's rare that agents will improperly represent themselves, but it does happen. If you find out somebody is pretending to be licensed when he's not, or pretending to be a member of any trade association when she's not, report it immediately to the appropriate authority. Make a lot of noise. That's the kind of thing that can adversely affect an entire industry as well as innocent members of the public. Everyone will thank you for your concern.

It's also entirely acceptable to ask for references from past clients, and to actually call some of them. Hawai'i residents, being friendly people in general, will usually be more than glad to answer your questions.

Beyond that, there are a lot of ways to go about the selection process. Some people have a great feeling about an agent upon first meeting. That's the luck of the draw—if the first agent you meet is a good "fit," works for a reputable company, and your conversation demonstrates she's intelligent and a good listener, you need look no further. Other people need to have lengthy conversations with several, or even many agents, before choosing the right one.

It's a very important decision. And it's also largely subjective. Some obvious factors are covered in the paragraph above: an intelligent, courteous person with whom you have rapport, who pays attention to your needs and works for a reputable company. Is there any more to it? That all depends on you, the client, your needs and requirements, and what you expect your agent to do for you. Especially if you are a first-time buyer, it's important that your agent is willing and able to give you hands-on guidance, teaching as you go along.

What Do All Those Letters
after an Agent's Name Mean?

Various letters may appear after the name of a real estate agent or on other printed material. Some frequently seen acronyms in residential real estate are as follows:

S – Salesperson: A licensed real estate sales agent. Must work under the supervision of a broker.

B – Broker: A licensed real estate broker. Requires a higher-level license, more education and experience. A broker need not work under anyone else's supervision, can open his/her own company.

PB – Principal Broker: The owner of a real estate company.

BIC – Broker in Charge: In charge of supervising the other agents in a company or a branch office.

You'll notice throughout this book, I customarily refer to real estate professionals as "agents" or "brokers," not as "realtors." That's because the designation "Realtor®" is correctly used only to refer to members of the National Association of Realtors (a nationwide trade association). In Hawai'i, such agents are also members of the Hawaii Association of Realtors® (HAR) and the appropriate affiliated local chapter (depending on where the agent conducts business, the Honolulu, Maui, Kaua'i, Kona, or Big Island Boards of Realtors®).

While all agents must be licensed by the state, membership in NAR (as well as HAR and their local chapter) is not required. Membership, however, includes participation in their Board's Multiple Listing Service—a database through which information about their listings is shared and publicized—that is not available to nonmembers. Members also receive other benefits that assist them in serving the public and are held to a level of practice that may be higher than that required by law, as stipulated in the NAR's Realtor® Code of Ethics. (In Hawai'i, that Code of Ethics is frequently used by the legislative and judicial branches of state government as a guideline for establishing correct real estate business practices.)

R – Realtor®: A licensed real estate broker who is also a member of the National Association of Realtors and its affiliated state/local chapters.

RA – Realtor® Associate: A licensed real estate sales agent who is also a member of the National Association of Realtors and its affiliated state/local chapters.

GRI – Graduate Realtor Institute: A designation given to Realtors® and Realtor Associates® who have completed a course of education beyond that required by state license law, provided under the auspices of NAR.

CRS – Certified Residential Specialist: A member of the RS Council, a more elite national trade association that requires membership in NAR and its affiliated state and local chapters. The designation requires a higher level of experience and successful completion of Council-required classes in residential real estate practices.

CRB – Certified Residential Broker: A member of the RS Council who has experience in and has successfully completed education regarding management of real estate companies and supervision of agents.

There are all kinds of agents. Part-timers. Full-timers. Newbies. Old hands. Star performers. Work horses. All have slightly different things to offer.

Part-timer versus full-timer

You wouldn't choose a part-time brain surgeon, so don't choose a part-time real estate agent. One may be more life-threatening than the other, but the reasons are the same. There's really no such thing as a competent part-timer—if you're talking about somebody who has another job as his/her primary source of income and does real estate as a sideline.

However, if you're talking about somebody who's semi-retired and just doesn't take on ten clients at a time—those can be some of the best agents around: they're not over-committed, have time to spend with you, love to teach people the ropes, and often guide their clients through the process with the care and concern of a parent. (This is one of the few businesses in which advancing age is not, repeat not, a detriment to success.)

Newbie versus old hand

Newcomers are generally eager to please, enthusiastic, and hard working. They need clients and will go the extra mile to prove themselves. All this is great and all of us were new once. But the blind leading the blind is not the best way to manage a real estate transaction, so if you decide to work with a novice, make sure his or her company provides experienced and competent backup. Good real estate companies give their less experienced agents lots of support. Visit your agent's office and ask to be introduced to the manager or principal broker. It's not regarded as rude or threatening, and it's good to show your face in the office, regardless. If your agent gets run down by an elephant on Kalakaua Avenue or just goes to the hospital to deliver her baby early, somebody in that office needs to know who you are and what's going on and to be ready to jump in and help you out.

What about a star performer?

Frequently, the owner of a real estate company is—or was before management duties intruded—a star performer. They are top sales agents. They drive good cars, dress well, and exude success. They obviously have to be very good at what they do, are successful business people, and are well-known in the community. You're likely to get a lot of respect when you're out looking at homes with a star performer because other agents know they're dealing with a real pro. You may feel very protected and comfortable if your agent owns the real estate company you work with. But is there a downside? It depends. Star performers are very busy people. If you need large amounts of time and personal attention, expect to have your calls returned instantly, and to have your agent on tap at any hour of the day or night, you might become frustrated. Some (by no means all, please note) extremely successful stars turn new or lower-end clients over to an assistant. Of course, if something goes wrong with the transaction, your actual agent (the star) should be there to put out the fire. And some assistants are extremely good agents in their own right.

Your best course

Meet the star performer at the office for a personal interview. This is common practice. Good agents are ready to face competition, so be straightforward about the purpose of the meeting. Ask questions and listen carefully to the answers. Check out the office; the way it works and its general atmosphere. Does the agent interrupt your meeting more than once or twice to take phone calls or deal with other business, or are you treated like a special person? If there is an assistant, what is his or her role? Is he or she a licensed agent who will show you property and handle the paperwork, or more of a secretary/coordinator? Do the other people in the office seem friendly, or is everyone in head-down mode? Do you feel comfortable there or intimidated? In short, would this be someone you'd like to do business with if he or she were not a top sales agent and/or the company owner? If, at the end of the meeting, you feel you'll get the service you expect and want, you've found yourself an agent.

What about a "workhorse" agent?

What is a workhorse agent, anyway? It's an agent who spends a lot of time working and so may not be very glamorous. It's an agent who loves the challenge of getting a difficult job done. (It's not an exclusive category; lots of star performers are also workhorses.) Workhorse agents are emotionally steady, stable, generally unflappable, focused on the job. They tend to be less excitable than some, but that's definitely not the same thing as being disinterested. If your workhorse agent appears to be interested in you, your needs, desires, and situation, you can be sure you'll have his or her full attention, and every aspect of your transaction will be managed carefully and well. But this type of agent is also very busy and probably will not sit with you for a two-hour afternoon tea. Socializing will be put on hold until after the closing. However, a two-hour (or four-hour) business discussion or property inspection is an entirely different matter. This agent will keep you on track, make sure you're not diverted by irrelevant factors, help you analyze agreements, property facts, and financial figures and make sure you completely understand what's happening and what you are expected to do. During the escrow process, you may feel as if your workhorse agent exists simply to give you instructions. If you selected her for qualities like personal rapport, reputability, and trustworthiness, it's best not to argue but do ask for explanations. (Asking is not the same as arguing.) Does it sound like you need a workhorse agent, whether star performer, newcomer, semi-retired or whatever?

Long story; short answer: Yes.

Workhorse agents come in both sexes, all descriptions, and all ages. They can be inexperienced; if so, they'll be ready to learn and willing to ask for help if they need it. And they have all kinds of qualities: Good at detail, good listeners, finance specialists, neighborhood specialists, construction specialists, creative thinkers, aggressive negotiators, and the list goes on. They all will have some of these qualities.

When not to work with friends, relatives, fellow church members, etc.

The most important factor of any agent-client relationship is trust. It goes both ways, but for now we're talking about your trust in your agent. That is usually a done deal when you do business with someone you already know. So, if you know a full-time agent with a good reputation, if you feel comfortable that she understands your needs and desires, by all means work with that person. The

10 Things to Expect from Your Agent

1. Has a current license to practice real estate and access to all available listing information on your island

2. Has intelligence

3. Is discreet and trustworthy

4. Communicates well and has excellent rapport with you

5. Respects your choices and budget; is focused on your needs

6. Addresses your questions and concerns directly; will turn over every stone until she finds an answer

7. Is solution-oriented; focuses on how to solve problems and challenges

8. Is available and offers you time and attention during reasonable hours on a regular basis, at least for the duration of your transaction

9. Is experienced in Island real estate or has experienced backing in her company

10. Is loyal (and expects loyalty in return)

same goes for an agent who is referred by someone you know well. (Our lifeblood is repeat business and referrals. We'll work harder and longer for a past or referred client than for any other kind. Past good rapport and a successful transaction makes it highly likely the same will happen in the future and will also happen with that client's friends. And, in the case of referrals, besides satisfying you, we have to satisfy the person who referred you or there will be no more referrals.)

So, is there any downside to this scenario?

Not if you heed the following rules:

The agent-client relationship should be based on trust.

✔ You are hiring an agent for your benefit. Make sure the agent is qualified, willing, and able to give the kind of assistance you need.

(**Note of caution:** If any agent tells you to drive by houses with for-sale signs in front and call if you want to see any of them, or tells you to look on the Internet and call if you find anything of interest, walk right away and don't look back. That agent, whether newly met or your own sister, is not sufficiently interested in you to be trusted with one of your most important life decisions. And furthermore, giving you back some of their commission is no excuse. None.)

✔ In the selection process, ignore pity or sympathy for the agent's personal situation, or how badly they need the work. Hiring an agent who's not up to the task is not helpful to them in the long run.

✔ If you are a recovering alcoholic, a recovering addict, or in a support group of any kind, it's tempting to want to help and support those who have helped and supported you. Don't write these people off, but do make certain that their problem, whatever it may be, will not affect your real estate transaction in any way.

✔ Although having things in common with your agent makes for better understanding and easier communications, do not assume a person who shares your religious or political views is a competent professional.

✔ If you have a sense of obligation to someone, think first. What if, in honoring that obligation, you make a decision that's seriously detrimental to your family's, or your own, well-being and finances?

✔ When the agent is a close relative, that's the hardest situation to deal with. If your relative is a competent agent, there's no problem. But if you have doubts, take control for yourself. Learn as much as you can about the process. Tell your relative you expect top-notch service. Be emphatic about it. You're family, you can be forthright. Be as specific as possible about what you need and expect, ask him for a definite commitment to get the job done. If all else fails, remember every transaction involves other allied professionals, from your relative's manager, to your mortgage loan officer, to your escrow officer. If you find yourself in real trouble, call for help. When and how to do that is dealt with later. Working with a relative will not necessarily save you money—there's no real savings if your transaction is not handled properly. You may get no house at all. If your agent is a close enough relative that he/she won't take a commission for helping you, there are some things to consider. Make certain—by way of your mortgage lender and your agent's principal broker—that it is legal and in accordance with the real estate company's policy. For instance, if you've hired your mother, and she intends to give you her commission as part of your down payment, there may be restrictions and rules on how it is handled, or if it can happen at all. And there's something else. What is your obligation to your agent-relative if you take assistance? There may be a payback somewhere down the road and maybe with interest. If that thought bothers you, tell your relative you want them to receive full and fair compensation for professional services. Trust me, they'll love you even more than they already do.

Many people prefer not to do business with friends or family. Why not? There are lots of reasons, some of them better than others:

I don't want someone to know my business, or I don't want everybody to know my business.

You certainly have every right to privacy, and you certainly shouldn't do business with someone who can't be discreet.

If they find out I'm buying a house, they'll think I'm getting uppity.

Please. Nobody who's in business scorns a customer/client on the basis that they're uppity! They'll just be happy that you are sharing your good fortune by allowing them to participate.

I know they expect me to do business with them, but I don't really think they're very good at what they do.

Excellent reason. Getting out of this implied obligation without hurting your relationship may require some finesse; perhaps telling them your policy is to never do business with people close to you would help.

I don't want to do business with them because I'm worried there'll be a personal falling out if things don't go well.

That's a little harder to deal with, depending on whether you think things won't go well because you don't trust the other person, or because you yourself are hard to deal with. If it's the former, refer to the paragraph above. If it's the latter, have a conversation with yourself. You may not be as hard to deal with as you believe. If you are, maybe you should try harder to maintain a businesslike attitude.

Is going through all this trouble to find a buyer's agent really necessary?

Why is it important to commit to one agent?

> *When I was fairly new in business, one of my associates— who was extremely successful and whose clients were fanatical in their loyalty to her—flatly stated she absolutely did not have time to deal with anyone who wouldn't work exclusively with her. I thought that was a very arrogant attitude. She thought I was terribly naïve. She was right.*
>
> *"You'll find out for yourself," she told me, "the first time you spend hours and days researching and analyzing properties and hunting for financing, and then you call your 'client,' to find out they just bought a house through*

10 Red Flags. Walk Away If:

1. An agent is unwilling to meet you at her office or introduce her principal broker or broker-in-charge

2. An agent appears impaired: Under the influence of drugs or alcohol or otherwise not focused on the job

3. An agent offers to break the law or violate ethical conduct or even hints at the idea

4. An agent tells you to look around on your own and call when you find an interesting property

5. An agent frequently interrupts your meetings and conversations or otherwise appears not to have time for you

6. An agent imposes her lifestyle on you or doesn't listen to your needs and priorities

7. An agent doesn't respond to questions with direct and appropriate answers or brushes off legitimate concerns without explanation

8. An agent's response to stress, complexities, or difficulties is to quit

9. An agent's sole recommendation is that she'll work for less or kick back some of the commission to you

10. An agent's sole recommendation is that you have an obligation to her

> *somebody else. We work for the best company on the island,"*
> *she went on. "I have no problem if people check my references*
> *before committing—and I do have one formal appointment*
> *before asking for it. You have to give people a chance to get to*
> *know you. But after that—well, how you work is up to you,*
> *but I prefer to deal with it up front and in the open."*
>
> *I decided not to argue further. She was the one with the*
> *heavy-duty success record. I've never been able to be as*
> *blatant as she was, but after a while I did learn to sense*
> *quickly whether a client was really a client or just game-*
> *playing—exploiting my expertise and using time I could have*
> *spent with a real client, or with my family.*

Pretend you are an agent and your entire paycheck depends upon closing transactions. You have been talking to two possible home buyers. One of them has said she will work with you and only you. The other thinks it's smarter to spread a wide net, and will work with the one who finds the right property. A home comes on the market that you think is ideal for both buyers. Which client would you call first? Will the other client eventually get a call from one of the many agents he's talked to? Maybe. But maybe not before you get your loyal client in to see that house and he decides to buy it.

Agents are human. We have personal loyalties and preferences like everyone else. And we work harder for people we know are loyal to us. Also, practically speaking, one of the ways we tell the difference is whether a buyer is willing to commit her loyalty.

Lots of people tell me they "don't want to make me work hard," or "don't want to waste my time." What is my answer? The truth: It's never a waste of time to work hard for a loyal, sincere client.

Also important, your agent needs to know a great deal about you, your family, and your finances. When we have an agency relationship with a client, it's part of our duty to keep personal information private and confidential. If it's necessary to divulge it to a mortgage lender or some other third party who has an interest in an actual transaction, we tell you first. If you don't want to share your information with everyone in town, choose one agent.

We won't establish an agency relationship with a person we know is dishonest, however. We won't help you be unethical. For example, we won't help you conceal bad credit or hide the fact that you have no job. However, we will take time and effort to help a loyal client solve problems in a straightforward manner.

Here's a wonderful example.

A Story of Two Strangers with a Very Happy Ending

A young man once walked into my office and asked me to show him and his wife some homes. I spent quite a bit of time with him, asked some pertinent questions about his job and his budget, and set up an appointment to see some appropriate homes later that week. He thanked me and left— only to return half an hour later.

He felt bad, he said, guilty because I'd been nice to him. There was no way he could buy a home. It was just that his wife wanted one so badly he'd given in and stopped at my office. No, he hadn't lied about the information he'd given me; he'd just failed to tell me he'd been forced to declare bankruptcy eleven months previously. He knew very well it would be a number of years before he could qualify for a mortgage loan. With embarrassment all over his face, he got up to leave again.

"Hold on," I told him. "Let's see if there's a way around this problem."

I called Mike, my favorite mortgage lender—who was really, really smart, and worked harder for me and my clients than anybody else did.

"What can we do?" I asked.

"I don't know," Mike replied. "But let's all get together and figure it out."

We had a meeting in my office. My client brought all his records and Mike brought his brilliant brain. (My role was to serve coffee, listen carefully, and learn how I could make a difficult transaction work.) Mike asked question after question, studied records, made lots of notes. Finally, he said he thought there was a chance my client could be approved for a particular loan program he knew of. Not a guarantee, mind you, but a chance. My client and his wife were so happy to have any kind of a chance, they just about jumped for joy.

"Go out and find a property, Fran," Mike told me, "I'll take it from there."

"Okay," I said, thinking that sounded far too easy. But we found a home they liked, put in our offer, and got it accepted. Then came the hard part—getting the mortgage approved.

"All right, what is it?" I asked when I saw him approaching my desk with a downcast look on his face.

"Well, your clients' jobs are verified, their income is sufficient. They have no debt because the bankruptcy wiped it all out, so they're qualified on that as well."

"So what's the problem?"

"I messed up," he admitted with great embarrassment. "I forgot the bankruptcy also wiped out all their credit. They don't have bad credit; they have no credit history at all, and I have to show some or our application will be rejected."

It was just like Mike that he accepted all the blame and never once mentioned that there wasn't another lender in town that would have even talked to these people, much less taken a loan application all the way through. That's when my own brilliant brain jumped in, however. "Sure, they have credit," I told him. "They've rented the same house for ten years. They've never once paid late."

"That's not credit," he argued. "Rent's paid in advance. I need something else."

"They've got ten years of receipts for all their utilities, their phone, and their TV cable service," I told him smugly after a moment's thought. "And those are paid after the fact, not in advance. I'll bet you'll find they've never been late once with those either."

"Underwriters don't accept utility bills as credit," he said, but I could tell he was thinking hard. Mike was not only very smart, he hated worse than anything to get a loan rejected—even if he thought it didn't have much of a chance in the first place.

I pressed the point. "But it is credit, no matter what they usually accept. They just usually don't need it because most buyers have lots of other things they can use. Go back there, yell at them if you have to, but make them see the point. I know you can do it."

"We better hope so," he finally agreed. "Okay, I'll give it my best shot."

> *Mike had to argue with mortgage loan underwriters three different times, finally went to their office in person and pounded on the desk, but in early December that year, I called my clients to tell them they'd be in their new home in time for Christmas.*

Would I have gone through all that with a client who wasn't loyal? Even if he were loyal, would I have done it if he hadn't come back and told me the truth that first day? No, I absolutely would not. (And there's no way, no way at all, I wouldn't have found out.) Would Mike have worked with them if I hadn't been loyal to him, referred lots of loans his way? He might have, because he loved a challenge, but chances are my client would never have met him. Would my client have set himself and his wife up for disappointment if he didn't trust we were doing the absolute best we could and were willing to go the extra mile? Would he have been willing to disclose his personal situation to just anyone? Or everyone? Would you?

Find a smart agent you trust and hang in there. It pays.

When you decide who will represent you, tell the other agents you've interviewed, and agents you meet for the first time. The same goes in the unfortunate event that you decide to change agents. It's a matter of business courtesy and respect. Also, one of the agents you reject could end up being the seller's representative on the house you ultimately purchase, so maintaining good professional relationships is very important.

Is it acceptable to use the listing agent as your (buyer's) representative?

Short answer: Yes.

Longer answer:

It is totally legal in Hawai'i for an agent to represent both buyer and seller (dual agency) as long as all concerned agree before anybody signs anything. If someone, anyone, tells you it is illegal, they are simply wrong. It is also totally ethical in Hawai'i for an agent to represent both buyer and seller, so long as everyone follows the rules.

What are the rules? Briefly, in a dual agency situation, the agent acts as an intermediary and advisor, and isn't allowed to give either party certain information. He or she isn't permitted to tell the seller, for example, the highest price the buyer will pay, nor is he or she permitted to tell the buyer the lowest price the seller will accept. A Dual Agency Addendum is included with the buyer's offer, and both seller and buyer must agree to the complete terms before the transaction can go forward. You'll find my company's addendum, which is similar to most and details all the rules completely, at the end of this chapter.

A listing agent will handle both clients with extra care because a lot is at stake in the transaction.

But, legal or not, doesn't the listing agent work for the seller? Not solely, if he agrees to represent you as well. Again, the requirement is disclosure. The listing agent must tell you ahead of time if you are going to be treated as a client, or simply as a customer. Obeying the rules, once again, protects everyone against real or imaginary bad things. And the ultimate decision, as always, is yours.

But what are the good things about buying through the listing agent?

Some sophisticated buyers have a personal broker who always handles their sale transactions, but they buy through the listing agent so long as they believe he/she is competent. Why? They believe they'll get a better deal if the listing agent is collecting both halves of the commission. Is that true? Sometimes. An agent may agree in advance with a seller-client that she will discount the commission if she ends up representing the buyer as well. What you can be sure of is that a listing agent will handle her own buyer-client and/or the buyer-client of one of her company's associates with kid gloves, and has a lot at stake in the transaction, both financially and in terms of her reputation.

Even if buyer and seller have their own agents, if those agents work for the same company, it's still a dual agency situation because, as you may remember, any client is officially represented by the agency, not the individual.

When handled in-house, transactions often proceed with far less difficulty. Why? Because the two agents know and presumably trust each other. And because problems usually come to light far sooner.

Some Dual-Agency Rules and Regs

✓ Dual agency is legal in Hawai'i.

✓ Dual agency must be disclosed to everyone before anyone signs anything.

✓ A dual agent has a fiduciary duty to both parties, except that a dual agent must remain silent on issues that would give one party an unfair advantage over the other. (Example: A dual agent can't disclose the seller's minimum price to the buyer without the seller's permission.)

✓ A dual agent cannot disclose information given in confidence by either party unless it affects the value of the property or the buyer's ability to perform his purchase contract. (Examples: A dual agent must disclose if she knows of hidden termite damage in a house she's listed, but may not tell the buyer that the seller has lost his job and cannot meet his mortgage payment. A dual agent must disclose what she knows about the buyer's ability to obtain a mortgage, but may not disclose that the buyer has a lot more cash than the down payment specified in his offer.)

✓ Ask for and review a "Dual Agency Agreement" before signing an offer with a dual agent.

✓ Agree on dual agency possibilities and procedures with your agent before signing a listing agreement.

✓ If you expect a commission discount if your agent sells your property herself, negotiate it in advance of signing the listing agreement.

✓ If you have revealed private matters to your agent before the dual agency situation arose, clearly state your expectations about confidentiality.

✓ Respect your agent's legal obligations and her ethical obligation to deal fairly with everyone.

✓ Unless you are confident that your agent can successfully manage a dual agency transaction in your particular case, do not agree to a dual agency situation.

The files are in the office, everyone reports to the same principal broker, everyone is motivated in the same direction, and, frankly, if one of the agents is weaker or less experienced, the stronger one can be relied upon to pick up the pieces if the ball drops and breaks.

The listing agent already has an excellent understanding of the seller's position, and knows what will and won't work. She also understands your position in advance; making a good fit between your needs and the seller's is easier. Getting details ironed out in advance, saving a lot of time and avoiding many misunderstandings works for the benefit of everybody.

But still, isn't it the listing agent's job to get the highest possible price for the seller? And isn't it the buyer's agent's job to get the lowest price possible for you? Does everything have to revert back to the dollars? So it would seem. But let's look at reality. Can a listing agent make you pay more than the property is worth by using aggressive sales tactics or wild promises? Not usually, no. That's why your bank hires an independent appraiser. That's why you hire a home inspector. That's why you collect data on comparable sales before you make an offer. That's why all promises are put in writing.

As far as getting the lowest possible price, here are the facts. Only you can decide how much to offer. In Hawai'i, all written offers, acceptable or otherwise, must be presented to the seller. Only the seller can decide whether to accept or reject an offer. His agent can only advise.

Bottom line: Choose an agent with whom you have personal rapport and who is trustworthy, interested in your well-being, and has the time to work with you. It's fine to work with licensed friends or relatives if they have a good reputation, but don't work with anyone solely out of sympathy or obligation. Dual agency is fine, too, so long as everyone follows the rules and you have personal confidence in your agent's integrity. Working with someone only because you think you might get a discount on the commission, or because you think he might slip up and divulge confidential information about the other party's position, is penny-wise and pound-foolish.

If You Insist
on Doing It Yourself

There always have been and always will be people who don't believe an agent will do the job they want, don't want to pay a commission, or both when they sell a home. If that describes you, this is your chapter. The following tips in no way constitute a comprehensive discussion, but may help.

Courtesy to brokers:

Customarily, buyers expect their agent's compensation to be included in the price. Include the words "Courtesy to Brokers," in all advertising material, accompanied by the percentage figure you will pay a buyer's agent. If you don't do that, it's a very rare agent indeed who will show your property and you'll be turning away the very people who can best help you. If the buyer's agent's compensation is far less than the norm, the same goes.

If you refuse to pay a buyer's agent you should say so up front on your advertising materials. That gives buyer's agents a heads up that they should make compensation arrangements with their clients; if the clients agree, they may still show your property.

Otherwise, you're on your own in persuading a buyer that you're so totally honest and forthcoming, so lacking in self-interest and so knowledgeable about every aspect of real estate transactions that they should go without representation and trust you instead (otherwise called "working the high wire without a net").

Determine your price

Be prepared to sell your property for less than the going rate in your area. Most buyers know the commission is built into the asking price for listed properties and will expect to save just as much money as you do.

Get the required documentation ready

Be knowledgeable about the legal requirements for Hawai'i real property transactions. Learn the roles of the various people discussed in "Who Does What," and collect names and phone numbers ahead of time of people you'll need help from during the transaction.

Know the necessary legal requirements for selling your property in Hawai'i.

The **Seller's Disclosure** is required by Hawai'i law. You can probably obtain a copy of the standard form used by real estate agents, but whether you use this, or another format, it must be comprehensive and detail everything you know about your property that might negatively affect a reasonable person's purchase decision. If you are in doubt about the need to disclose something, disclose it. If you simply don't want to disclose something, consult with your attorney before omitting it.

In addition to your personal disclosure, other documentation will undoubtedly be required.

If your property is a condominium, collect current copies of all pertinent documentation. This includes everything from the original Declaration to the minutes of the last three Board of Directors' meetings. Your building's management company will be able to provide these. There will probably be a substantial cost. Do not try to get away with the documents you received when you purchased your unit. Some things such as house rules, financial statements, and meeting minutes will likely be out of date. The management company should also provide a disclosure document called "rr-105c." There is a cost for this, too, but it is necessary for the buyer, and the lender will likely require it. It tells, among other things, whether or not there is any litigation pending against the owner's association or any other interested party. When you have an acceptable offer, copy these documents for the buyer and keep a set for yourself until the transaction closes.

If your property is a single-family residence, there are companies that research property and provide documents you may need, including all the building permits on record as well as everything about the property that's been recorded at the **Bureau of Conveyances**. They may also be able to provide copies of the

Serious Mistakes that Put Sellers At Risk

✔ Concealing or camouflaging property defects

✔ Failing to disclose "material facts," things that may affect the property's value to a reasonable person

✔ Providing inaccurate property fact sheets or other advertising materials

✔ Failing to recognize "red flags," such as unusual contingencies in offers

✔ Failing to thoroughly check a buyer's financial qualifications

✔ Failing to follow through with or enforce contract requirements

✔ Being ignorant of, or disregarding, their own or the buyer's legal rights

✔ Making any written or verbal statement that could be construed as discriminatory against any "protected class"

✔ Trying to enforce previous verbal agreements that are not included in the written agreement

✔ Trying to enforce changes to a written agreement after it has been fully executed

building plans if necessary. Two frequently used companies are **Hawai'i Real Property Research** and **Blue Sky**. If/when you hand out one of these sets, don't forget to retain a copy for yourself.

Have a marketing and advertising plan

Once you've taken care of the paperwork, it's time to start marketing.

Make, or have made, attractive handout sheets about the property. This should be only one page, should include all the basic essential information, including the price, perhaps a nice picture or two, and specific and accurate contact information.

Have a professional-looking sign made for the yard.

And put an ad in the paper.

The very best place for your advertising dollar is the local daily paper with the widest circulation. That is where serious home-buyers look for up-to-date information. The best time to run the ad is from Friday through Sunday. (Weekday ads have far fewer readers.) Magazines you may have seen require a great deal of advance notice; your property might have been on the market for six weeks before the ad appears. Advertising in the smaller weekly papers and on the Internet is fine, but don't do it if it means you must curtail weekend advertising in the major paper.

The ad doesn't need to be larger than one inch, but should include the number of bedrooms and baths, a brief mention of unique or distinctive features, and the price. If you're going to hold an open house, place the ad in time to be included in the Open House Guide and put the complete address in bold type. Include a phone number on any and all advertising material. If you're not having an open

---

Marketing Errors that Sabotage a Sale Before It Even Gets to Escrow

- ✓ Refusing to compensate a buyer's agent
- ✓ Making careless promises or misleading statements, either verbally or on written material
- ✓ Restricting showings or making phone contact difficult
- ✓ Allowing children to answer phone calls
- ✓ Allowing nonowners or children to answer questions or show the property
- ✓ Arguing with potential buyers or taking offense at their comments
- ✓ Negotiating verbally
- ✓ Failing to respond to written offers in a timely fashion

house, you may want to omit the specific address, but always indicate the neighborhood. (If you're not confident about how to write an ad, pick up a book on the subject and/or consult with the classified department at the paper.)

Contact and communications

Many people don't like dealing with recorded messages and children should not try to help by speaking with potential buyers. Once a sign's up and there's an ad in the paper, a responsible person should be available at all reasonable times. If that isn't possible, include "Call M–F 6–9 PM, weekends anytime," or whatever is appropriate in your ad, then make sure someone does, in fact, answer that phone during those times. Don't give out sensitive information—such as the times when no one is at home—to anyone who hasn't identified himself to your satisfaction.

If you're showing the property by appointment, make sure people know how to reach you if they are delayed and that you know how to reach them if you must change the appointment. (Don't do that unless it's a real emergency.) It's reasonable to wait half an hour or so after the time frame you've set up. Any more than that is abusive. If they're serious, they'll be on time or call you to reschedule.

If you're holding an open house, it's very important that at least one owner who can answer questions accurately is at the property for the entire time. If, for any reason, the open house must be canceled or interrupted, tape a large note to the For Sale sign.

In either case, you do not want to treat potential home buyers as potential thieves by following them around, so put all valuables and precious items out of sight and out of reach when showing the property.

Train yourself to communicate accurately, but not emotionally, about the features and benefits of your property when speaking with prospective buyers. Be available but out of the way when people are looking at the house and don't talk too much. Buyers are irritated by owners who follow them around constantly talking, trying to pitch the property. They want to look and discuss freely, without the owner interrupting, watching, or listening.

Do not argue with any comments made by a prospective buyer or agent. Why not?

A) They already expect you to be partial to the property, so your remarks are less significant and may even be suspect.

B) Often what sounds like criticism is actually an expression of interest. Arguing about it may turn off an otherwise interested party.

C) Prospective buyers are really and truly not interested in your unsolicited opinions.

D) If somebody has completely incorrect information, it's far better handled by presentation of the Seller's Disclosure or other documents that correct the error.

Answer direct questions truthfully and completely, but leave out all opinions—especially any opinion that implies the prospective buyer is stupid, ignorant, or ill-informed.

Don't be offended by what anyone says. Smile and remain silent if somebody is proposing to cut down your favorite tree, tear out that gorgeous carpet you saved for six months to buy, or says your wonderful master bath is absolutely not up to their standards. This is hard to do but very important. Remember your objective is selling the property. Releasing control of it is an essential part of the deal. The buyer needs to individualize it according to his needs. Your taste is irrelevant.

If you have non-negotiable requirements, disclose them immediately.

If you have non-negotiable requirements, disclose them immediately. The property handout sheet is best, but if not there, specify them as soon as possible to all comers. Such things as "The tenant has a lease until next July," or "This sale is subject to the seller purchasing a replacement property," are facts a buyer needs to know right away, before making any offer.

Do not negotiate verbally. That tactic is often tried by buyers who know they're speaking to an owner. It is entirely meaningless, except when the seller opens his mouth and blurts out more than a wise person would want to tell that buyer! Instead, politely and with a smile, say that you're not prepared to discuss money and terms unless they're in writing, but when they are in writing, you'll give them every attention and consideration. Do not fool yourself by imagining that when somebody says, "I'd pay no more than $450,000 for this house," it constitutes an offer. It doesn't. It's nothing but empty talk.

Dealing with offers

Before you receive an offer, review the do's and don'ts in the chapter "Negotiating the Best Possible Contract" and take them to heart.

An offer isn't an offer unless it's in writing.

When you receive an offer, do not reply verbally in any way.

If the offer is submitted by an agent, listen to the agent's presentation, but then review it in its entirety. Read every single word. Do not reply in any form or manner until you have done so.

Do not mark up the offer itself. If there are any items that need to be changed, make a list on scratch paper.

When you're finished with your review, if the offer is acceptable as written, sign it and get it back to the buyer or buyer's agent by the deadline written on the offer.

If you need more time, ask for it. Failure to reply on time without receiving an approved extension can make the offer null and void. It's also disrespectful and rude—not the way to set up a successful transaction.

If it's not acceptable on its face, make a written counteroffer specifying all changes.

Strategies for dealing with offers are discussed elsewhere, but this fact is worth repeating: Any change you make, even the most minor one, starts an entirely new contract. The buyer has no contractual obligation to continue negotiations, so be sure you're willing to lose that buyer if the changes you want aren't made.

After you've accepted an offer

Once you have arrived at a meeting of the minds and have a fully signed agreement, make a list of things that must be done, along with a list of who is responsible for doing them, and their contractual deadlines.

Hold the buyer to the timeline and keep your own. Real estate transactions are not casual and should not be treated as such. Pay particular attention to items that require written confirmation or approval from the buyer or his lender. Be reasonable if delays happen (and they will) that are beyond the control of the buyer, but don't be a sucker for a tall tale. One very important thing to watch out for is that the buyer makes any and all deposits on time and that his checks are good. Deposits are made to escrow and the escrow officer is responsible for keeping you informed, but don't take it for granted. Failure to make a required deposit may give you legal means to cancel a transaction, but if that happens and you decide to cancel, make sure the paperwork is handled exactly as the contract and escrow tell you it must be.

If you smell a rat, there very well may be a rat around somewhere. You don't need to be paranoid, but if you're getting "vibes" that make you suspicious of your buyer's sincerity, your best protection is an unbroken habit of performing your own duties correctly and on time and making sure the buyer does the same.

> *I once represented the seller of a very large property. We received an offer that appeared to be exactly what the seller needed, so it was accepted. The first red flag ran up the pole when the buyer's initial deposit was late. His agent said she had the check, but had forgotten to deliver it to escrow and would do so right away. All right, we said, let's not blame the buyer for his agent's carelessness. We let that error slide.*
>
> *When the due diligence process had been completed, another deposit was due—a very large one. We got a letter stating the buyer approved the property, but when I checked with escrow they had no check. Oops! I called the buyer's agent again, and this time let her know they were in violation of their agreement and the seller might cancel the contract if*

the check didn't get to escrow in twenty-four hours. She said she'd make sure the money got there, but by now I smelled a strong aroma of rat.

I called the buyer's lender (as seller's agent, I had the right to make sure the loan process was on track). The lender was vague and not forthcoming—a very bad sign.

Fortunately, I had one more call to make—to another prospect who had expressed serious interest. I alerted him that our existing transaction was iffy. Maybe he'd like to put in a backup offer? He appeared very happy that he might have a chance to buy the property after all and let me know he'd get the paperwork going.

Meanwhile, back at the ranch, when I got home that night, I found the original buyer's agent waiting on my doorstep— holding a large envelope. Her client had run into financing difficulties, she said, but he still wanted the property. Here was another offer which he hoped my client would accept in place of the original. A quick look told me this new offer was absolutely unacceptable and tied up the property while putting the seller at great financial risk. It's a no-go, I told the agent frankly. Even if the terms were acceptable, which they were not, my seller-client was now both angry and suspicious and unwilling to do any further business with hers. Eventually, the property was sold to the man who'd been second in line.

There are a couple of further points beyond the buyer's failure to meet time deadlines that gave my client legitimate cause to cancel the contract:

Neither party has any obligation to go along with changes made after the fact. Be fair but be firm. Insist that your business be handled in a businesslike manner. Red flags, hints, or implications that there may be a problem should be taken seriously.

Keep yourself fully informed about the transaction's progress. Do not assume that no news is good news. There is no sale until the check is in your hands. Keep names and numbers of interested parties and collect backup offers if possible until all is said and done.

If all this sounds like a lot of work, it is.

You may be beginning to get the idea that handling your own transaction is just about as smart as pulling your own teeth instead of going to a dentist.

There are, however, exceptional situations. A typical example might be selling your home to a parent or a sibling, also sometimes to an existing tenant who has lived in the property for a substantial time. If that buyer has submitted a written offer and is someone you know well and trust implicitly and is familiar with the property and all its idiosyncrasies, you may feel you don't need an agent. You still need to protect your own interests, however, and in this kind of case want to do so without offending a buyer who is close to you personally. You may want to ask an agent to represent you and handle all the formal details of the transaction for a discounted commission. Many agents I know are happy to provide this service and the discount can be as much as 50 percent, sometimes more. What's the benefit to you besides saving you a lot of work? Everyone involved can be confident that the transaction is done in accordance with the law and proper procedure. It puts a buffer between you and your buyer; any sensitive issue that may arise is then handled professionally, not personally.

And never say never. Close friends and relatives are often the very people who believe their relationship gives them license to take advantage in one way or another.

Another time you may feel you can sell on your own is if you're highly experienced, have done many other transactions, or perhaps are a real estate licensee in another state. If that's the case, I doubt you'll be reading this book, but if you are: Before you go it alone, check current practices in Hawai'i, and also current law, and if you're from out of state, don't assume the roles here will be the same as those you're used to.

What about buying property without an agent?

The only reason to do that is the hope of saving money—buying the house for less than the seller would otherwise accept.

You need to decide whether the potential saving is worth the potential risk. What risk? It depends on the honesty and good faith of the other parties involved. And it depends on your own knowledge and expertise. If you are not represented by a licensed agent, there is no buffer, no one to assume even partial liability for errors you may make, either in negotiating, in managing the transaction itself, or in becoming informed about the property itself.

Some buyers routinely purchase property through the listing agent. They believe they'll get a better deal if the agent is a dual agent compensated on both sides of the transaction, and some listing agents do discount the commission if they also represent the buyer. However, that discount is given to the seller because it's the seller who has signed the listing contract. Thus, it's up to the seller alone to decide if he wants to share the benefit of any discount.

> *Here's a mistake no one should make. But at least one person I know, a friend of mine, once did. He went to look at property with an agent who showed him several houses, including one of her own listings. He liked that one very well, but the price was a stretch for his budget. After going home, he got a very clever idea. He'd learned the owner's name, looked it up in the phone book and called him. "I saw your house today," he began, "and I'd like to buy it, but it's a little more than I can afford. How about we just make a deal between the two of us? That way we can save the six percent commission and I can afford your house." At that point, and to my friend's mortification, the owner had to explain that would be illegal. He had already signed a listing agreement and was obligated to pay that commission, no matter who bought the house. He then called his agent to ask that she stop crazy people from calling him directly. It's a great credit to that agent's tact and understanding nature that my friend eventually was able to make an acceptable offer—with her help and with no hard feelings.*

Most sellers, whether represented or not, are prepared to compensate a buyer's agent and have built that into their asking price. Sometimes, however, that's not the case. Then a buyer must decide whether to pay his own agent or go it alone. Normally, when compensation for a buyer's agent isn't already included in the asking price, it can be specifically added in the buyer's written offer. Again, this is a matter of individual choice. If you believe you are fully capable of managing your own purchase transaction, you may save some money if (and only if) the property is being sold directly by the owner or is listed with an agency under terms that do not compensate a buyer's agent. Before going into such a transaction, make sure you have correct and complete information about how the property is being marketed. Don't be bashful or make embarrassing phone calls—just ask!

Bottom line: Selling on your own is more difficult and complicated than buying on your own, but both require you to educate yourself beforehand and both involve a lot of work and certain risks. Before you decide if the potential savings are worthwhile, take a step back and look objectively at your own qualifications and abilities, then learn and follow the rules for a successful transaction.

6

The Numbers Game:
Real Estate Statistics

I've been asked about real estate statistics—what they mean and how they affect the average person.

Market statistics are gathered from the public record and from the **Multiple Listing Service** records. They are published monthly, quarterly, and annually and give general information about real estate trends. People who are numbers-oriented find them very interesting and useful. I'm not a statistician so the following should be taken with a grain of salt.

First of all, the real estate statistics in the paper are history, literally and figuratively. They're about the past. Their relevance in the present varies according to what's going on now and what's happened since the figures were gathered. For planning purposes, by the time major trends hit the paper, the horse may have left the barn.

As an example, say you're looking at quarterly numbers: the average price of a home, the average time it takes to sell a home, the average difference between asking prices and selling prices, and all the rest. If it's now November and the quarter you're looking at encompasses July through September (the most recent statistics), and a market-changing event occurred on October 1, the data may be of far less value because it doesn't take into account things that are happening right now.

In 2001, we experienced a market-changing event on September 11. The major bulk of data for the third quarter of that year (July through September) was from before the event, and didn't show much of an effect. However, the data for the fourth quarter (October through December) certainly did. Although everybody assumed the terrorist attacks would have a drastic effect on real estate, the actual numbers were not available until January 2002, so the actual-factual impact could not be evaluated until then.

But let's say a market-changing event had happened that was not general common knowledge. Before the public could find out about it and perhaps amend their decision-making, it might be four months after the fact. And as the September 11 example graphically demonstrates, statistical analysis certainly can't predict catastrophic—or any other exceptional—happenings before they occur. Statistics are only part of the entire picture.

There's another important thing about statistics: As my old sociology professor used to say, "You can't particularize from a generality." Just because there's a certain trend or tendency in the real estate market, doesn't mean it's valid to apply that tendency or trend to your own transaction. To keep it obvious, let's say during one quarter a home sold for $16,000,000 in a certain area. In the same quarter, thirty-two homes in a different area sold for $500,000 each. The total sales in both instances are $16,000,000. But are the markets comparable? I don't think so.

So we move on to another statistic: average sale prices. In the above example, those would be drastically different. Does it mean in the one case that all homes in the area are in the multimillion dollar category? No. Not at all. It just means that one very expensive home was purchased by one very wealthy buyer. In the other case, does it mean no homes in the area will sell for more (or less) than $500,000? No. It's possible a certain developer priced all his homes at that figure and sold thirty-two of them. Maybe he has two hundred available, or maybe he only had thirty-two and they sold out. Without knowing more, you don't know what those figures mean.

Moving on to the total number of sales in that quarter. This does give a person an idea of how active the market is, right? Yes, to a point. The number of actual sales compared to the number of available properties on the market can be important. The smaller that ratio, generally speaking, the more active the market. And the more active the market, in essence, the more competition for available properties. Say there were thirty properties available and twenty-eight of them sold. Very active market. However, if there were two hundred properties available and twenty-eight sold, that would be a very different story.

In general, when it comes to Hawai'i real estate, statistics for a specific area of interest are more meaningful than island- or state-wide numbers. For example, to the average home buyer or seller, homes on Moloka'i can't be compared with homes on O'ahu in any meaningful way. Nor can homes in Hale'iwa be compared with homes in Hawai'i Kai in any meaningful way. For any statistics to be meaningful to an individual, they must pertain as specifically as possible to what that individual is selling or buying.

When the figures are broken down by area and by category (single-family home, condominium, townhouse, etc.), they are much more pertinent—although, remember, they still reflect only the past. They don't tell you what's happening in the present, and they most certainly don't predict the future, except in very general terms and over very long periods of time. (As a hypothetical example, say you read that real estate prices over the last twenty years have averaged a 10 percent per year increase. It's foolish to imagine there's any guarantee that this year will see a 10 percent increase. Over those twenty years, there might have been a 25 percent increase one year, offset by a 10 percent decline in another, and any number of other ups and downs that ended up with that average 10 percent increase.

There's another statistic that the average home buyer finds important, though, and that's mortgage rates. For one thing, those figures are usually up-to-date and reflect currently available mortgages. Week to week, by reading the mortgage lenders' ads, it's also possible to discern developing trends. However, there's a very important **cautionary note:** The rates quoted in the paper are not applicable to all borrowers, nor to all properties, nor to all types of loans. Additionally, they don't necessarily all have the same closing costs. An advertised interest rate may also be what's called a "teaser rate," a loan that is available but only under extremely limited circumstances. So before you accept one lender's rate as better than another's, you need to be sure you're comparing apples with apples and not with oranges—or lima beans—and also that the loan program you're interested in is actually available to you on the property you're planning to buy. While simply scanning the rates and choosing the cheapest one would make life easier, that's not a good way to buy a mortgage loan. For more on how to properly analyze loan programs, see the chapter on "Doing the Math."

Mortgage rates are usually up-to-date but can be misleading if you're not comparing apples to apples.

Bottom line: Approach real estate statistics with an analytical and questioning attitude. What do they really mean, and do they have any relevance to you personally? Think about whether the person or agency who prepared them might have any bias. Remember that numbers can only reflect past history. Projecting them into the future is risky unless you're discussing trends over many years. Statistics are interesting and important to banks, economists, and large-scale investors, but those people are generally trained and experienced in their interpretation. For the average person who doesn't have such knowledge and experience, the numbers game is usually of far more limited value. Buying or selling a personal home is not the same as speculating in the stock market, nor should it be. And many factors in mortgage loans above and beyond simple interest rates require analysis in order to compare them correctly and decide which one is best for you.

How to Search for Property Effectively

The most common ways people look for property are: in the newspaper, through their agent, and on the Internet. Frequently, people also drive the streets of neighborhoods, looking for For Sale signs. Also, here in Hawai'i, a popular Sunday pastime is cruising open houses.

Plan Your Search

- ✔ Make a list of absolute requirements and be realistic.

- ✔ Make a list of desirable "bonus" features in order of priority.

- ✔ Establish a budget and verify it with a lender.

- ✔ Communicate all the above to your agent and anyone else you think might have helpful input.

- ✔ Using any or all of the search methods discussed, make a comprehensive list of available properties that meet your absolute requirements and your budget, put them in order according to which seem most appealing or have the most bonus features.

- ✔ Take the top five or six, verify they're still available and go look at them.

- ✔ Update your list at least every week; in a "hot market," update it every day.

- ✔ Keep working until you find "the one for you."

Which ways are effective, and which are a waste of time?

If you have NO PLAN, you are flying blind. That's the real waste of time. To make your search effective, first go back to the list of wants and needs you prepared earlier. Show it to all the people who influence your decisions and ask for their input. You may be surprised—even kids sometimes have valuable insight to put into the mix. And give a copy to your agent! Then start looking.

The newspaper

This is still the most popular place buyers look. A new listing will appear at least once in the paper with the largest circulation (unless it's sold before the paper's advertising deadline), whether it's a FISBO (for sale by owner) or sold through an agency. That first-time ad will normally appear in a Sunday edition, whether the property is an open house listing or by appointment. The ad will usually include critical information, such as location or address, number of bedrooms and baths, price, and who to call for more information.

Keep in mind that the newspaper normally doesn't include properties listed after the prior Wednesday (that's the usual ad deadline), nor can a listing be taken out of the paper after Friday at noon. Those big full-page ads that include many listings from a single company have a much earlier deadline. So—you may not see the very newest listings, and some of those you do see may already be in escrow. You may want to call the phone number for a particular listing to be sure it's still available.

Carry the paper with you if you go on an open house tour, and carry a map if you're not familiar with an area. We have lots of small streets and neighborhoods here in Hawai'i that may not be easy to find. If you get lost, you may find the agent's cell phone number in the ad. Don't hesitate to call for directions.

The Internet

Listings online may include a lot more information than those in the paper and plenty of pictures. At this writing, a popular Web site is **www.hicentral.com**, but there are certainly others. Looking online is a great way to search for property anonymously. If you have your wants and needs clearly in mind, you can find properties that fit without using a lot of gas and energy.

Among the drawbacks: Many Web sites are not kept current on a regular basis. I recently received a call about a listing that sold and closed two years ago! What a disappointment for that buyer who thought she'd found a "steal." It wasn't on my Web site, nor was it on my company's; someone had gratuitously advertised my listing. Agents don't necessarily even know if someone else has posted their listing.

Additionally, the Internet listings are not comprehensive; not all agents post there. Surf the web but don't rely on it exclusively.

Cruising open houses and streets

"They're out there for a reason," my principal broker Jean Wade used to say. And she was right, of course. People who spend their Sunday looking at homes are, by definition, real-estate minded and interested in property.

In twenty years, I sold my listings at an open house twice. In that same twenty years, I've probably met fifty clients for the first time at an open house. So are open houses beneficial to buyers, to sellers, or to the agents tending the open houses? The answer is all of the above. Buyers are getting educated; sellers are getting exposure for their property; agents are meeting new clients and expanding their reputations and sphere of influence.

Open houses are far more entertaining than efficient but can be a lot of fun, and sometimes you do find just the right house.

If you know the specific street or neighborhood you want to live in, check for For Sale signs regularly. However, don't just do that. Many people, for whatever reason, don't want a sign up in front of their house. Also, while a sign may go up before a listing is in the computer, the reverse is also true.

Do tell all agents you meet at open houses who your agent is. Also, ask your agent to call the numbers on signs rather than doing it yourself. Both of those simple courtesies will garner you a great deal more respect. Your interest will be taken seriously, your questions will be answered carefully.

I'm told some people sign into open houses with a fake name or phone number. To be frank, I haven't experienced that. If you don't want someone to call, tell them not to, or don't leave a number. If you do want information but don't want calls, leave your email address instead.

Have your agent contact the buyer's agent if you see a house you like.

If you want to do what one of my clients did, and interview agents by visiting their open houses or talking to them on the phone, that's just fine. Be honest, though. There's no reason why you shouldn't tell an agent your true objective. When someone who's unrepresented calls me or comes in to my open house, I always feel it's a great opportunity to "show my stuff" and hope they'll like me well enough to ask me to represent them.

Friends, relatives and neighbors

For some reason, many house-hunters keep their search a secret. Why? Heaven knows. You shouldn't, because your own circle is a very valuable source of information. Your friend or coworker may know someone who has just put his house on the market. Your husband's sister-in-law's second cousin may know (or be) the best real estate broker in town. And if you already know people in the area where you want to move, for goodness' sake, tell them! People talk to each other, and real estate in Hawai'i is a favorite topic. Get the word out. It never hurts and often helps.

Your agent's research

All members of a local Board of Realtors, on all islands, have access to their island's MLS (Multiple Listing Service) database on their computer. At this writing, it is not open to public access on the Internet. It is as close to a comprehensive list of what's available as you can get and is more accurate and current than any other database. Members are required to add their listings promptly, and we pay fines if we fail to keep information current.

If the Plan's Not Working

If you've looked at more than a dozen homes (actually gone inside them and looked) and haven't found one that suits you, something is wrong.

- ✔ Reevaluate requirements that are breaking your budget. (That's usually where the problem is, so do that first.) Are they all true requirements, something you must have in any home you live in? For example, if you have three children, four bedrooms would be nice, but is it an absolute must? Only you can decide, but be objective.

- ✔ Search out any modifications or compromises that will change the picture of budget vs. requirements.

- ✔ Consider other financing options. Is there a different loan program that might also change that picture? (This is where working closely with a highly skilled team of agent and lender can make all the difference.)

- ✔ Have you communicated your needs accurately to your agent? If not, regroup and start over. (If you have, and you believe your agent isn't listening to you, find another agent.)

- ✔ Are you living in the past? Memories of last year's prices— or a home you could have purchased last year and didn't— may be affecting your ability to make a good decision. Accept that you cannot move backward and must deal with what's available now at today's values.

- ✔ Are you indecisive because of some personal situation or fear that you're not disclosing, either to yourself or to others involved? Ask yourself if you truly want to buy a home and pay attention to the answer.

We have cooperative agreements among ourselves to share our listings and make them available to agents from other companies. It is not necessary to check with every company to see what they have listed; your agent has access to it all, with the exception of for-sale-by-owners properties and listings of nonmember agents. For those, you and your agent will both have to read the paper or look for roadside signs.

Note to sellers: When you're deciding on a listing agent, make sure your home will be adequately advertised. A full-service brokerage company places all of its listings in the MLS, and should, and normally does, pay for advertising in the newspaper and on the Internet. We pay the hefty fees because that is where agents look first for properties.

Bottom line: All search methods can be useful. Use the ones that feel comfortable. The most important thing in a constructive and effective search is that you work with your list of needs and wants, communicate them to everyone involved, and use them as you evaluate the homes you see.

8

Only in Hawai'i

There are a few significant things about home-buying here that usually don't apply in other places.

Leasehold property

This means the owner owns the building and other improvements, as well as a long-term lease on the land. He does not own the land itself.

There are a lot of myths that can distort the facts. You should be concerned with facts.

Myth: All property in Hawai'i is leasehold.

Fact: Today, most single-family homes are fee-simple, which means the owner owns both the land and the improvements. There are still, however, many apartment and townhouse projects that are leasehold.

Myth: The monthly lease (rent) payment is the same as rent-to-buy. At the end, you'll own the land.

Fact: The lease payment is just that—rent. At the end of the term, the lessor (landowner) gets the land back unless he has sold the land to the lessee (owner of the building and tenant on the land) for an additional sum of money. This purchase of the land by the lessee is called "fee conversion." If the lease, as many do, has what's called a reversion clause, the owner of the land also gets all the improvements (buildings, etc.) when he gets the land back.

Myth: Buying leasehold property is always a bad idea.

Fact: Buying leasehold property can be a good idea—but only if you clearly understand the concept, as well as the particular lease in question, and know what you're doing.

Here are the basic facts you need to know:

Owners and agents must disclose if the property they're selling is leasehold.

"LH" after the asking price on the property information sheet or in advertising material means the property is leasehold and the purchase price does not include the land. The land may or may not be available to a buyer for an additional amount. If you don't see a fee purchase price, ask if the fee is available.

"FA" means that purchase of the fee interest—the land—is available to the new buyer. The price of the land may appear separately under the heading "fee purchase," or something similar. To determine the entire cost of land and building (or apartment unit), add the two together.

"FP" means the fee purchase is presently pending—in escrow, but not yet closed. However, the cost of the land is not automatically included in the asking price. If you don't see a clarification on the information sheet, ask.

You may want to walk away from the property if the fee purchase isn't available, or if the price isn't known. Many people simply aren't willing to deal with that insecurity, even though leasehold prices are substantially less than fee-simple. To find out if you're one of those who might benefit from buying leasehold property, read on.

Required information also includes:

Monthly lease rent amount: There may be one or more "step-ups" in lease rent; the dates for when those will occur should be included.

Renegotiation date: The point when the lessor can raise the rent.

The renegotiation date is very important for a couple of reasons. First, since most leases originated many years ago, the current fair market rent for the land in question is likely to be very high by comparison. It's not unusual for lease rents to go up 1,000 percent on renegotiation. Also, since lenders know that can happen, the number of years until renegotiation affects a buyer's ability to get a

Hawaiian Kuleana

Occasionally you'll discover a kuleana on property you're interested in buying, or you'll find out that the property abuts a kuleana. Without getting into any lengthy discussion, a kuleana is a piece of land that native Hawaiians have a permanent right to access and to use. The tradition goes back to the time of the Hawaiian monarchy, and kuleana rights "run with the land." That means the rights apply to the land itself. Land may be used for religious or agricultural purposes or may not be used at all. A kuleana may be right in the middle of someone's land; it can also be surrounded by private properties with no means of access except across one or more of those private properties. Sometimes a stream runs through a kuleana, and native Hawaiian use of that stream may affect adjacent property owners in various ways.

Sometimes, although the kuleana remains "on the books," nobody ever wants to use it and the entire question is moot. Sometimes a property owner has absolutely no problem with allowing either access or use. Other times, an owner may be in for a surprise when he learns people plan to access the kuleana by way of his backyard or when he finds somebody planting taro in a spot he thought was his to use as he wished.

While the chances you will encounter kuleana land are remote (it is extremely rare to find kuleana in developed residential areas), it should certainly be disclosed in advance to any buyer. The title search is where its existence will be revealed.

mortgage. If renegotiation is very soon, the buyer may be strapped. Most lenders require at least ten years of fixed lease rents.

Expiration date: That means just what it says: the lease is over on that date and the land goes back to the landlord under terms that are detailed in the lease itself—reversionary clauses and the like.

If you buy leasehold property, you must be given a copy of the lease as well as a **Plain Language Lease Disclosure**, often but not always prepared by an attorney, that discloses all the important facts in regular English, before you're bound to your contract. **Note:**

With leasehold condominiums, there is both a primary lease and an apartment lease. Frequently, if you're not careful, you'll receive only one, not both. It's a very good idea to require both in writing on your initial offer, and don't take no for an answer.

This is already pretty scary, right? You're picturing yourself on the street or living in your car, while the lessor walks off with your stove and fridge. So why would anybody ever buy Hawaiian leasehold property?

It depends on a buyer's personal needs and situation, on the term of the lease, and on whether the fee purchase is now, or is expected to be, available. The lease disclosure gives you the term of the lease. Your agent or the seller's agent can provide the facts about future fee purchase, as well as brochures with expert detailed information about Hawaiian land leases in general.

Match the facts up with your personal needs:

If, for instance, the lease term has forty years to run and you're already seventy-five, purchase of the fee may not matter to you.

If the fee is, or soon will be, available, and you're a younger person with a steadily rising income, buying leasehold property may let you acquire a nice lifestyle now, and deal with the land cost later when you can better afford it.

If you are buying investment property, owning in leasehold may give you tax advantages you wouldn't have otherwise. Discuss and confirm possible deductions of lease rent payments and depreciation of the entire purchase price with your tax expert.

These are personal decisions that can only be made when you understand exactly what is involved.

Conditions, covenants and restrictions (CC&R's)

These are not unique to Hawai'i. Many communities have rules for homeowners. Find out from your agent or the seller if there are

CC&R's on a property you're interested in, and make sure descriptions are provided by escrow right along with your title search. Make offers contingent upon review and approval of CC&R's if they exist.

New subdivisions frequently have CC&R's, and usually everybody knows about them. However, if you're buying fee-simple property that once was leasehold, the original land owner may have recorded CC&R's at the time the land was first developed. These are probably still in effect today, even though that lessor is no longer in the picture and nobody's thought about them in years. Some argue that while they still exist, they can no longer be enforced; it's a gray area. Most often you'll find they are aimed at protecting property values, and you'll feel very comfortable accepting them but there may be exceptions.

So make sure you read them before accepting a property.

> *For example, my own property sits on 10,000 square feet of land that once was leasehold. The zoning in my area requires a minimum lot size of 5,000 square feet per house. It appears that I should be able to legally construct a second dwelling on the property. However, when the subdivision was constructed, the land owner recorded CC&R's that stipulate only one dwelling per lot can be built. Those CC&R's "run with the land" (apply no matter who owns it). I'm personally content to accept this restriction, but someone who wanted to build another home, and concluded from the zoning regulations that he could, might feel differently.*

Other things "only in Hawai'i"

It's the only place in the country where people worry about buying property on top of an active volcano. (No, I'm not kidding. Some people do worry, and if anybody told you that's what you were doing, you'd worry, too. So I'm not ridiculing anyone.) Let's replace the myth with the facts.

Fact: Only one inhabited Hawaiian island has any active volcanoes. That is the Big Island of Hawai'i.

Fact: Hawaiian volcanoes are not the same geological type as Mt. St. Helens and do not have a high risk of explosion. (The University of Hawai'i and the state library system are great sources of authoritative information on our volcanoes.)

Fact: Some lands and homes in certain Big Island areas have been overrun by lava. So use common sense. Don't buy land without seeing it and finding out for yourself whether it's in a vulnerable area. It's just as safe to live in most Big Island places, though, as it is anywhere else.

But then there are also tsunamis (tidal waves) and hurricanes, aren't there?

Yes, tsunamis have occurred here once in a while and might again. And hurricanes happen—not often but with fair regularity.

It's also possible for mud slides to occur in certain areas with or without either a hurricane or a tsunami.

In the front of the phone book, you'll find maps showing flood inundation areas. That is just a starting point, though. Check on the Flood Designation for your property. That is required information for any listed property, and very easy to discover. It tells you the likelihood that your property will be affected by flooding. (And it's not always obvious, either. For instance, although I live in canal-front property, it is not in a designated flood area.)

If you select property in an inundation area, your lender will require flood insurance. However, anyone can purchase flood insurance, regardless of where the property is. The only question is price. Insurance agents are the best people to consult about your needs.

Important note: Flood insurance and hurricane insurance are not the same things. Make sure you have satisfactory coverage for all the eventualities you are concerned about.

Totally apart from weather and land conditions, there is also:

Our cultural heritage

Hawai'i truly is a multicultural society. Many, if not most, families have a mixed ethnic heritage. What mainlanders understand as cultural or ethnic "minorities" are not regarded as such here, and they don't regard themselves as such either. There's an entirely different prevailing attitude among and toward our many diverse cultures. We've all managed to get along so well over all these many years because everyone respects everyone else's different ways of doing everything, including business.

When you do business in Hawai'i—and purchasing or selling a home certainly qualifies—these things must be taken into account.

For instance, some people, among them those from Japan, are accustomed to doing business on a handshake and expect their word to be accepted as their bond. They often don't consider written agreements as important as Americans do. Occasionally, someone might become offended if asked to sign something or make a deposit in order to bind an agreement. Extra tact and explanations may be called for.

Local people of Japanese ancestry, however, are Americans and have for the most part adopted American customs. They do expect a formal agreement and, once it's been reached, expect meticulous adherence to both letter and spirit.

The point: It can be important to know if you're negotiating or working with someone whose *name* is Japanese (or Chinese or Hawaiian or Filipino or European or whatever), or someone who really *is* Japanese.

For an agreement to be binding, both parties must know what they've agreed to do. Communication is key.

Some cultures also have entirely different ideas as to what constitutes a negotiation. For some, including most Americans, a signed contract is the end of the road—the deal is set, the agreement done. For those from some other places, though, it's only the beginning. They expect negotiation to continue until closing has happened. This can be very disconcerting both for the person who expects that a deal's a deal and for the person who is told they must do exactly what they've agreed to do or the other party can cancel the agreement. A clear understanding of expectations is crucial—and even then there may be difficulties.

Of course, this is America and the laws of the state of Hawai'i generally reflect American culture. But relying on legalese and the letter of the law without taking someone else's cultural values into consideration can very definitely be a losing strategy.

It's also important to be sure that both parties understand the details of an agreement. And it's not only a matter of courtesy. For an agreement to be binding, the parties must both know what they've agreed to do. It's more common here than in some other places that you'll do business with someone who's knowledge of English is limited. Sometimes a translator or interpreter is necessary; sometimes a friend or relative with a better understanding of the language is sufficient. Either way, all concerned need to take language and cultural differences into consideration.

> *I recently was involved in a transaction with a buyer who'd been born in Korea. She had a real estate license here in Hawai'i and therefore had to know enough English to pass the state licensing exam and likewise had to be familiar with our standard forms and state laws. I made the mistake of assuming that familiarity constituted agreement.*
>
> *It didn't: She was still accustomed to taking a contract as a starting point because that's how contracts are treated where she's from—all her past experience told her it was not only acceptable, but expected, to argue over contractually required items after agreeing to them. Without those nitty-gritty discussions, she felt there wouldn't be any mutual respect. We worked everything out in the end, but not without a lot of stress and difficulty. The important lesson for me was that I learned the difference between a person who is simply looking for a way to avoid keeping her commitments and a person for whom negotiating after the fact is a cultural imperative—a necessary and essential part of doing business.*

Ultimately, remember: It's more important to know where an individual is coming from in his mind than it is to literally know where he comes from.

And then there's our beloved Hawaiian pidgin

Don't make the mistake of assuming that because an individual uses pidgin English in ordinary conversation, he or she doesn't know and understand the more formal language. Many, if not most, Hawaiians and kama'āina (locals) scatter pidgin phrases throughout their speech. And many who use it as their dominant form of communication are highly educated and extremely sophisticated in their business dealings; they understand absolutely everything. Pidgin is often used simply as a graphic statement of local pride that says, "I'm from Hawai'i," in an unmistakable and unique way.

Love of the 'Āina

There is something else unique to Hawai'i that has to do with cultural attitudes toward the land. I don't pretend to have the complete understanding of the concepts that Native Hawaiians do, but I do get that in the eyes of ancient Hawaiians, and many of those living today as well, the land has a soul and it belongs to God, not to people. People can use it, but it isn't theirs in the way other Americans understand ownership.

Hence, when the first haoles (foreigners) came to the Islands, the natives thought they were stupidly paying money for land they could have used freely. They took the money, but had no idea those haoles were going to take the land—permanently. Perhaps just one

Author's note: Haole is not now, and never has been, racist terminology. Its use is not considered rude or insulting unless it's accompanied by uncomplimentary adjectives such as "dumb" or other more unprintable qualifiers. While in the past, the term denoted "foreigner," in today's idiomatic speech it means simply "white person."

of many mistakes that occurred, at least in part, because neither party understood the cultural beliefs of the other.

Today, many Native Hawaiians don't own their homes. It's not always because they can't afford to buy one, although that certainly can be the case. In my experience, however, I've met many people who still don't deeply feel and understand the importance of property ownership and thus aren't willing to make the sacrifices home ownership involves.

Here's why I care and one of the reasons I've been in the real estate business for such a long time: I believe in the importance of home ownership as part of our American way of life. I believe it's essential to our individual freedoms and, as a group, to our political clout in many ways. And I also believe that permanent residents of Hawai'i, whatever their ethnicity, need to own, at the very least, the home they live in, or they will one day be forced to leave the Islands we all love.

Along with Hawaiians of all eras, both native and adopted, I also believe in good husbandry. Whether you believe God or people own the land, taking care of it is important. Those who share a deep love for the land will tend it in the best way possible and make sure it's not wasted or badly used. Making sure our paradise remains heavenly is up to us.

Bottom line (and editorial comment): It's not possible to go back in time and undo what's been done. We can only deal with today. And today if the people for whom Hawai'i is home don't control the use of the land (and ownership does give people at least some control over its use), somebody else will. I think that's a bad thing. Therefore, I want to help as many local permanent residents achieve home ownership as I possibly can and through this book encourage people to reach out for the right kind of help to achieve it.

9

Choosing
Your Home in Hawai'i
(Sellers, You Should Read This, Too)

It's time to actually look at homes you will seriously consider purchasing.

You may find one on your first day out.

Do not, repeat not, be intimidated or reluctant if that happens. If a thorough job of research has been done and you and your agent have clear communications, it's a likely possibility. It is not necessary to look at ten, or even five, homes if you already know which one you want. Just get the offer in before someone else does.

But let's assume, for discussion purposes, there are three homes you like, any one of which will meet your needs.

Choose the one you like the best. It's that simple.

It is? Of course it is. Don't feel nervous about that, either. Here's why.

This is going to be your home. It is to be expected that your choice will be based on many subjective things that we lump together under the category of "emotional appeal." If you are fortunate enough to find an affordable home you love, grab it! Looking gift horses in the mouth has never been a good policy.

But we do have to consider practicality as well as emotional appeal, don't we? Yes, we do.

And that is why, here in Hawai'i, we have some time after an offer is made and accepted that we call "the due diligence period." It's usually ten to fourteen days, although that's a negotiable factor. During that time, you will be given written information that falls under the general heading of "disclosures." You will order, pay for, and be present for a professional physical inspection of the home, after which you will receive a written report about its condition.

You will have the opportunity to ask any and all questions that may be important to you and to get satisfactory answers. All of this happens before you are legally bound to your contract. If you discover negative factors that change your mind during the "due diligence" period, you may cancel with no risk to your deposit funds and without being in breach of contract. (This subject is dealt with in greater detail later in the book.)

The most common situation is that you will find a home you like a lot, or even love a lot, but that is not perfect. Here's the plain truth, and the sooner you accept it the better for your satisfaction and ultimate happiness: There will be no perfect home unless you build it yourself, and even then there will be something about it you'd have done differently after the fact.

These imperfections can be broken into two categories: Things you can change and things you can't. Be careful with "can't." Almost anything can be done, up to and including tearing the whole thing down and starting over. Maybe a better expression would be "things that can't be changed without unreasonable time and/or expense."

Here's where you need to have a clear understanding of yourself and the others who will be living in the house, as well as a clear grasp of your personal capabilities.

Don't let the state of replaceable items in the house such as appliances adversely affect your decision.

Sometimes the analysis is easy. You love the house, hate the carpet. Or the house is great, but the fridge is ancient and rusty. Never select a home based on the condition of appliances; the color, type, or condition of carpet or vinyl flooring; or the color of the paint. If you love those features, that's a great bonus. If you don't, take them into consideration on the purchase price, of course, but don't, for heaven's sake, reject the property. Things like this are called "cosmetic" for a reason. Learn to look past the cosmetics and evaluate the house on its more substantive merits. It's just as silly to base a $400,000 purchase decision on a refrigerator that may have cost $2,000 tops, as it would be to marry a woman because you like her shade of lipstick.

If you love the house, can live with the rug/fridge/paint/whatever until you have time/money to change them, fine. Buy the house.

If you love the house but feel changes must be made immediately, take them into consideration when you make your offer and get actual estimates during the due diligence period.

Note 1: Do not put the home inspector on the spot by asking him to estimate costs. He may not be qualified, certainly is not hired to do that. Get an actual quote from someone who can guarantee it. It's likewise not recommended that you get a contractor to do an as-is home inspection. His desire for work may impact his objectivity.

Note 2: Try to discover whether the seller has already taken damaged or defective items into consideration in the asking price. Do this by analyzing comparable sales and discussing the features in question with your agent.

Note 3: Understand the drastic difference between something you don't like and something that is damaged or defective. One is a matter of taste, the other a matter of value. Make your offer based on value. Don't, for instance, expect a carpet credit of $10,000 when the carpet is brand new but you don't care for the color.

If you want work done on the house, make sure you know which building permits will be required.

What if you want to change things that aren't cosmetic, maybe something expensive or involving major work, but you still love the house?

This is where the nitty gets gritty. So here's how you figure it out.

If the work you want done requires a building permit, make sure the changes can be permitted under the governing building codes. (Think twice before you do "renegade" construction—and then don't do it. It affects your resale value later on, and the work itself may be substandard—a prime example of penny-wise-pound-foolish decision-making.)

What if some feature of the house did not have a permit when one was required at the time it was done? This is sometimes complicated. Building codes change over time, and lots of improvements need a permit now, but did not in years past. In Hawai'i, if an improvement was permitted or allowed to be done without permit at the time the work was done, it is considered "legal" now even if the same improvement would be treated differently now (the abbreviated term is "grandfathered"). A typical example is lānai enclosures done years ago. Another is GFCI (ground fault circuit interrupter) outlets in kitchens and baths. Before you get agitated over a missing permit, make sure a permit was needed at the time of construction. If so, then decide whether it is important to correct that now.

If there are substantial unpermitted improvements—an entire bathroom, for instance—you may also want to consult a contractor as to whether a retroactive permit can be obtained. (It will require that the improvement be brought up to current code.)

Unpermitted and un-grandfathered improvements do affect the property's value and should be taken into consideration on the price. See Note 2 on page 69.

When considering a property such as this, remember you may have as many different types of inspections as you want during the due diligence period, so long as you pay for them. (What about asking the seller to pay for them? Bad idea. You want inspectors who are hired by you and are responsible to you. The only exception is the termite inspection. Customarily, that is the seller's responsibility to pay for, but you select the inspector.)

I once represented the buyers of a home that was a serious fixer-upper. My clients loved the lot and the bare bones of the house. They also wanted to live in this particular upscale neighborhood, but their budget put them out of the running for other homes there. They believed they had a good eye for beauty, good fix-up skills, and several friends and family members in various building trades who could help them if they needed it.

However, three general contractors had already looked at this house with an eye toward remodeling for resale and decided it was a tear-down. The roof leaked, which had caused dry rot. Termites had been dining in the beams. Tree roots had undermined the concrete slab foundation in a couple of places. This had caused the walls to shift, creating a gap in the walls at one corner of the kitchen through which six inches of daylight was visible. The appliances were antiquated, as were the bath fixtures, and there was only one bathroom—for this family of four.

And my clients loved this house! On top of that, they knew it was probably their final opportunity to get a foot in the door of this neighborhood. What were we to do?

Don't take the unsubstantiated opinions of those contractors, I advised, but do protect yourselves. Get it inspected by people who work for you, and let's have enough time for due diligence that we can have follow-up inspections if need be. You'll have to pay for them, I added, but better you spend several hundred now than find out you've wasted multiple thousands later. Okay, they said, let's write it up.

First, we had a general home inspector. As I recall, we then had two roofers, an architect, a general contractor, a painting contractor, a structural engineer, a plumber, and an electrician. As buyer's agent, I was present for all nine separate and independent inspections that were done on that property before my clients proceeded with their purchase, feeling they now knew everything that could be known about what they might face in the remodeling.

The house is just lovely now, and my clients netted something like $300,000 when they sold it a couple of years later to "move up."

There are several points and lessons to be learned from this story, but they all boil down to the need to intelligently analyze the facts. The emotional decision, "we love this house" was tempered by rationality. This couple knew, no matter how much they loved the house, if it could not be saved, it would not be to their ultimate benefit to buy it; they had enough self-discipline to trust that they would not make a bad decision if that were the case. They also knew they didn't know it all and understood that good professional advice does not come free and were willing to pay fairly for it. (Actual cost estimates are usually free, but that's when the contractor knows you're going to buy the house and hopes for actual work to result. Inspections prior to purchase are an entirely different animal.) They also knew their budget and spent hours carefully evaluating their costs. These people were not gambling. They bought a substandard house in a great area, knowing their intelligence, ingenuity, creativity, and hard work would add to its value. It's called creating "sweat equity."

Lots of people have made lots of money this way, and/or been able to live in a neighborhood they could not otherwise afford. But fixer-uppers need a certain kind of person. You need to know if you are that kind before you get involved in a major project.

First decide what the term fix up means to you. Depending on the individual, it can be anything from changing carpet and paint or remodeling a bathroom to a top-to-bottom renovation or a substantial addition. Discuss this with your spouse if you have one. You may be surprised to find out that your partner has an entirely different concept—and maybe a totally different level of tolerance. After you've come to an understanding, communicate carefully and clearly to your agent just how much of a fixer you are willing to handle.

Then objectively and logically decide what your personal skills and capabilities are. Do you have a great eye for décor, but fall down when it comes to budgeting? Are you a champ at finding bargains, but not so great at figuring out how to put them together so they look nice? Does tearing down walls scare you? Is plumbing one of the world's great mysteries? Determine what kind of help you're going to need and realistically figure it into your budget.

And what about your family's tolerances? How long is this fix-up going to take? Living in a construction site may not be safe for small children and almost certainly won't be comfortable. It's probably not a good trade-off to sacrifice your marriage for the sake of making some money on a house remodeling. There are many considerations. Only you can know what they are.

 Now here's a tip for bargain hunters: Dirt and damage are not the same thing.

When I hear a buyer say, "What a shame. This would be a nice house if only it weren't so filthy," I just cringe. I know that buyer's attention is not focused where it belongs.

Of course, everyone notices if a place isn't clean. People react negatively to a dirty house and it drives its sale price down. Sharply. I've seen simple dirt and grime cost sellers as much as $10,000 in the ultimate price. That's a lot to lose for the sake of saving the cost of a cleaning service!

What to Expect (and Not to Expect) about Hawaiian Home Construction

✔ Central air conditioning is very unusual, especially in older homes.

✔ Heating is practically nonexistent. (A fireplace is a huge luxury feature.)

✔ Insulation is unusual, too: It's never been important for houses to be "tight" because climate control on the interior has never been important.

✔ Washers and dryers are often found outside the back door or in the carport, rather than inside the house.

✔ Single-wall construction was the norm here for many years, although new homes must now be built with double walls.

✔ While pitch-and-gravel roofs have now been largely replaced with newer, longer-lasting types, they may still be found.

✔ Attics are usually just crawl spaces above dropped ceilings.

✔ Basements are also very uncommon.

None of the above are considered "defects" or "substandard" in Hawai'i. When unexpected items are present, they do add value to a home.

Other things to keep in mind in Hawai'i:

✔ Many wonderful homes don't have any particular street appeal, and all of their great features are inside or in the back of the house. Go inside! Don't reject a home from the street unless it's incurably terrible.

✔ Many homes in excellent areas are relatively simple in terms of construction, fixtures, and cosmetics.

✔ Year-round outdoor living makes spacious interior areas relatively less important and outdoor space, privacy, and amenities relatively more so.

When you are looking at property as a buyer, try hard not to consider whether a house is clean, whether it has a lot of clutter, or whether the furniture is placed nicely or whether you like the furniture or art work or anything else that's going to be removed when the seller leaves.

The neighborhood question

Why haven't I yet mentioned the standard real estate statement— "The three most important factors in choosing a home are location, location, and location"?

Well, it's trite. But let's say it anyway:

It's better to buy the cheapest home in the best neighborhood you can beg, borrow, or bargain your way into than a great house in a lesser area.

Period.

Taking that as a given, how do you know which neighborhoods are great? Your selection of a neighborhood is as personal to you as is the house itself and maybe even more important. Decide what neighborhood factors matter most and communicate this to your agent. You may be surprised at what you learn about yourself in this process. A wealthy, or wealthier, area may be far down on your list after careful analysis. Schools, parks, churches, shopping, family atmosphere, executive homes, beaches, fishing grounds, convenience to work, etc., may be of much higher priority.

Watch and observe. Drive around interesting areas, or areas your agent has shown you. See what's generally going on. Does everyone bar their windows and keep big dogs? Do the children play outside freely? Do you see neighbors visiting and talking with one another? Look for signs of a place you'd like to call home, a place where you'll be comfortable.

Familiarize yourself with local customs and lifestyle. Mainlanders are often surprised to discover that what we tolerate with a grain of salt is totally unacceptable where they come from and vice versa. That which we would see as a warning sign (bars on the windows) may be the rule rather than the exception where you come from. Signs of a blighted or deteriorating area where you come from (broken-down vehicles on the road or in driveways, for instance) may only be an indication of disposal difficulty in Hawai'i. Nobody's trying to make you change your standards. It's just important for you to realize that signs and symptoms may have different meanings here, and you need to interpret them correctly.

Here's something else in Hawai'i that may be very different elsewhere: Newer is not necessarily better. First, because a new area may not have had time to become established, it may not be possible to tell how successful or desirable it will become. But mostly, the very best land for housing was used up long ago. And land here is very, very expensive, relatively speaking. (On O'ahu it is reported that an average 60 to 75 percent of the sales price of an existing home represents the value of the land.) Therefore, you may discover that newer subdivisions have smaller house lots, are inconveniently located or have topography that makes construction difficult, expensive, or both. Remember, you can change just about anything you choose in your home or rebuild from scratch—but you can't change the land it sits on and where that land is located.

Check out schools and talk to authorities such as the police.

Meet a few people who live there: Maybe you can strike up a casual conversation, maybe your agent or friends know someone to introduce you to.

Ask your agent about "turnover" and the ratio of owner-occupants to tenants. Low turnover and high ratios of owner-occupants are good indicators of a stable neighborhood.

Ask friends and coworkers what areas they consider desirable.

Condominiums may be neighborhoods unto themselves. You can learn a great deal by reading the minutes of owner association meetings (which should be provided to you as part of the "condo docs" after you make an acceptable offer). There you should discover any problems serious enough to warrant association concern—a rash of burglaries, car thefts, excessive noise complaints, etc. More subtly, you'll get a general sense of "what kind of place it is." The financial

Location, Location, Location

The factors that contribute most to the monetary value of property may differ in Hawai'i, too. What are those factors?

✔ Land area: In Hawai'i the proportional value of land vs. improvements (house and amenities) always favors land; an estimated 60 to 75 percent of the value is usually in the land.

✔ "Usable" land area: Land that can be used for buildings, pools, gardens, etc., has more value than land that simply distances you from your neighbors.

✔ View.

✔ Privacy.

✔ School district. (Even if you don't have children yourself, or if your children go to private schools, schools matter to many buyers and do affect property values.)

✔ Proximity to the ocean, especially a good swimming beach.

✔ Proximity to church, shopping, university, work, medical and/or emergency facilities, and other highly used amenities.

✔ Parking.

Some factors that can negatively affect monetary values are:

✔ Flood inundation or tsunami areas.

✔ Unstable or filled land.

✔ Lack of connection to a sewer system.

✔ Bad traffic.

statements and operating budget (also provided in those "condo docs") will tell you, among other things, where the association chooses to spend its money and what items it considers important to the general welfare of the building or townhouse project.

> *There's one final note that I was hesitant to include, but decided I must. Once, long ago, I received a call from a potential home buyer, a woman who had just moved here from the mainland. "Can you find me a white neighborhood?" she asked.*
>
> *I almost dropped the phone. "I beg your pardon?" I made my voice cold, hoping she'd back off. She didn't.*
>
> *"A white neighborhood," she insisted. "You know what I mean. I want to live with the right kind of people."*
>
> *"I can't do that," I told her then. "I'm sorry." And I hung up. That was the first and only time I've ever hung up on somebody. Thankfully, it's also the only time anyone has ever asked me to do that—either baldly, as she did, or even implicitly.*

I was offended, yes, but that doesn't matter here. The point is, it's completely unethical and simply wrong to ask an agent to commit illegal discrimination, so don't do it.

Your home as an investment

The investment aspect shouldn't be ignored. A home is, after all, the most important and expensive purchase most Americans make in their lives. And, strangely enough, the things that make a home work for you usually also make that home a good investment.

Clients have a habit of asking, "So, how much do you think this house will be worth next year?" (Or in two years, or five, or whatever.) I can't answer that question. No one knows. The actual dollar value of appreciation of a particular home at a specific time is largely influenced by economic factors we can't control and trying to predict them in advance is—well, risk, is an understatement. Hawai'i's real estate cycles are discussed in the chapter on buyer's and seller's markets, though, and may give you a good sense of how to time your transactions.

But, your home is worth far more than the appraiser's dollar-evaluation: It satisfies the fundamental human need for shelter. Other assets may be reflected only on pieces of paper such as stock certificates or bonds, and sometimes can become completely worthless. Not so with residential real estate in Hawai'i. If you don't need to use your property yourself, someone else will gladly pay for the privilege. Rental markets in many areas in Hawai'i have had "zero-vacancy factors" for years and years and will continue to be that way for the foreseeable future—as long as more people want to live here than can fit on our Islands.

So keeping your property in good order pays off big-time for many reasons and certain things will maximize its value regardless of the economy.

Keep your home well maintained, in good repair, and clean outside and in.

Buy in the best neighborhood you can afford.

Don't overbuild. There is usually a "neighborhood ceiling," or a price point above which homes in a given area do not sell. The dollar figure changes over time, but the principle does not: If a home is much larger or more elegant and upscale than homes in the surrounding area, it will not sell for the same price as a comparable house in a better area. If you are considering buying a home that you will sell in order to move up, it's more sensible to keep your upgrades and improvements in line with what's around the neighborhood. If you must make enlargements or improvements that violate this principle, go ahead. Just don't expect to regain the entire investment if you sell the property any time soon. (There are certain improvements that can be relied upon to increase your property's value, though; those are dealt with elsewhere.)

Bottom line: Selecting a home for emotional reasons is natural and important. You should never disregard those reasons, but you should back them up with sound and rational thinking. Your home can be much more than just a place to live, and as with any investment, careful management and logical financial analysis pay very big dividends.

10

Negotiating the Best Possible Contract

It's time to make that offer

You've thought, planned, hunted, and found a home you love. You want to buy it. You have an appointment with your agent to write an offer. Actually sign something. Wow! Is that scary, or what? Maybe you should pull out now before it's too late.

Oh, for goodness' sake! It's the only way you'll ever get what you want. Besides, everybody on the face of the planet gets nervous buying a home. Why should you be any different? If you've done your job and followed the steps, you've made a good selection and have every right to feel confident about your decision.

The offer will probably be made on a standard form. "DROA," **Deposit Receipt Offer and Acceptance** is used in Hawai'i. Your agent will fill it out for you, review it with you, and make sure that you understand it and that it reflects your intentions accurately. If you and your agent have communicated clearly, you can sign with confidence.

A note of warning: Do not negotiate verbally or make a verbal offer, no matter how tempted you may be to display your wheeling and dealing skills. We have a saying in Hawai'i real estate that probably is heard often elsewhere as well: An offer that's not in writing is no offer at all. Despite any and all legal opinions about verbal contracts, a verbal offer will not be taken seriously. If you are a buyer, do the paperwork. If you are a seller, demand it.

With the initial offer, you are opening the negotiation phase of your transaction. Whether this phase ends quickly or goes back and forth with counteroffers multiple times, you no longer solely control

Considerations for Negotiating with "Smarts":

✔ What is the present market climate? Is it a strong sellers' or buyers' market?

✔ Is there a lot of inventory on the market?

✔ Are defects or problems reflected in the asking price?

✔ Is the asking price logical in terms of the above?

✔ What negotiable issues besides price may make an offer more or less acceptable?

1. Closing date.

2. Occupancy date.

3. As-is condition.

4. Building permits.

5. Repairs or credits for repairs at closing.

6. Inclusion or exclusion of appliances, fixtures, furnishings, or items of personal property.

7. Closing costs.

8. Seller financing. (See "Doing the Math")

9. Tax issues. (Structuring a transaction so the parties can take full advantage of available tax breaks is up to the experts, but willingness to work with the other party to accomplish that is a great negotiating tool.)

10. Indications through behavior that the other party will perform obligations in a timely and responsible manner.

what happens. The seller's decisions—and your best guess as to what the seller's decisions will be—now come into play.

To negotiate the best possible contract, you need to be clear in your own head about your own needs. And it will be to your significant benefit if your offer reflects an understanding of the seller's point of view. So, put yourself into the other side's shoes, and when you make your offer, use your insight to make it as enticing as possible to the seller while it simultaneously satisfies your own requirements.

On the face of it, you're negotiating for the highest possible price if you are the seller and for the lowest possible price if you are the buyer. But most transactions end up with both seller and buyer obtaining a "fair value," and most negotiations have to do with more than simple price. Why? Because people are emotionally involved with their homes and there's more involved in "fair value" than money.

Most transactions end up with both the seller and buyer obtaining a "fair value."

But let's deal with money first.

Fair dollar value

Fair dollar value is established primarily by current economic conditions that no individual controls. Last year doesn't matter; neither does tomorrow. Today is all that counts.

If you need a home now, you need it now. If you can afford to buy one now, you should do so. Cycle after cycle, over many years, has proven that waiting for the market to drop is a losing strategy for buyers and home ownership is a winning one. Likewise, if you need to sell now, you're going to have to deal with today's values.

Here are the facts that real estate brokers and sophisticated real estate investors already know and that you should take to heart when negotiating.

If a seller has correctly priced his property for the current market, he will get that price, or close to it. He will not have to consider unreasonably low offers because he will receive better ones in a reasonable period of time. If a seller has underpriced his property because he is "really motivated," he will probably get more than one offer and at least one of those offers will reflect the fair market value.

There's no harm in trying a lowball offer on a correctly priced home—except wasting your time and being disappointed. You probably won't get anywhere; if you do, consider it your lucky day and grab that property while you can.

Look for a property that's priced fairly to begin with.

But if you make a lowball offer on a home that's priced too high for current conditions, it's not really a lowball offer, is it? If the comparable sales for the area are far below the asking price, then you are probably dealing with a seller who isn't realistic or isn't really motivated to sell. There are people who put their properties on the market just to see what will happen, but this is rare. There's so much work involved in marketing a house that most people only do it if they're serious. More likely, the seller has rose-colored glasses when it comes to his own home, or his agent hasn't correctly advised him. This can be due to inexperience, inadequate research, or just wanting the listing so badly that the agent makes irresponsible promises in order to outdo the competition. It really doesn't matter to you as a buyer.

Whatever the reason, if an agent advises her client not to accept a low offer, that client most likely will listen. Unfortunately, human psychology is such that if that same agent urges her client to take a low offer, he probably will not listen. Either way, the buyer is fighting an uphill battle.

It's a better strategy to look for a property that's priced fairly to begin with. Then, if, after studying the comparable sales data and closely looking at the house itself, you feel a fair offer would be something less than the asking price, at the very least your offer should be dealt with seriously and respectfully and a meeting of the minds may result.

So, what are the other negotiating points besides price?

Here's where you need to know something about the seller's needs.

Buyers usually try to find out why a seller is selling to determine motivation—a backdoor strategy to find out if the price can be pushed down. I usually say motivation doesn't matter and under normal circumstances, it doesn't. (If you're dealing with a distressed property or a foreclosure, read that section for the rules that may apply.)

However, certain other specifics do matter, and here are a few of them.

Closing date is a biggie. If a seller needs his transaction to close by a certain deadline, he'll be more likely to negotiate with a buyer who can accommodate him. The best strategy in this case is to be up-front. Have your agent ask the seller's broker when the seller wants to close and whether the date is important. Let the seller know you'll cooperate if you can, and keep your word. This sets you up as a good guy, and greases the wheels for getting some perks that may matter to you.

The ubiquitous "as-is condition" addendum (discussed at length elsewhere) is another significant factor that can work two ways, depending on the seller's circumstances. It can be very important to some sellers to have a deal that doesn't involve repair issues, while others are willing to bend over backward doing repairs and fix ups in order to get a better price. Sometimes the seller's position is evident: The listing offers credits for such things as new carpeting or roof repairs; or, conversely, a house in perfect order. Other times a discreet conversation between your agent and the seller's agent can be very enlightening and beneficial in determining the seller's preferences and attitude.

Finding out just what the seller prefers before making your offer may allow you to use that as-is addendum to your best advantage

---

Never Negotiate Away

- ✔ A specified period of time in which to conduct any and all inspections and research, as well as to review documents (the due diligence period).

- ✔ A specified time for review of the seller's disclosure.

- ✔ A provision that should either diligence or review fail to satisfy the buyer *for any reason*, he may cancel the contract without penalty, even when an as-is condition addendum has been signed.

when negotiating the price. If, for example, you observe that the house may need a new roof in the next couple of years, you can specifically refer to that item in your offer. Including something like, "Buyer is aware house may need a new roof and specifically accepts the existing roof in its present as-is condition," lets a seller know you will not try to renegotiate the price or cancel the contract if your home inspector reports the roof is in marginal condition. Directly addressing obvious issues at the initial stage of negotiations may make a lower offer more palatable to a seller and identify you as an up-front kind of person who isn't playing games.

As a note of caution: A successful strategy depends not only on the attitude of the seller, but also on tact and diplomacy.

> *One of my associates recently received an offer on one of her listings, accompanied by a strongly worded cover letter from the buyer's agent that itemized at least ten negative features from worn carpet to an ancient ceiling fixture in the kitchen, everything the buyer didn't like. It appeared the agent thought pointing out all those things would make the seller more amenable to the offer, which was on the low side. The seller's broker shared that letter with several of us before presenting the offer.*
>
> *"If they see this, they'll reject it out of hand," she said. "Do I have to show it to them?"*
>
> *After some discussion, we decided the agent had good intentions—wanted the seller to know the offer was "as-is" and the buyer wouldn't ask for repairs or replacements later on. But it was phrased in such a negative, insensitive way that the agent was undermining her own clients—and herself. Ultimately, before she presented the offer, the seller's broker asked the buyer's agent to rewrite the letter, saying simply that the buyer loved the home, was aware of various old fixtures and cosmetic items and was accepting them as-is. Eventually, then, after some negotiation, the offer was accepted.*

Negative comments can blow your offer right out of the water. Or if condition issues have already been taken into consideration in the asking price, trying to push the price even lower may make you

Ten Tips for a Successful Negotiation

1. Make all proposals and counterproposals in writing; do not respond to verbal proposals.

2. Reply to written offers and counteroffers within the required time frame.

3. Make intelligent offers and counteroffers based on current market facts.

4. Include a lender's credit preapproval letter with all offers.

5. Accede to issues that are insignificant to you but meaningful to the other party; it will strengthen your position on other, more important points.

6. Make sure all special conditions are truly essential; i.e., you will not transact without them.

7. Make certain all contingencies are included. For example, if the down payment is coming from proceeds from a property that's in escrow, give particulars. (Don't ever leave out a contingency that might make you unable to perform your contract as it is written.)

8. Remember, you can raise the down payment amount at your own discretion, but reducing it requires the seller's permission.

9. Omit or rephrase any language in offers, counteroffers or cover letters that might be personally offensive to the other party.

10. Submit a good cover letter indicating you're interested in taking a cooperative approach.

appear aggressive rather than straightforward. Also, a seller who is emotionally attached to his property (and most are) wants to sell to someone who loves his house. So make certain all criticism is stated tactfully and balanced by a complimentary statement.

Many negotiations begin long before an offer is put in writing.

Many negotiations start long before an offer is put in writing, and neither the buyer nor the seller is aware that that's what's happening. Be very careful of what you say any time you are in the presence of the seller. The idea of setting a seller up to accept a lower offer by talking about what's wrong with the property or saying what modifications must be made in order to suit your needs, or even discussing how you'd remodel the kitchen, is 100 percent a very bad idea. Antagonizing a seller may make him decide he doesn't want to do business with you under any circumstances. And it's equally bad for a seller to allow a potential buyer to hear him say anything about his "bottom line." This is why most agents try not to allow sellers and buyers to meet at any time prior to closing. Be totally frank with your agent but only when you are in private.

Before we leave the subject of attitudes, there's one more hint that may help you if you are a newcomer to the islands. In Hawai'i's multi-ethnic culture, people give the greatest respect to other people who are perceived as humble, or who do business "with a lot of class." The higher your position in society, or the wealthier you are, the more important it is to project an attitude of humility. Arrogance does not pay, nor does a flagrant display of wealth or influence, nor do tactics intended to intimidate. Hawai'i folks are generally soft-spoken. They say, "I don't think so" when they mean "No way," and "I think so" or "Probably" when they mean, "You can take that to the bank."

To obtain the best possible price and terms, don't use bulldozer tactics. Using honey instead of vinegar is the best way to get the most consideration from the other party.

Closing costs are another area that may be important to you. If you don't have a lot of cash, you can ask the seller to pay them for you. This amounts to something like three percent of the purchase price in the average transaction. It doesn't sound like much, but stating it in dollar terms—$10,000 to $12,000 on average—shows you how big a bite that can take out of your available cash. You will undoubtedly have to offer more for the property if you expect the seller to do this. How much more depends upon, among other things, whether the asking price is correct in the first place. If it is, then you may have to add the entire amount on top. However, if the asking price is on the high side, offering full price, or nearly full price, and including your closing costs may salvage both the seller's ego ("I got full price for my house") and your savings account. If the seller absolutely must pay your closing costs for you to buy, your agent needs to know that well in advance of showing you property.

There are many ways smart agents and intelligent buyers and sellers can negotiate an agreement that satisfies all concerned. What must be discovered is—what does the other party want or need besides cash? And then everyone must come to a meeting of the minds as to what those things are worth.

A carefully worded cover letter is essential, especially when price is an issue

In addition to setting a favorable overall tone for a transaction and telling a seller how motivated and qualified you are, it can also initiate other ideas that may lead to a meeting of the minds that have not yet become apparent.

> *I once wrote an offer for a buyer who wouldn't be making her permanent move to the islands for nearly a year after closing. She intended to rent out the property until she was ready to move in. I made a major point of that in the cover letter because her budget was slightly less than the asking price, and I thought it might help if the seller knew how much she loved the home: She was going to buy it a year before she needed it and go through all the potential hassles and expense of being an absentee landlord because she didn't think she'd find one she liked as well if she waited. Little did I know . . .*
>
> *The listing agent called me within hours of receiving the offer. The seller had received three offers, she told me. Ours was the lowest in terms of price. But she added before I could even take a long and disappointed breath, if my client would sign a formal lease agreement with the sellers for an entire year, they would accept our offer. It turned out that the sellers' planned move had been delayed; they were going to take the property off the market altogether and reject all the offers until they read my cover letter and thought there was a chance for a win-win after all.*

Cover Letter Tips

The cover letter is an extremely important tool that almost always leads to smoother and more successful negotiations. It contains information that doesn't belong in the offer itself, but may be very important to a seller. If you are the recipient of a cover letter, read it carefully for "make-or-break" clues and hints about the buyer's sincerity and qualifications. If you are the writer (or your agent is writing it), make sure it is carefully phrased.

1. Make all statements positive. Your offer presumably is based on your perception of the property's condition and speaks for itself.

2. Include some mention of what you like about the property and why you are making the offer. ("The Smiths feel this spacious home will be ideal for their growing family.")

3. Include some personal comments to humanize the negotiation and induce the seller to like you as a person. ("Your home has obviously been well cared for by a happy family. The Smiths want you to know they'll love it as much as you do.")

4. Include something about your job or finances. ("Mr. Smith is a financial analyst who has worked for XYZ company for ten years; Mrs. Smith is a teacher at ABC school.")

5. If this is your highest and best offer, say so. ("The Smiths' lender has informed them this is the best offer that they can responsibly make.") If your offer is an opening move, say nothing.

6. If you have something to offer but you're not sure whether the seller wants it, the cover letter is the place to mention it. ("The Smiths would be glad to rent back the home to the sellers for a month after closing, if that's important to them.")

What To Do When in Doubt About a Condition Issue

Perhaps you've seen a home you want, but there's a question about its condition or some other factor has been discovered during the due diligence period—after the contract has been negotiated. Say the issue is serious or expensive enough to materially affect what you're willing to pay, or perhaps would change the purchase decision altogether. You can choose among several courses of action that will both protect you and allow the seller an opportunity to clarify or solve the issue.

✔ There's no rule that says you can't have a property inspection before you make an offer. (However, most Hawai'i buyers don't choose that option, because while the inspection is being done, the door is open for the seller to accept someone else's offer, and most buyers want to "tie a property up" before spending out-of-pocket funds.)

✔ Ask to see the seller's disclosure before making your initial offer and look for any reference to the issue you're concerned about.

✔ Mention the issue specifically to the seller or his agent and ask for further information before making the initial offer.

✔ Make satisfaction a specific condition. ("This offer is specifically subject to buyer being satisfied that apparent swimming pool cracks involve the plaster coat only, and/or that tree roots have not compromised the pool's integrity.") This tells the seller there's a potential deal-buster. It also gives him a "heads up" about an issue of concern while negotiations are still in process. He may then choose an appropriate action such as: **1)** give you a counteroffer accompanied by a pool inspection report or an estimate of repairs from a licensed pool contractor; **2)** tell you the pool repairs are already arranged at his expense; **3)** tell you he's taken the pool's condition into consideration in the asking price; **4)** tell you the pool's condition is as-is and he doesn't know anything about it. In any case, bringing the issue out in the open doesn't harm your position in any way. Here's why: According to law, the seller must tell buyers everything he knows. If inspections uncover a previously unknown condition, he must disclose it to all subsequent buyers, so he has absolutely nothing to gain by refusing to address the issue with you.

(**Note to sellers:** A primary factor leading to low offers is a buyer's doubt. Don't market a pig in a poke! Be aware of all serious issues with your property, even if you can't afford to fix them before the sale.)

✔ If you'll want repairs made at the seller's expense, it's usually better to ask for a credit at closing so they'll be done by somebody you hire and according to your standards.

✔ Exception to all of the above: Foreclosure homes or bank-owned properties are usually conveyed absolutely as-is, with up-front notice that the seller knows very little about the property and assumes no liability if the buyer later finds an undisclosed defect. These homes are far more likely to be in less-than-ideal condition than other homes. Most often the asking price is calculated using market statistics and an appraiser's or real estate agent's opinion as to what it will bring—without the benefit of a professional inspection. If there's an "upset price," a minimum acceptable dollar amount, it will usually be disclosed prior to offers. Offers are usually treated as take-it-or-leave-it and special conditions or terms are not acceptable. Whenever possible in these cases, do get a home inspection before submitting an offer. If that's not possible, you're forced to make a "best guess." Pencil out the figures and estimate how much you might spend to put the property into acceptable condition, add that to the purchase price and determine if the property is still a good buy. Depending upon how badly you want it and how much competition you anticipate, you may want to offer on a worst-case-scenario basis.

Are there any different negotiating points if you are the seller?

If you are the seller, the first move is made by a potential buyer. Your starting point in negotiations is determined by what that first offer says.

Here are a few seller's strategies to keep in mind:

The most important rule

While I'm sure you've already heard the message that a verbal offer is worth zero, it's more dangerous for sellers to negotiate verbally than it is for buyers. The buyer only risks being disregarded or ignored. The seller who takes a verbal offer seriously risks discouraging other, more sincere buyers. And the seller who discusses price informally with anyone risks that his statements will be misconstrued. Refer buyers who want to engage you in conversation to their agents or yours. Tell insistent buyers politely, but frankly, that they must put their proposal in writing to get a response.

Often the first offer you receive will be the best one.

Often the first offer you receive is the best one you'll ever get. During the first few days or weeks of marketing, all the motivated buyers who have been waiting, and all the agents who have been looking for the right house for their clients will come to see your property. The motivated buyer who truly feels an emotional attachment when he sees it is most likely to make an early offer and to offer more money. If the offer is unacceptable as written, make a counteroffer.

Counteroffer strategies

In fact, it's smart to counter all offers, no matter how unacceptable they may be to begin with. You really can't know whether a buyer has made his best offer until you present him with a written counteroffer detailing exactly what you will accept. The manner in which you counter may give the buyer an idea he hadn't thought of that allows you both to arrive at an agreement.

Ignoring written offers is unacceptable. It identifies your agent as unprofessional and you as rude. (Also, the buyer's agent may ask your agent to prove she showed you that offer.) Besides, what if a buyer makes his best offer today, you ignore it tomorrow, and the day after he comes into money that would allow him to buy your house after all?

Jean Wade used to give us all a very good piece of advice. It was meant for us as agents, but buyers and sellers would be wise to heed it also. "If you have to lose a transaction, let it go," she said. "But do everything you can to salvage your relationships with the people involved. You'll be doing business with them again, one way or another."

Hawai'i law says agents must present all offers, no matter what the circumstances. Period. If you receive an offer after you've accepted another, you may reject it with thanks. However, if the offer would have been acceptable, asking if the offeror would like to be in a back-up position is a far better strategy.

If you have received multiple offers, you may want to accept one as primary and one or more as backup offers; reject any that are unrealistic. Handling multiple and backup offers correctly is dealt with in detail elsewhere.

What about countering the price?

First of all, you need to know what the offer price actually is. There may be more to it than the dollar figure on the first page. If you are asked to pay closing costs for the buyer or make repairs, your actual net price is reduced. Before you decide how to handle an offer, your agent should provide you with an estimate of your total costs that comes very close to what you'll actually see on a closing statement.

Secondly, take careful note of the following: Any time you make a counteroffer, you are opening up a whole new ballgame. The buyer has no obligation to you whatsoever unless you accept his offer as written and on time.

If the price isn't even nearly what you'll take, you have nothing to lose by countering it. In a counteroffer, you may change any and everything, so make sure the other aspects of the proposal are acceptable and amend them if they're not. If you suspect the buyer is sincere but has a budget crunch, you may want to explore ways and means of helping him pay more, such as the closing costs

Early Occupancy

Early occupancy involves a buyer moving into a property before escrow has closed and is sufficiently common that, at least on Oʻahu, the Board of Realtors has prepared a standard form to cover the situation.

It is generally considered a bad strategy. Agents don't like it, do everything they can to avoid it, and for good reason. Among the many possible problems:

✔ If the transaction fails to close, all signed documentation notwithstanding, getting the buyer to move out can be a nightmare.

✔ If something breaks down, or the buyer discovers a problem he didn't notice before, or says he didn't, serious disputes about who is responsible for repairs can arise.

Unlike the seller rent-back, with early occupancy, most of the risks accrue to the seller. If you can avoid it, don't do it.

If you can't avoid it, or at least have good and compelling reasons for allowing it, make sure the buyer has signed a *completely filled-out standard early occupancy agreement*, and don't let him occupy the property under any circumstances until:

✔ The down payment is in escrow.

✔ You have received a copy of the lender's final loan approval document.

✔ The buyer has completed all inspections and has signed off unconditionally on all due diligence issues.

✔ The buyer has done anything else you may require to make you feel secure about allowing him to occupy your property when he doesn't yet own it.

Seller Rent-Back

A very useful strategy when closing date and moving date don't match up, the seller rent-back is usually a short-term agreement, specifically not intended to create a landlord-tenant relationship.

Because that relationship is not established, and the people involved don't usually know each other, caution is appropriate when agreeing to this. It's usually a concession—a favor—granted to the seller by the buyer and the biggest risks are also to the buyer: That the seller won't move out when he promises, that he won't pay any additional rent, or that when he does move out, the property won't be in the promised condition one way or another. A thoughtfully prepared written agreement should take care of most of these concerns.

The rental amount can be anything the parties agree upon, but most often the new owner expects the amount to cover his entire monthly payment, which is broken down into a daily amount and multiplied by the number of days the seller will remain in the property after closing. Commonly, the entire rent-back amount is paid to the new owner at closing, although other arrangements are certainly possible.

A rent-back agreement does not relieve the seller of any responsibilities in the DROA, such as leaving the property clean and in good order, removing all personal belongings (including trash), or making repairs he has agreed to make. It simply delays the time in which he has to do them. If the seller has obviously cared well for the property up to now, that's probably not going to be a great concern, but asking for a refundable deposit to make sure these things are done isn't unreasonable.

If you, as the new owner, are seriously concerned about the seller moving out as promised, you should think twice about permitting a rent-back in the first place. If it's essential to the seller, perhaps he'll agree for escrow to withhold some part of his proceeds until all his contractual obligations have been met. You should consult with your agent, with escrow, and maybe also with your attorney to be sure all your serious concerns are dealt with appropriately.

(For the protection of all concerned, if you're going to rent the property long-term, you should use a standard rental agreement form.)

discussed above or even seller financing. Here is where smart and creative agents on both sides can make all the difference.

What if you receive an offer that's marginally acceptable, but you'd like to see if the buyer will pay a little more? This is tricky because in countering such an offer, you may lose the transaction entirely. Whatever you do, don't ask your agent to find out in an informal manner whether the buyer will pay more. That's the mark of a novice, but more importantly, the buyer is not bound to any agreement unless it's officially signed. Your intuition, or sometimes things you've overheard in conversation, may give you a clue as to whether the buyer is able to come up with more money. Also, whether your property was priced right in the first place is key to whether you should counter a good offer. My advice: If there's been a lot of interest in your property and your agent believes you'll get more offers relatively soon at or near the offered price, try a counteroffer. If not, think hard about whether you're being penny-wise and pound-foolish.

Bottom line: *For buyers:* The most acceptable offer to a seller will be one that reflects and respects his needs, and it's not always all about the money. Anything you can do for him that does not work against you will make your offer stronger and more likely to succeed. Find out what the seller values that you can add to the pot and present yourself in a manner that makes him like you and want to do business with you. Fair initial offers work better than ones that are too low. If negotiations reach the point where you don't want the property if you have to pay even a single dollar more, have your agent tell the seller's agent this is your highest and best offer and stand firm. If that offer fails, move on.

For sellers: Get an accurate estimate of the true offer price and your true net proceeds before accepting an offer. It's best to counter all offers, no matter how unsatisfactory, unless an offer from someone else has already been accepted. Find out the buyer's financial position to the best of your ability and, if you're anywhere near a meeting of the minds, try to find a creative way to make the transaction work. Remember the most motivated buyers show up early in the marketing process; your first offer may be the best you'll receive. Listen to your agent's advice about the likelihood of better offers before countering small differences in price or other nonessentials.

Disclosures
and Due Diligence

First, my own disclosure: I'm not qualified to give legal advice. I'm a realtor, not a lawyer. This chapter won't tell you how to litigate your way through problems. Its intent is to provide basic general information for laymen who are transacting in good faith and to offer advice gained from my own experience. You should discuss specific issues with your agent. If you are not satisfied with her answers, contact a real estate lawyer before closing on a property.

Basically, the law is this: A real property seller in Hawai'i is required to disclose everything that may affect the value of the property in the eyes of a reasonable person *before* a buyer is contractually obligated to complete the transaction.

Agents provide sellers with a form—a checklist to be filled out that covers most common issues—that is reprinted in the chapter on "The Paperwork." If a seller knows something pertinent that isn't covered by the form, he is also required to disclose it. It's important to remember, unless otherwise stated, that the seller is making the disclosure as a layman. (If he is a contractor, a real estate agent, or other professional who would be expected to have more extensive knowledge, he is required to disclose that fact.)

Note: It's perfectly acceptable to ask for the disclosure before making an offer. But don't be surprised and don't worry if you're told it's not ready yet. The law says it must be given to you, and you must be given a specific number of days afterwards in which to review it. Until that has happened, you won't be bound to a contract unless you unwisely give away your rights. (See box on following page.)

Due Diligence Do's

✔ Read the disclosure carefully with an eye toward areas of special concern to you.

✔ Question gray areas and red flags in writing *before* the deadline for acceptance.

✔ Ask for clarification of anything you don't understand. (There's no such thing as a stupid question, but failing to ask it may not be too bright.)

✔ Make sure all condominium documents are the most recent available.

✔ Read the meeting minutes, house rules, bylaws and financial information with particular attention.

✔ Determine what areas of responsibility belong to the condominium owner as opposed to the owner's association.

✔ Attend the formal inspection(s) of the property, pay attention to the inspector's verbal commentary as he walks you through, ask as many questions as you want, take as much time as you need.

✔ Read the written report carefully; don't hesitate to call the inspector if you have more questions.

✔ Verify questionable information with the appropriate authorities.

✔ Pay attention to your deadline for due diligence performance and ask in advance for extensions if you need them.

What do you look for? How much can you rely on the disclosure? How can you tell the difference between what's important and what's not? What do you do about questions?

First of all, look for how long the seller has owned the property and whether he has actually lived in it. If it's been fifteen years and the seller is an owner-occupant, it's likely the disclosure will have much more detail and useful information than if it's only been a year or the seller is an owner-landlord. In the latter cases, you will need to rely more heavily on your own investigation.

You will have a specific period of time to investigate and inspect the house.

What's important is that beauty is in the eye of the beholder—or the buyer. Most people would say disclosures about the roof are important, or about the swimming pool, the foundation, maybe the plumbing or electrical systems. However, your personal needs and requirements might necessitate a hard look at something other people would find relatively insignificant. Read the whole document carefully. In particular, note things you did not notice when you looked at the property, or things that were not on the fact sheet or otherwise disclosed before you made your offer.

You have a right to a full and complete disclosure about anything the seller knows, but he may not know all there is to know. That's where "diligence" comes in. Basically, that means you (with the help of your agent) are responsible for confirming statements the seller has made, and also finding out for yourself things the seller may not be aware of. You will have a specific period of time to complete that investigation. Do not ignore either the investigation or the time frame.

A very important part of due diligence involves a professional home inspection. You, the buyer, will have to pay for it. As I write this, an expense of between $300 and $450 is common, depending on the size of the home. Many buyers are reluctant to spend that money or think substituting a personal friend or relative who knows something about construction is just as good. Others think a licensed contractor is a better idea. However, a friend or relative may not have comprehensive knowledge and a contractor may be more interested in obtaining work than alerting you to issues that may affect your decision to buy. Also, many contractors are specialists only in certain areas: A roofer, for instance, may know very little about electrical or plumbing systems.

You can have as many inspectors as you want but waiving inspections altogether is foolish in the extreme. If you don't have one in mind, your agent will provide you with names. Call them, talk to them, then hire the one you feel most comfortable with. He or she will inspect all the visible and accessible areas of the home in a non-invasive manner. The inspector should have access into all the rooms, the attic and basement if those exist, and to the plumbing and electrical areas. However, he is not permitted to poke holes in walls, pull up installed carpeting, or do anything else that might be regarded as destructive. You will receive a written, detailed report of everything found and will walk through the house with the inspector as he itemizes the details.

After that is done, you may have questions about some of the findings or want more detailed professional inspections of specific items. You can have more inspections (my personal record is nine on a single property), so long as you pay for them and they are completed within the time frame spelled out in the DROA.

If a "red flag" appears, and you cannot obtain satisfactory answers on time, instruct your agent in writing to defer approval of the physical condition of the property. The seller is not required to give you additional time, though, so negotiate a comfortable amount in

---

Warning

As of this writing, the standard DROA form indicates that a buyer *must notify a seller by the stated deadline if he does not approve the results of his due diligence inspections and research.* Silence, in this case failure to tell the seller of a question or problem, means the buyer has approved the results and waived his right to cancel the contract based on them.

Most agents do provide a written approval letter, but it is not required for a contract to become binding upon the buyer. Don't unknowingly give away your rights.

the first place. Ten to fourteen days is common in Hawai'i, but if the property is large, complicated, or very expensive, you may want or need more. If you request a time extension, make sure it's for an important reason and be prepared to make a difficult decision if your request is denied: Either cancel the contract or proceed without a satisfactory answer.

For townhouses and condominiums make sure to inspect it's building permits.

Another important thing to examine in single-family homes and in townhouses and condominiums that have been renovated is building permits. Frequently the seller's agent provides a "package" for the buyer of the entire public record regarding the property. All the building permits ever obtained for it will be included. You may want to request that package as part of your offer, especially if you have observed modifications to the original home or apartment. (These are fairly expensive—$75 minimum at this time—and consist of many, many pages, so they aren't normally handed out until there is an actual contract in escrow.) The standard DROA requires the buyer be given the latest copies of condominium documents if those are applicable. However, in practice I've found management companies sometimes don't update those packages as they should. If any dates look old to you, verify that you have received the latest documents available and also that the rr-105c (management company's disclosure) has been updated.

What other issues should you pay special attention to? If you plan to make changes to the property once you own it, it would be wise to make sure they are possible and permissible before you accept the results of your due diligence. The list of possible alterations is limited only by your imagination, but here are a few examples.

Say you would like to install central air conditioning. You might like to have the appropriate contractor inspect the property and let you know just what would be involved and what it would cost. The way many of our homes are built makes central air impractical, so you might need to look at alternatives, such as split-system air conditioning or even window units. If you're considering window units in a condominium, you'll need to know if the owner's association allows them.

Or, say you'd like to add a bathroom to the home you're buying out in the country. Some country areas are not connected to a municipal sewer system. In that case, you may not be able to get a building permit unless the property has a private septic system or you install one. In that case, it's important for you to know what kind of waste disposal is already in place, and the total picture of the expense and work involved in adding that bathroom. You'll also need to know where the present plumbing lines are. The home inspection and the disclosure should give you most of the information you'll need, but you still might want to call a licensed plumber for additional advice and cost estimates.

If you're planning an addition or a swimming pool, you need to know the general rules that apply in the area you're buying, and it would be a good idea to have some inkling of the dollars you're talking about, even if you have experience with building in other areas. Building codes here may be very different from what you are accustomed to. Construction costs and practices may also vary widely. Calling in a licensed general contractor or a swimming pool contractor during the due diligence period would then be appropriate unless you are going to buy the property regardless.

Important note: In most cases, the seller is selling the property as it stands. With the rare exception of property sold together with building plans, it is not reasonable to expect a seller to read your mind, be aware of your budget, or know the rules and practicalities surrounding future improvements. It is your job to find out these things.

The following example is oversimplified, but makes the point.

A property that had a main dwelling and a guest cottage was sold to a buyer who intended to "legalize" the cottage—make it a second permitted dwelling unit. After the purchase was complete, the buyer found out he couldn't get the necessary permit because the property did not have room for the required number of parking spaces—in that case, four. The angry buyer wanted to sue the seller. No dice, said his attorney: The seller had never promised that permit could be obtained. It was the buyer who had failed to a) make his offer contingent upon legalizing the second dwelling; and/or b) ascertain the rules that needed to be followed in so doing.

Diligence—Doable When Due

Several years ago, I represented a buyer who was scheduled to be on the mainland, traveling the country on business during the entire due diligence period. He'd found a home he wanted badly, but it was old and several red flags had been disclosed, including termite damage and a forty-year-old cesspool. Despite its condition, the house was in a particularly desirable location and my client knew it would not wait on the market until he returned to the Islands. Common sense said he couldn't allow his emotional attachment to the property to sabotage a good investment decision. What to do?

We did several things: First, we specifically stated in our initial offer that certain important issues had already been disclosed, that the buyer's inspections would determine whether he accepted them or not but that he'd considered them to the best of his layman's ability in making the offer. (This told the seller we weren't intending to claim surprise in order to drive the price down after inspections, unless there really was a surprise.)

Then we negotiated up-front, from the beginning, for a longer-than-usual due diligence period, specifically explaining we anticipated times when the buyer might not be reachable. (Because the due diligence period ties up property, it was important that all concerned be aware that we weren't playing games or trying to take undue advantage.)

Once the offer was accepted, we hired an inspector who made detailed written reports. We made sure he didn't mind allowing more time than usual on the phone to answer questions and reassured him that his phone bill would be reimbursed. No problem and no extra charge, he told us, which made the buyer happy.

Then the buyer asked a relative to accompany the inspector and me during the physical inspection. It's not a good idea to substitute any nonprofessional judgment for your own, but in this case, it was unavoidable and better, in the buyer's mind, than nothing.

We arranged for the buyer to receive the written report by fax and he gave us a list of phone numbers where he could be reached at certain times, along with notations as to time differences in various places. (This would be a lot easier now than it was then, in pre-cell-phone days.)

Finally, the buyer gave me written permission to order additional inspections by other professionals in his absence if issues arose. (I did order one additional inspection—of that old cesspool—and the inspector later told me he'd had about five long-distance phone conversations with my client.)

You may never be in a similar situation, but the story demonstrates key factors that benefit any transaction: Clear communications (both verbal and in writing), straightforward negotiations, and a win-win objective on the part of all concerned. Here's how those factors worked specifically in this case.

✔ Potentially serious issues were disclosed from the beginning, increasing my client's confidence in the seller's honesty.

✔ That was confirmed when the seller respected the buyer's need for extra time and didn't try to curtail or circumvent his evaluation of the property.

✔ Mentioning previously disclosed issues in the offer told the seller that the buyer was negotiating openly, using a logical and rational approach.

✔ The inspector was patient and generous with his time, far beyond the usual three or four hours of a physical inspection.

✔ The seller's agent and I had a trusting relationship based on reputation and past transactions: We each knew the other would make sure the written agreement reflected our principals' true positions clearly and completely.

✔ The seller's agent had a trusting relationship with her client, as did mine with me.

With a win-win objective as top priority for all concerned, my client closed on the house and lived there happily for several years.

Other issues that might influence your decision: View planes or road widening. If your view is important, and you want to be sure nobody can block it, check the rules. If you're concerned about public projects such as road widening, ask the authorities if any are planned.

Confirm any potential deal-busting information during the diligence period. It is your sole responsibility to decide what the issues are and to inform your agent and other involved parties. Don't officially accept the property until you are satisfied. Once you have closed, going back to the seller or your agent, or to anyone else, is difficult, expensive, time-consuming and usually has a negative result. The exception to this, of course, would be if you received actual misinformation of a material nature.

Confirm any potential deal-busting information during the diligence periods.

How and where to dig beyond inspections and records

Many buyers like to hang out in the neighborhood of the home they're considering, talk to neighbors, get a feel for what's happening in the area. Many times neighbors do have plenty of interesting things to tell a buyer. The danger, of course, is confusing rumor with fact. Many people think they know all there is to know about their neighbors and their neighborhood. You'd be surprised how seldom that is really the case. If neighborhood research gleans anything alarming, don't panic until you confirm the facts.

Depending upon your concerns, a few other places to go and people to talk to might include:

> The police department
>
> Neighborhood school principal(s)
>
> Board members of any neighborhood or condominium association
>
> The Department of Planning and Permitting
>
> The Department of Land Utilization
>
> Any authority or expert on a specific subject of concern

There are "gray areas" in the entire disclosure process. Each and every time I've given paperwork to a seller with instructions to "Fill it out completely and accurately to the best of your knowledge," I've been asked, "Do I have to say anything about . . . ?" at least once. In general, the answer is, "If you thought of it, it's important enough to disclose," or simply, "Yes." But many items on the form are subject to at least some interpretation.

Concerns about "notorious incidents" are a conspicuous example. Just what is a notorious incident? How long ago must a notorious incident have happened before you don't have to mention it any more? Certainly a murder in the master bedroom six months ago is more notorious than a burglary five years ago or a homeless man peeing on the sidewalk outside last week. Where can a seller draw the line? Basically, that's the wrong question. If a seller knows something, he needs to disclose it. Whether in his opinion it's significant isn't supposed to matter. It's the buyer's opinion that counts.

Where things get sticky is when a seller thinks something is so innocuous or insignificant that it doesn't need to be mentioned, or when he thinks something is common knowledge and therefore, ditto, or when it's so unimportant in his own eyes that he didn't even notice it happening at all. That homeless man? Might be nothing in the seller's mind. But one man's nonissue can surely be another's deal-buster. What if you, the buyer, have a phobia about homeless people? That sure would change the picture in your mind, wouldn't it? And you'd probably feel used if the seller didn't tell you about it.

So here's what I'd advise buyers: When you read the disclosure, take note of those gray areas. Ask specific questions—in writing—about things that are important to you and insist on written, equally specific, and complete answers. It's better to be a pain in the neck during the due diligence process than to be stuck later on. All the agents I know would agree with me.

Bottom line: Trust but verify.

You may have any professional inspection you want, and any number of them, so long as they are performed at your expense and in a timely manner. Get opinions from qualified experts on significant issues. Actual lies on a seller's disclosure are rare, but there is no guarantee that any seller knows all the facts. The disclosure is usually a layman's opinion and may be only a starting point for your own investigation. If the seller doesn't live in the property or there's something unusual or eccentric about it, dig a little deeper. And do the same if you intend to make changes to the property that require permission from any authorities. Allow enough time in your original agreement to complete that investigation, as the seller has no obligation to give you extensions.

Renegotiating
After the Inspection

There are two reasons buyers try this strategy. One is legitimate; the other not so.

If a buyer discovers a problem during the due diligence period, he often wants the seller to correct it before closing. Sellers try to deal with this in advance by incorporating a document into the original agreement called **The Existing As-Is Condition Addendum**. The addendum is designed to make all concerned aware that the agreement does not include repairs at the seller's expense. If, after his inspection(s), the buyer is unhappy, he may cancel the contract, but he may not demand the seller correct anything. This doesn't mean the buyer can't ask.

Very frequently, right after the formal home inspection and despite the existence of an as-is addendum, the buyer's agent delivers a list of requested repairs to the seller's agent. So: Does the as-is addendum really mean anything?

The answer is simple. Asking for repairs amounts to renegotiating the contract. The seller's bottom line will change. He may or may not find this satisfactory, and he cannot be compelled to make those repairs. In practice, it should come down to common sense and usually does.

Most often, sellers accommodate small repairs. A typical example would be something like a leaking pipe under the sink. If you, as the seller, refuse to fix it for the buyer and the buyer walks away, you'll have to fix it anyway. So fix it now. If there are a lot of small items like this, though, that can run into some money. There are some further strategies that clarify the issue for all concerned.

If you're the seller, take care of as many items as you can before putting the property on the market. If a home appears generally run down, buyers will make lower offers even if each item isn't particularly expensive to repair. Buyers generally estimate repair costs much higher than they are. They may think that if they've seen many small defects, there may be a large one hiding somewhere. And a lot of small repairs add up to a large pain in the neck.

If you are selling the property as a fixer-upper and aren't willing to take care of repairs or delayed maintenance issues, list them on your disclosure statement and also on the as-is addendum. This alerts the buyer to the facts up front and simultaneously tells him there's no point in bringing up the subject later. If he's not willing to accept your position, you can move on to other buyers immediately.

Take the home's condition into account in the asking price. You want buyers to say to themselves, "Even with the cost of repairs, this house will be a great buy and I'm going to love it." You don't want them to say, "This guy is dreaming!"

Agents can arrange for what used to be called a **home warranty**, now referred to as a home maintenance contract or something similar. It generally covers repairs to all major appliances, plumbing, and electrical fixtures for one year after the sale has closed. It's also available to sellers, from listing date until closing. If a covered item breaks, the company will send someone to repair it for a set fee—currently about $50. If the item can't be repaired, the company will either replace it or offer a credit toward the purchase of a new one. This is extremely helpful both in relieving buyers' concerns about older fixtures and appliances and also in minimizing sellers' expenses during the marketing period. Many agents provide this maintenance contract at their own expense, but even if you have to pay for it yourself, the one-time charge of between $350 and $450 can buy you peace of mind. Obtain one and make sure it's noted on all marketing information sheets. Ask your agent for a copy so you can review what's covered and what's not.

What if issues come up that seller wasn't already aware of? Unless the contract includes an agreement to the contrary, the buyer has the right to walk away—whether or not the seller is willing to make repairs. And the seller has the right to refuse to make repairs.

But the buyer or the seller may want to salvage the transaction. Renegotiating the agreement at that point is legitimate and appropriate.

A number of questions must be answered by both buyer and seller before deciding how to handle the situation:

- ✔ Is the "cost-to-cure" substantial?

- ✔ Is it a problem that can't be cured?

- ✔ Does the problem detrimentally affect the value of the property for this particular buyer, or for any buyer? (Remember, once a seller knows about a problem, he has to disclose it to all future buyers.)

- ✔ Is there general agreement about the nature of the problem?

- ✔ Is there general agreement about what the cost-to-cure will be?

- ✔ Does the seller have the funds to make the repair?

- ✔ Is the buyer at the end of his financial resources?

- ✔ What are the attitudes of the principals? Does the buyer think the seller tried to deceive him? Does the seller think the buyer is nit-picking?

- ✔ Is the property as-is still worth what the buyer has agreed to pay, or will the bank's appraisal be low?

- ✔ Will the lender still approve the buyer's mortgage when he learns of the problem?

As you can see, some of the answers are subjective. Others can be handled by research and fact-finding. Still others require creative thinking. Both parties need to use common sense and remain focused on the true issues. Successfully renegotiating an agreement at this point is where a good agent really shines.

In the end, whether or not the transaction proceeds, if all concerned have been fair and equitable, the due diligence and inspection periods have served their purpose.

Strategies to Discourage Buyers From Renegotiating after the Fact

✔ Make all intended repairs before the home is shown to buyers.

✔ Take care of as many "little things" as you can afford.

✔ Include a home warranty at no extra cost to the buyer.

✔ Even if you're not going to make repairs, investigate and know the condition of your property before marketing it, and obtain a realistic estimate of the "cost to cure" any material defects (that may affect the property's value in the eyes of a reasonable person).

✔ Price the property accordingly.

✔ Don't wait until you receive an offer to disclose material defects. Do so immediately, especially if they're not readily visible.

✔ Include detailed records of dates, expense, and extent of all material repairs as part of your disclosure, even if they were made a long time ago.

✔ Specifically address material issues within the contract itself. ("Seller has disclosed and buyer understands that the roof is twenty-five years old. Seller is specifically conveying the roof in its current as-is condition and will neither make nor pay for any repairs.")

✔ If you're willing to contribute toward some repairs, cap them by stipulating a specific credit amount and purpose in marketing materials and the contract itself. ("Seller will give buyer $3,000 as a credit at closing to apply toward floor coverings.")

✔ Continue to show the home until the current buyer has accepted all contingencies.

✔ Seek backup offers and make sure the buyer knows if one is accepted.

The second reason buyers try to renegotiate after the fact is entirely different. Once a property has gone into escrow, it's off the market for all practical purposes. A buyer can then hold a seller's feet to the fire by threatening to cancel the contract during the due diligence period unless he's given further concessions. The alternative—cancellation—may be highly detrimental to the seller's plans and cost him a lot more in the end than giving in.

The ploy works because during the due diligence period, the buyer can cancel his contract for any reason whatsoever. It doesn't have to be a good reason.

Sellers can't stop buyers from trying this ploy. And, no, it's not fair. There are, however, smart ways for sellers and agents to discourage the practice.

Disclose as much material information as possible before buyers make offers, especially things that might normally be regarded as important. Get that **Seller's Disclosure** ready early and give out copies freely.

Include specific mention of problem areas in the original agreement, on an **Existing As-Is Condition Addendum**, worded to indicate that the buyer already knows about the issues and is accepting them up-front.

Read the cover letter prepared by the buyer's agent with an eye toward getting a feel for the buyer's sincerity and motivation. Agents often have a good sense of their clients' attitudes and that may come through between the lines.

Have your agent talk to the buyer's agent. How well does she know the buyer? Is he a past client with a track record? Is he still looking at other homes or does he appear committed?

If possible, and especially if you are suspicious for any reason, find out how long the buyer has been looking for property and if he's made other offers or backed out of other agreements. After the property goes to escrow, continue showing it and ask for backup offers. Better yet, have a backup offer in place and make sure the buyer knows about it.

If a buyer requests an unreasonable and unacceptable price reduction after the inspection, keep in mind that if he really wants to cancel, he will find a way. Cut your losses. Release him immediately and start remarketing. If he's just trying a manipulative ploy, he may back down when his agent tells him you're not willing to renegotiate.

All of the above assumes no legitimate problem has come to light. If something materially detrimental has been discovered, you, the seller, will have to disclose it to every other potential buyer. You may be better off trying to come to an agreement with the one you have.

As a buyer, why shouldn't you try this strategy, and why do I, as a buyer's agent, refuse to use it?

Hawai'i's real estate community is a small one in many ways. Agents know each other. I have to work with my associates year after year. I may also ask other agents to take my word for things from time to time and to cut my clients some slack over one issue or another, and I expect them to accommodate my requests to the best of their ability. If I become known as a "chiseler," for lack of a better word, I can't expect that. Professionally, it's a losing strategy.

Also it's not a great idea to be the buyer who cried wolf. If I (or you, as a buyer) beat a seller up over trivial issues, we may well be brushed off if a truly serious one arises. And, worse, if my client runs into some difficulty and really needs some assistance—an extension of time to close, for instance, or a place to store two containers full of furniture that arrived two weeks early, or whatever—just how likely do you think it is that the seller will do anything he doesn't have to do?

I must trust my client's integrity to represent him in a community where I both live and work, among people upon whom I rely for all my future business. Questionable transactions do become known. Even one can wipe out all memory of ten—or a hundred— straightforward ones. If you, as a buyer, want to establish your own place in your new community, you may want to consider how you'd like people to regard you before trying any less-than-honest strategies.

My other reasons are ethical. I simply believe in fair play and am not interested in participating in the game under any other circumstances. And I've learned my attitude leads my clients to trust me. If I won't help them cheat someone else, I'm highly unlikely to cheat them.

Bottom line: Renegotiating a signed contract is not fair play unless some new material fact has come to light. When that happens, solutions are reached on a case-by-case basis. Many buyers try to negotiate with no valid reason, however, and there's little other than good faith to stop them. Sellers can discourage the practice by disclosing in advance, carefully writing as-is clauses, and learning as much as they can about their buyer before accepting an offer. Sellers can feel more confident when they're working with agents whose integrity is assured and who know their clients well, but there is no guarantee that a buyer won't try renegotiation because buyers are free to cancel a purchase contract for any reason during the due diligence period.

13

Buyer's Remorse:
To Be or Not to Be a
Pain in the Neck

Purchasing a personal home (and selling one, too) can be extremely emotionally charged. But that's natural: How could you be cold-blooded about something as important as your home? Being emotional during the buying process is a good thing. You should care deeply about making the right choice, and nobody with any sense is going to tell you otherwise.

Most people are nervous—afraid of making mistakes or bad decisions—when they're involved in something they don't fully understand, and most home buyers, especially first-timers, feel they don't understand at least some part of what they're involved in. Sometimes they're so anxious they can't even bring themselves to make an offer. Even more often, they become worried and distraught after an offer has been accepted. Did they make a mistake? Is the house really right? Can they really afford it? Have they failed to notice some critical detail that would change their mind? What's the worst-case scenario? This is Buyer's Remorse.

It can take several other forms as well. During the escrow process, nervous buyers may constantly harass their agent, their lender, their escrow officer, and anyone else they can find over small or imaginary problems. Others feel compelled to talk to lender after lender, shopping for more favorable rates, points, and closing costs long after it's possible to change loan programs and still close on time.

Still others keep looking for homes long after their offer has been accepted and put into escrow, afraid to miss out on "something better" that might come on the market.

Have I described you in any of the above? I'll bet I have. So, when is it okay, and when is it not, to be a pain in the neck?

First of all, you need to pay attention to the facts. It's important that you understand yourself well enough to distinguish between irrational panic and concern over real issues. And to avoid that panic in the first place, it's essential to know what to do—and what not to do—to get out of a situation if you must.

If you've honestly and diligently assessed your and your family's serious, no-compromising needs, and the home you're considering meets them, then it's fine to base the rest of the selection process on your emotional reaction: If you love it, buy it. If you don't exactly love it, but you can't find anything better, buy it and remember you can make improvements and/or move up later.

If you've been truthful with yourself as well as with your agent and lender about your budget and your monthly expenses, you can afford the house or your agent wouldn't have written the offer. How can you be sure of that? It's simple. We make no money negotiating offers that fall through because the buyer isn't qualified.

Your due diligence period gives you time to find out all the details, real or imagined, that keep you awake at night worrying.

Beyond that, you need to decide: Do you want to buy a home or not? Asking yourself the following question will let you determine if your concerns are realistic or if you're just having the normal case of nerves all buyers are plagued by from time to time: Would I be worried if I were buying *any* home, or am I just worried about *this* home?

The best strategy in dealing with potential nerves over your offer is to work out your game plan before you look at even a single house. Make sure all involved in the transaction know the necessary essentials for any offer, whether it's price, size, neighborhood, or whatever. Then when you do look at homes, you won't waste time on those that don't meet your needs; more importantly, when you are called upon to make a decision, you will be able to do so with confidence.

If the finance aspects worry you, do your homework ahead of time, take the actions discussed in "Doing the Math" and talk through all your questions with your loan officer at your first meeting. If the lender doesn't have time to satisfy your concerns, find someone who does. Ask what will happen if rates drop during the processing of your application. Ask about discounts for closing costs. Read the truth-in-lending statement you are given. Deal only with reputable lenders who have track records in Hawai'i and get commitments in writing. If you've done all this, you've done everything a knowledgeable and responsible person can do. It's reasonable to expect progress updates every week or so, and if this is happening, you can be sure everything's on track as it should be.

No mortgage is forever, and lenders are very competitive. Reputable and competent loan officers will offer you the very best loan program they have available, for which you and the property qualify. If you think you've found a better loan, make sure you qualify, that it's available in Hawai'i for the property you want, get a written commitment, and then ask your lender to match it, tell you why he can't or prove it's not going to work in your case. Then act accordingly.

If you find a home you like better than the one that's in escrow, yes, you can cancel the escrow during the due diligence period. You'd better be sure that your offer on the other house is accepted, though, or you could lose both. And even so, who's to say you won't find something wrong during that due diligence period? (Oh, by the way, if you have two accepted offers in escrow, you better be sure you have the legal right to cancel one of them or you may discover you've bought two houses.)

It's very common for buyers, especially during an aggressive seller's market, to feel pressured into making quick decisions. That's because agents know the hesitant client doesn't get anywhere. It's extremely tempting to use the available due diligence mechanisms just to get your foot in the door on a transaction. However, it isn't fair, and can backfire to your disadvantage. A far better strategy is to be very clear about your needs and desires in the first place. Then you won't need to use your right to cancel for anything other than its intended purpose.

Don't succumb to unfair tactics. Real estate is a game at which everyone wins only if everyone follows both the letter and spirit of the rules. Make your offer promptly but thoughtfully, after considering all of your options. If it's accepted, keep your end of the agreement and insist everyone else keeps theirs.

When Is Buyer's Remorse Probably All in Your Head?

- ✔ When you can't identify the specific factor that's making you nervous.

- ✔ When you've made and followed a well thought-out advance plan.

When Should You Listen to Yourself?

- ✔ When there's been an abrupt and significant change in your personal or financial circumstances.

- ✔ When you learn new and significant factual information about the property or the area.

How to Avoid Buyer's Remorse in the First Place

Make a fact-based plan that also takes your emotional needs into consideration:

- ✔ Establish a realistic and honest budget and stick to it.

- ✔ Establish your nonnegotiable parameters (the needs your purchase must satisfy) and stick to them.

- ✔ Don't waive any of your contractual rights; conduct due diligence diligently.

- ✔ Don't allow yourself to be pressured

- ✔ Don't make an offer on any property you wouldn't live in if you had to.

- ✔ Communicate your true and honest concerns to everyone involved before getting involved in a purchase contract and during negotiations.

Validate your own emotions:

- ✔ If you're the type who is always nervous, acknowledge and understand that. You can ask others to be understanding and have enough discipline not to victimize them with your fear fantasies.

- ✔ If you're the type who only gets nervous for a reason, but you can't figure out the reason in this case, slow down. Revisit events, figure out what actual fact or piece of information triggered your nerves, and take appropriate action.

A Pregnant Pause

A young couple with one child had worked hard and long to move up from their rented house to a first home, then moved up to a second home, and later purchased another small house for investment. Now, with their second baby on the way, they wanted to purchase a multiunit investment property. They'd planned it well: They wouldn't have to sell either of their two properties and could borrow the cash down payment from the husband's mother. The mother could live in one of the new units, near enough to see her grandchildren regularly but still having a home of her own: compensation for the down payment she provided. The other three units would be rented for almost enough to cover the mortgage payment. The appreciation potential in this extremely popular area near Honolulu was tremendous.

The property inspection went well, I thought, but late that same evening I received a frantic call from the wife. "We can't afford it, Fran! It's just too much risk. Can we still get out of the deal?"

Well, they still could, I told her, but was that a good idea? We knew there was a backup offer in position; there would be no going back if they canceled, and properties like the one they were considering didn't come along very often. After a long conversation in which I reviewed with her all the factors that had led to the purchase decision in the first place, she still couldn't get past her fear. Finally I told her I'd write the cancellation letter in the morning.

Disappointed, I went to bed wondering what I'd done wrong. I didn't think I'd pushed too hard—they'd found the property themselves, had called me. I hadn't miscalculated the income potential either; I was sure I'd estimated the rents on the low side rather than the high. And this had been a long-standing plan, not spur-of-the-moment wishful thinking. We were in a "down market," to be sure, but these were by now sophisticated buyers. They knew this was a good time to buy. Had they just succumbed to fear, thinking the down market would never rise again? Truth to tell, upset over what I was going to have to do first thing in the morning, I didn't get much sleep that night.

> *At eight in the morning, my phone rang once more. It was the wife again. "I'm sorry I did that to you, Fran."*
>
> *"Don't worry about it," I said, trying to keep my voice cheerful. "If you have to change your mind, it's better to do it now."*
>
> *"That's not it," she said. "I mean I'm sorry I put you through that for nothing. We want to buy the place. I'm just pregnant, that's all. I had a 'pregnant moment.'"*

Worst-case scenarios

Your contract is in escrow, you have every intention of keeping your agreement, but your attack of buyer's remorse actually has a foundation: You've discovered something you didn't know before, or your circumstances suddenly change, making you feel your decision was unwise. What to do?

First, tell your agent immediately.

If the problem is financial, you can also call your lender and disclose the change of situation. If you no longer qualify for the loan, you will probably be able to get out of your contract by way of the loan approval contingency. It will undoubtedly be a disappointment to all concerned, but in a true emergency, that can't be helped.

What not to do:

> *A locally famous athlete once contracted to buy a very expensive home on the beach in my town. Everything was concluded and it was time to sign. At the closing table, he made an offhand remark about the Lear jet he'd just purchased. The lender abruptly put down the papers, saying, "Did you finance it? It wasn't on your application."*
>
> *"No," the athlete replied, "I just took that loan out yesterday."*
>
> *Everything stopped. The mortgage loan was denied, and the transaction was canceled on the basis that the buyer didn't qualify.*

I don't know if the athlete thought he could safely go ahead and acquire further indebtedness once his loan received written approval or whether he actually wanted to cancel the purchase. On the one hand, had he discussed it with his agent, she would have warned him not to buy the jet until the day after recording. On the other, he simply manipulated things to get his own way—definitely dirty pool but technically legal.

That's a terrible strategy, and no one should use it. I cited the example only to demonstrate that changes in your finances can be reported at any time until the loan has closed; if they're severe enough, your loan can be denied, thus ending your transaction.

If it's a personal thing—you're going to get a divorce, your mother on the mainland is ill and you have to leave—again, tell your agent immediately.

Let's say you learned of your mother's illness after you'd completed your due diligence, your loan was approved, maybe even after you'd signed the documents, but the transaction has not yet recorded (closed). That is definitely a sticky wicket. You'll need all your resources and all your agent's expertise and objective advice to get out of your contract with a whole skin—but maybe you can.

The possibility of a real emergency is the most significant reason in the world why you should always be honest with all concerned. What you will need most in any worst-case scenario is goodwill. If you have been a pain in the neck, you may not have that goodwill. But if you do, and you have an intelligent agent, you may just bring off a win-win situation.

There are several possible options besides cancellation to manage legitimate emergencies. If it makes you feel more secure to think them through now, before you're into something you can't handle, then the rest of this chapter is important.

Whether some of those options are feasible depends on your financial capability. If you can afford it, the best thing may be to close your transaction, then either rent the property or put it back on the market. Have your agent do a rough estimate of the costs of both these options—there won't be time for a precise one. If the figures are close to working out, go for one of those options.

If that isn't possible, ask your agent to contact the seller's broker, explain the situation, and beg for mercy. (Here's where you really need a highly reputable agent.) The attempt may not work but should be made. Perhaps the seller has a backup offer. Perhaps the seller has changed his mind about selling. (There's such a thing as seller's remorse, too.) In a strong seller's market, he might even get a higher price for his property now.

Failing all of that, have your agent find out what the seller would charge to cancel the contract and decline to exercise his right to sue. Yes, that will probably cost you real money, but we're talking about a real emergency.

Your agent may suggest other options. If you have told her the truth and done everything in good faith up to this point, she will help you to the best of her ability.

There are several possible options besides cancellation to manage legitimate emergencies.

You will probably never need this information, but just in case: So long as the transaction has not yet been recorded at the Bureau of Conveyances, you can most likely successfully instruct the escrow company to cancel it, or at least delay it. This is drastic and not without risks and potential high financial cost, so it certainly should not be undertaken on any kind of whim and without good, solid legal advice.

Say everything you've tried has failed. You're stuck in a contract you can't perform, with no way out that's not going to cost you tons of money you don't have. I really hate to say this, but it's time to call a lawyer—a real estate lawyer—and explain the situation. Your agent can recommend one who can advise you whether or not to call the escrow company and cancel the recordation of the transaction.

Enough of disaster scenarios. If you really believe something like this could happen, you may want to reconsider your decision to buy at all right now.

Let's take a different hypothetical situation: It's the same eleventh hour, but in this case you find out something about the property that makes you change your mind. Assuming this is something that materially and negatively affects the value of the property in the eyes of a reasonable person, you are then dealing with an after-the-fact disclosure issue. At that point, you are probably rightfully entitled to the number of days called for in your contract to review any newly discovered information. There are a couple of very important things to keep in mind about this scenario.

First, it doesn't matter who discovers the new information. The rules apply whether the seller knows about the problem or not. Here's a real life example.

The pest inspector found evidence of live termite infestation, and treatment is required. An exterminator is hired to tent the house, but he's on a tight schedule and can't get to the job until two days before recording. You have already signed your escrow and mortgage papers, authorizing recordation conditional on the tenting being completed. When the men go to put the tent on the house, one of them falls through the roof, initiating discovery of severe structural damage that nobody was aware of before. This constitutes a new disclosure. You and your agent have to handle the paperwork correctly, but it normally would mean you have time to reconsider your position. Then you can go back to the same options you had during your initial due diligence period—ask for compensation, decline to proceed, or whatever's appropriate.

Note to sellers: Had the seller in this hypothetical case disclosed that he suspected there might be termite damage to the roof structure, and had the buyer accepted the property as such, chances are this would not qualify as newly discovered information.

A second thing to remember in cases like this: You must be pro-active. Everyone in the transaction from the seller's broker to the lender to the escrow officer needs to be notified immediately in writing that something has come up. Do not handle a situation like this verbally or informally.

Bottom line: If you have pangs of remorse, know yourself. Understand and recognize when you are having a fear fantasy as opposed to legitimate concern over significant issues. Disregard fear fantasies. Deal with legitimate concerns as follows:

1. Plan ahead. Make basic buying decisions before you look at homes, share them with all concerned, and stick to them.

2. Take your personal circumstances into consideration before you decide this is the right time to make a purchase.

3. Understand the contingencies in your contract before you sign it, and know and use the formal procedures for dealing with the unexpected.

Remember, being reasonable and fair in all your dealings usually leads others to treat you the same way.

14

The Paperwork

Now here's a fearsome topic. Perhaps you'd like to avoid it.

Yeah, right. But we can try to keep it (sort of) simple.

You will have somewhere between one and two gazillion pieces of paper before you're done with any transaction. Some of these will be critical to your transaction, and none should be ignored. But many, including, but not limited to, the title search, survey, termite inspection report, and home inspection report are prepared by professionals hired by one party or the other. This section deals with paperwork that *the buyer and seller are required to prepare and sign personally.*

There are two basic documents that are critical to every buyer, and three basic documents that are critical to every seller. Everything else ties into one or more of them one way or another and is used case-by-case.

For a buyer, the two documents are the **actual purchase agreement and the Seller's Disclosure**.

The purchase agreement (contract, DROA, offer, whatever you choose to call it) itemizes the promises made between you and the seller, which you are each legally required to perform. It also specifies jobs to be done by others (inspection, survey, etc.), who is to order and pay for them, and when they are to be done. Finally, it outlines both the consequences (or penalties) if one or the other party fails to keep a promise and the procedures for handling deal-busting circumstances.

The Seller's Disclosure gives you facts about the property, as well as clues to things you may want to investigate. The seller must tell you the truth to the best of his knowledge, and you must be given time to review the disclosure before your agreement is legally binding.

The three documents critical to sellers are the two above, plus the **Listing Agreement** (the contract between the seller and his agent's company).

It is very important to read all of these through at least once word-for-word, line-by-line. Having a clear understanding of their contents goes a long way toward telling you which of the other many pieces of paper you also need to read (or fill out) carefully and which are simply legally required forms. (Of course, you should read every word of every paper all the way through, but in the real world, most people do not do this.)

Here's something basic about the paperwork to keep in mind: Handwritten insertions supercede anything to the contrary that is typed in, and all typed insertions supercede anything preprinted on the form that contradicts them. If you familiarize yourself with the standard statements, you'll easily find things that have been added or changed when reviewing actual documents.

The Hawaii Association of Realtors' standard forms current at this writing are reprinted here, but they are frequently amended to reflect new laws and changing situations in our market, so may be out of date even before you buy this book. Ask your agent for current forms and see what, if anything, has changed. (Using non-standard forms may be legal, but since that means reinventing the wheel with every transaction and leaves everyone open to errors and misunderstandings. Almost all of us use the standard forms.) These have been composed and reviewed both by real estate attorneys and a committee of Hawai'i Association of Realtors agents. All worked hard to make the forms clearly understandable. There is even a section of "definitions" in the DROA and the Listing Agreement to help avoid misunderstandings. But, since they become legally binding contracts when signed, a certain amount of wordiness is unavoidable and maybe intimidating. This book explains general ideas and gives general information with a minimum of legalese and trade jargon. My language is therefore not as precisely worded as the actual documents. Also, to get deeply into specific cases is beyond the scope of this book. And, quite frankly, if I try to interpret specifics for you, without knowing you, your situation, or your concerns, I might create an error and misunderstanding. If you want to go beyond generalities, ask your agent to make the time for a thorough discussion, sign up for a class in real estate, or read other books on real estate contracts which are available in the library or at bookstores.

That said, here goes.

The Listing Agreement

This is a binding contract the seller makes with his agent.

In it, he certifies that he has the legal right to sell a specific property, and agrees to sell it for a specific price during a specific time period. The fine print itemizes what services he will receive from his agent and the real estate company, what he will pay for these services (the commission), and when he must pay it. It describes what he will do to cooperate with marketing efforts. It also states how and when the listing can be canceled, by either the seller or the agent, before the end of the listing period.

Sounds pretty simple, and it is.

If you're the seller, you'll confer with your agent about the basics— price, commission, and beginning and ending dates—come to a mutual agreement, and then proceed with marketing. But before you do that, there are a few less obvious things to know about that are a common source of misunderstandings between owners and agents.

The listing agreement is, strictly speaking, a contract between you and the real estate company your agent works with, not between you and your agent personally. Any verbal agreement you may have with your agent should be included in writing (because if your agent goes out of town, quits, or, heaven forbid, even dies, your contract with the realty company still stands). Don't expect the company to abide by, or even know about, verbal agreements between you and your agent.

The positive aspect of contracting with the company is that there will be backup in case your agent isn't able to perform her duties. Ask your agent who her backup will be in case of emergency and keep that person's contact information, as well as the contact information for the principal broker or broker in charge.

All owners of a property must sign the listing agreement or it isn't valid. (That goes for all other documents involved in the sale of property, too.) If you list property and accept an offer without the signature of everybody named on the title, you may be required to pay a listing commission whether or not the sale closes. You also might be open to legal action by a disappointed buyer. If any other person is listed on the title who cannot or will not sign the listing agreement, you must have written authorization (power of attorney, court order, whatever) for the listing agreement to be valid. If you have any doubt about who is listed on the title, your agent or title company can get the facts.

All owners of a property must sign the listing agreement to make it valid.

Most residential listings in Hawai'i are **Exclusive Right to Sell** agreements. This means you agree to pay the commission to the company you've listed with, no matter who finds the buyer (even if you find one yourself), for any offer accepted during the listing period that results in an actual sale. (The commission includes compensation for a buyer's agent also, which you already know if you read the section on how agents are paid.) So if your neighbor has expressed interest in the property and you don't intend to pay a commission if that neighbor buys it, say so up front and ask your agent to put your neighbor's name on the listing agreement as an exception. Be prepared for your agent to tell you she won't help you facilitate that sale without pay, and to negotiate fair and reasonable compensation in the event your exception actually buys the property. Also be prepared to pay a commission to your neighbor's agent as well, if he decides he wants representation. In my experience, the exception rarely actually buys the property.

There is also a protection clause in your listing contract that states a period of time—commonly 120, even 180 days—during which you still must pay your agent's commission if the buyer saw the property during the listing period.

The fine print below the signatures itemizes the services provided by your agent, such as advertising, signs, lockboxes, open houses, etc. It also grants permission for the listing to be publicized in various ways and for the sale information to be included in the Board of Realtors' Multiple Listing database. If any of the standard clauses present a problem—for instance, your tenant won't allow open houses—discuss these things during the listing interview and agree in advance as to how the sale process will be managed.

About tenants: Their legal rights are specified in the **Landlord-Tenant Code**. It's part of Hawai'i law, so familiarize yourself with it if you haven't already done so. Selling a property does not cancel a lease or otherwise allow you to trample on your tenant's rights nor does your tenant have any obligation to help you expedite the sale. Ask your agent for suggestions and advice about your particular tenants and their particular situation and deal with them before putting the property on the market.

Selling a property does not cancel a tenant's lease.

The listing agreement also itemizes what you will do to move the sale forward, such as giving your agent access (keys, etc.), making the property available for showings, notifying tenants, and keeping the property clean and in good order. If any of your responsibilities pose a problem, work out a solution before the property goes on the market.

In fact, any unique situation that may affect your agent's marketing efforts needs to be handled and planned for in advance. So read the fine print about who's responsible for what and customize your agreement accordingly. If you and your agent thoughtfully prepare the listing agreement, you'll have a great start toward a successful and relatively stress-free marketing process.

But what if something unexpected comes up? How do you handle trouble? Here are some situations that sellers often worry about:

✔ You change your mind about selling and decide to keep the property before the listing period expires and before you have accepted an offer.

That's not trouble, that's a phone call. In Hawai'i, an owner can't be forced to sell just because there's a listing contract, even if a buyer offers full price and meets all the seller's terms. You can take your property off the market at any time, for any reason.

If, however, you receive an offer within the listing period that meets your full price and terms and then refuse it and take the property

---

For a Trouble-Free Listing

✔ Clearly communicate your wishes and expectations about service to your agent before signing a listing and coming to an agreement.

✔ Frankly disclose and discuss any unusual circumstances that might affect your decision to sell or in any way deter your agent's marketing efforts, and agree how they will be handled.

✔ Make sure the signed listing reflects all of the above.

✔ Take responsibility for any decisions you make contrary to your agent's advice, and for any marketing restrictions initiated by you or your tenants.

✔ Expect regular feedback from your agent and pay attention to it.

✔ Openly discuss with your agent anything that changes your position (or your mind), and/or any problems that arise.

✔ Know and understand the rights and obligations spelled out in the listing agreement.

✔ Adhere to those rights and obligations and expect the same from your agent and agency.

---

off the market, you may owe your agent a commission. (In practice, most companies don't charge if that happens, but it is a possibility.)

✔ You want to change the listing price or other terms of sale.

That's not trouble either. All it takes is a signed note of instruction to your agent. Period. She may or may not argue, but you are the owner and you control that. Her option is to drop your listing when the contractual time is up (see the part of the listing agreement that states when and under what conditions either party may cancel the agreement).

✔ You discover your agent isn't doing a good job, isn't doing what you expected, or you've got some good and sufficient cause for dissatisfaction.

Now that is trouble. Your listing is a contract, which means that both parties have obligations. So, what's appropriate if your agent hasn't held up her end of the deal?

Before we get into that, read the following carefully:

During a buyer's market, most agent-client problems happen because the property has not sold in the time frame the client expected or the agent is asking for a price reduction. But before you blame your agent, think honestly about whether you followed her advice on pricing and helped her to market the property correctly.

In hot seller's markets, sellers may feel their property was underpriced because multiple offers came in or offers came in far above the asking price. That is a much happier problem and also 100 percent under your control. Remember, agents don't decide the price, sellers do. So long as the paperwork is handled properly, there are several strategies: You can raise the price, or you can instruct your agent to collect offers for a specified period of time before accepting any of them.

Note: Decide this in advance, not after the fact. You can even counter the best of several offers by stipulating that if the lender's fair market appraisal comes in a lot higher than the offered price, you can renegotiate it.

Most agent-client difficulties involve the price. A smart agent and a smart seller will discuss the price and have a clear understanding of each other's attitudes and strategies long before a listing is signed and a property is put on the market.

✔ But let's assume you are justifiably dissatisfied with your agent. What then?

Your first step is to have a frank discussion with her. Tell her that you will cancel the listing if things don't change. Be prepared to be specific, factual and reasonable and to follow the agreements in the listing contract you signed. That's usually sufficient. Our livelihoods depend on a continuing stream of clients, which in turn depends on our reputations. An agent who gains a reputation for not doing her job will soon have no livelihood.

If things still remain unresolved, contact the principal broker or broker in charge of the company and have the same frank discussion. That broker is ultimately responsible for the company's performance and for your agent's.

If you're still unhappy, ask to be released from the agreement. The broker will most likely agree. If the problem is serious enough that you believe you've suffered actual damage, you can also contact the Board of Realtors, the Real Estate Commission, or your own attorney to find out what recourse you may have beyond what that fine print in the listing says.

Bottom line: The listing contract details what the agent and agency will do for you and what you agree to do in return. By signing that contract you are authorizing the agent and agency to act on your behalf according to your instructions. A full-service brokerage does just about everything except make the critical decisions about price, terms, accepting offers, and signing the required documents. You agree to cooperate with marketing efforts and pay the commission when the sale closes. Most full-service brokerages do not charge a dime unless and until that happens and then only the agreed-upon percentage of the sale price, nothing more.

So, to list successfully, choose your agent carefully, then put all agreements in writing, know what you're agreeing to, keep your end of the deal, and expect your agent and realty company to keep theirs.

The DROA* *(Deposit Receipt Offer and Acceptance)*

The DROA is the deal between buyer and seller. It is twelve pages long as I write this. It may be intimidating when confronted for the first time and all the more nerve-racking because you'll most likely be doing business with a total stranger as the other party.

But rather than a worry, the length should be reassuring. It takes a lot of words to explain things clearly, completely, and unambiguously. As you read through the DROA, you'll realize that there's nothing in it that an ordinary person can't understand. You'll see how it's geared to reflect both the letter and the spirit of fair and straightforward dealings.

Be aware that the standard form changes with fair regularity in Hawai'i, to reflect changes to the law as well as changing topics of concern to buyers and sellers.

Your agent should go over the offer with you, paragraph by paragraph, at the time you fill out the form, explaining in detail anything you're in doubt about.

What I will try to do here is to give you an idea of some of the choices and options you'll have about important issues in general, as well as things that may apply to your own case.

Agency Disclosure identifies whose agent is who. Under Hawai'i law, you must be given that information before you sign an offer. If you are purchasing a property listed by the same company your agent works with, or if the company you have listed your property with also represents the buyer, you will also be asked to sign a Dual Agency Agreement.

Deposit Receipt shows the amount of the earnest money deposit the buyer has provided and the agent has signed as recipient. There may be a copy of the check attached. It's usually a relatively small amount—$1,000 to $5,000 is common. Here are the rules about earnest money deposits:

---

* The standard DROA is most commonly used by private individuals. If you are buying new housing being sold by a developer the form may be different, although it will cover all the above topics and be explained by the developer's representative and/or your own agent.

✔ The check should be made out to either an escrow company or the buyer's agent's company, not the agent personally. It will not be cashed until/unless the offer is accepted.

✔ For a contract to be valid, there must be some consideration, which is usually money.

✔ If, for any reason, the check isn't good, the transaction can be canceled.

✔ **Sellers:** if there is no check, find out why not before considering the offer and know that the offer is not valid without it. This section of the DROA outlines exactly how that money is to be handled.

✔ Normally, it becomes part of the down payment if the transaction closes, and is returned to the buyer if the transaction does not and the buyer is not in breach of contract.

✔ **Note to buyer:** You must make an earnest money deposit even if you intend to get 100 percent financing. In that case, make sure the contract stipulates what will happen to that deposit upon closing.

✔ Nonrefundable deposits are highly unusual in Hawai'i, but they do exist. If you are the buyer, read the section on the circumstances under which you might forfeit your deposit before writing that check.

✔ There is a check-block if the earnest money is to accrue interest. This is not usual unless the escrow period is longer than usual or the amount is very large.

The Offer comprises most of the rest of the document:

The Addenda section lists other pieces of paper that will become part of the binding agreement between buyer and seller. Pay special attention to their contents and understand that anything you want incorporated in the agreement must be listed in this section.

Purchase price and financial terms

✔ Most sellers ask for an additional deposit after the buyer has performed his due diligence investigation. Note when that additional deposit will be due.

✔ Make sure the loan amount specified matches up with any prequalification or preapproval letter your lender gave you.

✔ If you think you may want to change the down payment amount later, understand that you can always raise the down payment at your own discretion but cannot reduce it if it will jeopardize your loan approval.

Strategy tip: This section will be closely scrutinized. As the buyer, make yourself look as good as you can, but don't promise what you can't deliver.

Inclusions and Exclusions are self-explanatory but merit careful attention to avoid problems later. Buyers, make sure everything that you expect to receive with the property is on that written list. You or the seller may attach an inventory. If there's any doubt in your mind, or you think the other party may have any misunderstanding, write the item in one list or the other. Confirm all verbal agreements in writing.

Both the seller and buyer need to be clear when listing what is and isn't included with the property.

Sellers, make sure anything you intend to remove that an average person might expect you to leave behind is listed in the exclusions section. Things like antique chandeliers that are wired in or stained glass windows that are installed in the window frame will be included unless you say otherwise. (Normally in Hawai'i, sellers include major appliances, including washers, dryers, refrigerators and air conditioners. Small appliances, such as microwave ovens, that aren't built in and can be removed simply by unplugging them, will be excluded unless listed otherwise.)

Strategy tip: When a real estate sale includes a lot of items that are not strictly speaking real estate, such as a completely furnished apartment, the lender's appraiser may reduce his evaluation accordingly because thirty-year mortgages aren't available for a couch or a bed, etc.; these items are considered personal property, not real estate. If those items have substantial dollar value and may affect the amount the lender will lend, do the following:

1. Find out in advance how your lender will treat the situation and prepare the paperwork according to his advice; and/or

2. Make a large enough down payment that the loan amount won't be affected if the appraisal is lower than the sale price; or

3. Arrange to purchase the furnishings separately; or

4. Arrange a personal loan for the furnishings after the sale has closed (not before, unless you are completely certain the additional debt won't affect your ability to qualify for the mortgage).

The Closing Date (recordation at the Bureau of Conveyances) must be a business day when the Bureau is open.

Remember, closing day is moving day in Hawai'i. Unless other written arrangements have been made, the seller must have moved out, leaving the property clean and otherwise entirely as agreed to in the DROA, by the time the buyer receives the phone call saying the sale has been recorded.

Normally, the seller must move out, leaving the property clear by the closing date.

Strategy tip: If you can be flexible, it's a good idea to find out in advance whether any particular date is important to the other party. It can sometimes make or break an offer and also save lots of potential hassles and stress on both parties.

If, as the seller, you are reluctant or unable to make moving arrangements adequately in advance of closing, stipulate in the original DROA that you'll require a seller rent-back.

Extensions of Time to Close: Most agreements allow some flexibility when there's a delay beyond the control of either the buyer or the seller. But if time is of the essence, know that you may be in violation of your agreement if it doesn't close by the date specified.

The Escrow Company is initially specified by the buyer. Selection of the company is usually not a material (deal-buster) issue.

However:

✔ You may be informed that the other party wants to use a particular escrow company and/or officer. Sometimes one or the other party may be eligible for a discount at a particular company. Discounts may be offered to senior citizens, military personnel, people doing multiple transactions, etc. Ask, if you think you might qualify for a discount.

✔ Sometimes a developer has an arrangement with a particular company to handle their entire project.

✔ Most agents have a couple of favorite officers or companies based on past good service.

 Strategy tip: The small courtesy of allowing the other party to select the escrow company may make for a smoother transaction when you ask for some other small concession.

Prorations refers to things the seller has paid for in advance, such as property taxes or maintenance fees.

✔ If a seller has paid for six months' worth of property taxes, for example, and sells the house three months into that period, then the portion of taxes that apply to the latter three months are collected from the buyer at closing and the seller is reimbursed.

✔ The buyer should include proration costs in the estimate of cash needed at closing.

Closing Costs specifies most normal and ordinary items and identifies which party customarily pays each. Escrow will compute closing costs for both buyer and seller according to this paragraph unless the contract specifies something different.

Assessments identifies who is responsible for paying any assessments that may exist. (In this context, assessments have nothing to do with property taxes.)

- ✔ Assessments by condominium associations for improvements to the property, such as new roofs, should be disclosed in advance of a contract. Assessments by utility providers have become unusual, but to avoid surprise, fill that section out to say that the seller will pay any that exist.

- ✔ Assessments that crop up after the contract is signed but before closing are open to negotiation. If no agreement can be reached, the transaction can be canceled.

Strategy tip: An assessment by any other name, be it a "loan" or "additional temporary maintenance fee" or whatever, still amounts to an assessment. Make sure you've received the latest copies of all owner's association documents and carefully look through them for such references.

Consents is a statement that if either the buyer or the seller needs to get consents from any third party to close, he won't drag his feet in doing so. Here, a third party means anyone not a party to the transaction—either buyer or seller—from whom permission is required in order to close. This clause is especially pertinent to leasehold property in Hawai'i; sometimes the lessor (owner of the land) must sign a "consent," permitting the sale to take place. The agents or escrow will tell the seller and/or buyer what paperwork is necessary to get this done on time.

Strategy tip: Delays on the part of lessors are common. Making allowances in advance (at least a 45-day escrow period) is a good idea.

Tenancy and Vesting identifies the buyer(s) and states their marital status. It also contains a space for filling in what kind of tenancy the buyer wants.

There are four different ways a buyer can take ownership in Hawai'i depending on whether you're buying alone or with a spouse or partner. If you're in doubt, check off the block that says "tenancy to be determined" and ask escrow for the literature detailing each type.

Tenancies in Hawai'i*

By the Severalty: Contrary to how it sounds, this is how title is taken by a sole individual.

By the Entirety: Reserved for married couples in Hawai'i, this is the most common way those couples take title. If one spouse passes away, the other owns the property in its entirety.

Joint Tenancy: Similar to Tenancy by the Entirety, two or more people may own property jointly, regardless of marital status. In joint tenancy, if one owner dies, the other(s) then own the property in its entirety.

Tenancy in Common: Two or more people may take title this way, in equal or unequal shares. If one owner dies, his heirs inherit his interest (percentage of ownership) in the property.

*For a complete description of tenancies, ask your escrow company for literature. If you're in doubt about the best tenancy for you, consult a real estate attorney or your financial advisor.

Sometimes a buyer wants to add other people to the title at closing, or even assign the contract to someone else entirely. Writing "to be determined" where the names of the buyers belong, or including the words "or assigns," indicates the buyer's identity may change during the escrow process. For example, a mother going on a trip might tell her son, "If a one-bedroom apartment becomes available in XYZ building, please buy it for me; I'll be back in time for closing." The son might obtain a power of attorney from his mother, but he might also sign an offer in his own name, accompanied by the words "or assigns."

Strategy tip: It should go without saying that signing a contract on behalf of a third party can be risky. You may still be responsible for performance if that third party later changes his mind. If this is a matter of concern to you, consult with your agent and perhaps also a real estate attorney before becoming involved.

Contingencies are things that must happen before one party or the other is required to close. The DROA details correct procedures for terminating the contract in the event one of those contingencies becomes a deal-breaker. There's a lot of legalese here, but it's important for you to clearly understand how you must proceed if that happens, because you will be held to the rules.

Strategy tip: Be alert if you suspect the other party to your contract is unhappy and will cancel if they can (for example, if a seller receives a higher offer after accepting yours, or if a buyer finds a house he likes better during the escrow period). Your failure to follow even the tiniest, pettiest, and most inconsequential detail of the rules about contingencies may give that person an escape route. Your agent will advise you and most escrow companies provide everyone with a time-line of deadlines. However don't assume someone else is looking after things or that nobody can make an error. Track the transaction carefully and do everything you need to do on time.

Strategy tip: The cash funds for the down payment are contingent if they will come from the sale of another property or if they're dependent on any other circumstance beyond the buyer's direct control. Buyers should be forthright in disclosing this. The seller has a right to know if there's anything that might prevent the down payment from being available in time for closing. Failing to disclose might just put you in breach of your agreement should anything go wrong.

Financing Contingencies include time frames by which the buyer must complete the loan application and get loan approval. It's very important to pay attention to these dates.

Strategy tip: Submitting a credit preapproval letter from your lender at the time you make the offer demonstrates your credit-worthiness, indicates you've already given the necessary information to the lender, and strengthens your overall offer.

This section of the DROA also includes a paragraph about assumption of the seller's mortgage.

Strategy tip: Most modern mortgages are specifically not assumable and, if they are, the interest rate may escalate. Before entering into such a contract, verify with the lender that assumption is possible and find out if the interest rate will change.

In this section, the buyer also authorizes the lender to give information to the seller and/or the seller's agent about the progress of the loan. You are not authorizing the lender to tell the seller or his agent any personal financial details, just how the loan process is coming along.

Buyers often are reluctant to divulge financial details to sellers. Why does he need to know, they ask? Sellers need to feel confident in your ability to close and assured of your sincerity before they effectively take their properties off the market.

Strategy tip: The best way for buyers to assure sellers is to completely disclose the details of the planned financing and to authorize the lender to confirm those details to the seller. Understand that this is not prying into your personal business.

Default Provisions and Mediation and Arbitration sections outline the rules for handling defaults and disputes between the parties. There aren't any blank spaces to fill out or choices to make here; the rules simply tell you what your recourse is if things go wrong and what will likely happen if you're the responsible party.

Strategy tip: Most agents aren't lawyers and aren't qualified to give legal advice. If you want advice or an in-depth interpretation about these sections, consult with a real estate attorney before making any offer.

Title: This section is short, but very important as it deals with what will happen should there be any "defect" in the title or should the buyer be dissatisfied with the title report for any reason.

Strategy tip for the escrow period: The title report is a critical document. When you get it, read it. Do not feel ignorant or foolish if you don't fully understand it. Agents take hours of classes on the subject, and we don't necessarily understand everything! Ask your agent and/or escrow officer to explain anything that's not clear.

Title Report Summary of Contents

- ✔ The legal description of the property.

- ✔ Identifies all owners.

- ✔ Discloses any and everything that's recorded as an encumbrance on the property (such as an easement for a utility pole, or the right of someone to use the property as access to an adjacent property).

- ✔ Lists recorded mortgages and/or other liens against the property or the seller that must be paid before the title can pass to the buyer.

- ✔ Lists any recorded liens against the buyer. Such liens can affect the buyer's ability to complete his purchase.

- ✔ Lists commitment for title insurance and any exceptions or exclusions from this coverage.

You'll be asked to sign an approval of the title report along with your other closing documents. Don't sign it unless all your questions have been satisfied.

Transactions involving foreign or non-resident buyer and seller

HARPTA and FIRPTA are acronyms for state and federal laws respectively about withholding tax from sale proceeds if the seller is foreign or a nonresident of Hawai'i. Those regulations can affect a seller's net proceeds at closing. Currently the federal withholding amount is 10 percent, the state 5 percent of the gross sale price, although that's subject to change.

Strategy tip: If this section applies to you, consult with a tax expert to find out if and/or how you'll be affected before selling your property, or at least before calculating what your bottom line after closing will be. Don't forget to file timely tax returns for the year you sell.

Wow! We're about halfway done and a lot of the good stuff hasn't even come up yet. Moving on . . .

Staking and Survey (usually not applicable to condominiums) is ordinarily a seller's expense. The buyer selects either staking, in which a surveyor establishes the property boundaries and marks them with stakes or pins or, more commonly, survey, which includes a little map graphically showing what the surveyor has found. The latter will also note any structure or improvement (fence, wall, etc.) that encroaches (butts into somebody else's property or meanders along the boundary line). These are very common in Hawai'i—so common, in fact, that a law was passed a few years ago, referred to as the "de minimus rule," that specifies how many inches a boundary line can be "off" without creating an encroachment. Rules and a time frame for handling anything that does constitute an encroachment are spelled out.

Unless otherwise specified, the survey will not include the footprint of the house unless the house itself is somehow encroaching. If you want the footprint of the house included, you can either negotiate with the seller or ask the surveyor to provide it at your expense.

Strategy tip: Surveys of remote places, large or irregularly shaped properties, or areas that are difficult to access may take more time and/or be more expensive than anticipated. If you're the seller, it's a good idea to get an up-front estimate both of cost and of the time necessary to complete it.

Now, finally, we get to the good stuff!

Disclosures, inspections, maintenance and warranties

Most of the subject matter covered in this is discussed at length in other chapters. In summary, this section establishes and enumerates many important rights and obligations of both buyer and seller. You should read every word of this section carefully and insert time frames that are reasonable and realistic.

Strategy tip: A timely inspection is critical. Failure to do it within the specified time limit can mean you've waived your right to cancel based on its results.

Paragraphs regarding asbestos, hazardous waste, mold, and sex-offender registration are required by law to be mentioned. They provide general information about these topics. They are not an indication that any of the problems addressed pertain to your property.

Other paragraphs clarify practical matters about property maintenance until closing, final walk-through, any warranties the seller may have, cleaning responsibilities, and removal of the seller's personal belongings.

A timely inspection is critical.

Termite provisions

The termite inspection is distinct from the general home inspection and is normally paid for by the seller. The buyer usually selects the inspector.

Unless otherwise agreed, the seller will kill all live termites but will not repair any damage. (Other states may have very different rules about this.)

Termites are a common problem here, sometimes serious, sometimes not, but almost all wood-frame homes that are more than a few years old have some evidence of termites at one time or another. If significant termite damage is found during the inspection (current language says the damage must "directly, substantially and adversely" affect the value of the property), that opens up a new disclosure issue. Remember, a buyer has a stipulated time to review and consider a new issue, *no matter who discovers it*.

Strategy tips: Select an accredited entymologist instead of an exterminator for the inspection. Two reasons: Entymologists have no vested interest in finding live bugs, and their reports usually include valuable information about termites in general and "conducive conditions" (termite attractors) that you can remove or avoid once you've concluded your purchase.

Do not rely on the termite inspector to assess damage. He is probably not qualified to do so. If the inspector reports damage you don't already know about, extensive enough to open up a new disclosure issue, get it reinspected by an appropriate professional before deciding what action to take.

Rental Property Matters apply if the house is rented out and are largely self-explanatory. (References to leases in these paragraphs refer only to the lease of a home to a tenant; they do not refer to property that is leasehold.)

Strategy tip: Getting an unwilling tenant to move out can become a nightmare. Sellers, if you're selling the property empty, make sure you and your tenant have come to an agreement. Do whatever you have to do, including financial enticements if necessary, to get the tenant's cooperation. Buyers, if you don't want to inherit a tenant, make sure you can't be required to close the transaction before the tenant is gone.

Condominium/subdivision/homeowner organizations

The list of documents the seller must give you, particularly if you're buying a condominium, is another specific contingency. You must receive, review and approve everything checked off before your contract is binding.

In Hawai'i, a property can be a condominium whether it's an apartment, a townhouse, or a detached dwelling.

In Hawai'i, a property can be a condominium whether it's an apartment, a townhouse, or a detached dwelling. The letters CPR stand for Condominium Property Regime, and if you see them anywhere in a property description, that means the property is a condominium, regardless of its physical configuration. There will usually be a CPR number included as the final four digits of the tax map key number. However, if a CPR is newly created, that number may not be assigned until closing. If you are buying a condominium, check all the boxes. You'll be informed if some of the requested documents don't exist.

There is also a statement that sellers aren't responsible for, among other things, repairs to the common elements of condominiums. However, if the common elements don't meet with your approval, you can still cancel the contract during the due diligence period. For example, if you discover that the lānai railing's about to fall off, and it's the association's responsibility to fix it and repairs aren't planned for six months, you can walk away. More likely, however, the current owner will be able to galvanize the association into action.

There is also a check box to request the CC&R's discussed elsewhere as well as any other applicable documents. Check this. If documents don't exist, you'll be informed.

Other Special Terms cover unique situations and requirements and anything not dealt with elsewhere that the buyer or seller wants to clarify or emphasize.

Strategy tip: This paragraph is scrutinized by agents and sellers; it is where we look for "weasel clauses," indications that the buyer is insincere or unreasonably nit-picky. If there is any competition for the property, a bunch of relatively insignificant issues itemized under special terms may put your offer at the bottom of the list. So use special terms judiciously and only when absolutely necessary or to confirm verbal agreements that aren't mentioned anywhere else.

The balance of the offer portion of the DROA is comprised of disclaimers, explanations, and definitions for your information and use. Read through them to avoid confusion later.

Finally, we are at the end of the buyer's part: The signature lines!

Strangely enough, while all the sellers must sign for a real estate contract to be binding in Hawai'i, only one of the buyers—no matter how many there are—need do so. However, it's best to get the signatures of all buyers as quickly as possible.

The document concludes with the ***Acceptance or Counteroffer*** section, which the seller completes appropriately.

Bottom line: The DROA tries to cover all common situations and concerns and refers to all other pieces of paper (addenda) that may be part of the offer. Read through it in its entirety. Once accepted and acknowledged, it overrides any previous agreement or verbal understanding. When you fill it out, make sure it's consistent, that it includes everything you intend, says exactly what you mean, and confirms all verbal understandings.

The Seller's Disclosure

The Seller's Disclosure is a checklist comprised of about four pages, with blank lines for explanations and details. The form also includes statements about the law and about how sellers and buyers are to treat the form. All sellers in Hawai'i must fill out the disclosure statement, with rare exceptions in cases where nobody involved has any knowledge about the property—such as a bank that is selling a foreclosed property or a trust company that is acting on behalf of a deceased owner. This information itself then constitutes the disclosure, however, and buyers will be told in advance and in writing that they need to depend solely on their own investigation and inspection.

Agents are not permitted to complete the disclosure for sellers. It must be filled out by you, personally, in your writing, and you alone are responsible for its statements.

Important note: If your agent becomes aware of a "material fact" about your property, whether she found it out from you or from somebody else, she is required to disclose it.

Tell the truth, all the truth. It is extremely foolish to avoid mentioning facts you know about your property in the hopes that they're not important, or won't be noticed by a buyer. Everything you disclose truthfully protects you. If you question whether something needs to be disclosed, it probably does. Explain the facts as you know them in sufficient detail to give the buyer a clear understanding.

Though the above may sound simple, there are lots of gray areas regarding disclosures.

It is expected you will have layman's knowledge about your property and that you are not a contractor, a realtor, or any other professional who would have expert knowledge. If you are such a professional, you are required to say so, and your disclosure should reflect any special knowledge you have.

If you haven't lived in the property, or haven't been there in a long time, and your information is limited, say so on the form. Do not fill out the blanks based on what you remember or assume. Report what you know. You may, of course, use information that has been provided to you by a rental property manager or a tenant, but you are still responsible for the truthfulness of the statements, so you should include a note on the information's source and let buyers know who to contact for further details.

If you know something that might affect the property's value in the eyes of a reasonable person, but it's not specifically mentioned in the form, you should still disclose it. Just because the form doesn't address it doesn't mean you can ignore it.

You're not required to report rumor and gossip on a disclosure. But if you've heard rumors about anything you would care about if you were purchasing a property—further development in the area or proposed road-widening, for example—try to find the facts and disclose them.

There are always a lot of questions about notorious incidents: What is a notorious incident? How long afterward do you need to disclose it? Do you have to report things that have happened in the neighborhood? And so on. A notorious incident usually refers to a felony, a murder, or a suicide. You are required to disclose these things. As far as how long ago it happened or negative happenings in the surrounding area: Don't second-guess the rules. Disclose things you know about, but do leave all dramatics and opinions to TV and news reporters. Leave it to the buyer to decide whether it's significant. (If you were personally involved in a notorious incident, don't discuss it with potential buyers under any circumstances. Say what needs to be said on the disclosure and leave it at that.)

Here in Hawai'i it may be important for a buyer to know if anyone has passed away on the property under any conditions, notorious or not. Common courtesy and common sense make disclosure appropriate if that has happened. It is also common sense to disclose all important or critical facts immediately, preferably even before a buyer has made an offer. The best strategy is to deal with major issues upfront. It wastes valuable marketing time to work with a buyer who cancels the contract after reading the disclosure. Also, when a buyer thinks a seller has tried to hide even one thing, he may regard the entire disclosure with suspicion, and the importance of the nondisclosed item may become exaggerated in his mind.

When the disclosure law was first passed in Hawai'i, all agents were required to be educated about its use. Of course, everyone wanted to know how to advise clients on what they needed to disclose and what they didn't. It quickly became clear that what was supposed to be disclosed was everything and what could be omitted was nothing. That is still true today.

Bottom line: Disclose, disclose, and disclose again. It's in your best interest and it's the law. Do not try to decide whether something's important enough to mention; if in doubt, mention. Disclose obviously significant items before a buyer makes an offer.

Disclosure and Agents' Dilemmas

A Short Conversation Overheard at Broker's Open House
Buyer's Broker to Listing agent: "My clients have small children. I'm worried about the house across the street. Are the same tenants still there?"

Listing Agent: "My sellers don't know for sure. Things have been very quiet over there ever since they bought this house five years ago or so, and they hardly see anybody going in or out."

Buyer's Broker: "The same owner's still on title, though. I checked."

Listing Agent: "Right. So did I. We just don't know if the tenants were there before or not."

Buyer's Broker: "I don't know what I should do."

Listing Agent: "It's getting harder and harder . . . We need to get this house sold, but… not badly enough to risk anything like what you're thinking. Here's what I think: It all depends on whether you trust your clients. How well do you know them?"

Buyer's Broker: "Pretty well. They're not personal friends or anything like that, but I know they're very family-oriented. This would be important to them."

Listing Agent: "Yeah. It would be to me, too. Look: You're going to have to make a judgment call. If you trust them, just let them know, and tell them we're not sure if the tenants are the same or not."

Buyer's Broker: "We can't put anything in writing, can we?"

Listing Agent: "Uh-uh. No way."

Buyer's Broker: "Okay. Guess I'll just go talk to them. I'll let you know if they're still interested after."

And A Long List of What-Ifs

What was all that about? I still don't know.

But sometimes the rule that says, "When in doubt, disclose," can be seriously problematic.

When agents know "material facts," they're required to disclose them. But whether they can do that legally isn't always clear. Even when the facts are certain, disclosure requirements can conflict with laws regarding civil rights, privacy, confidentiality, fiduciary duties, and other legal issues. Agents can be held to a higher standard of conduct than "civilian" sellers. And we usually aren't lawyers. So deciding whether a situation must be disclosed or can't be disclosed is sometimes a very sticky wicket.

What if disclosing what you know violates a third party's right to privacy? What if making the disclosure is somehow interpreted as discriminatory against a protected class of people? What if the entire issue has been set up, the client is bogus, or a member of some activist group who's trying to entrap either the agent or the seller? What if making the disclosure is contrary to the client's instructions and/or his best interests? Even if the agent knows the answer to that last question (and we all do), what if there's some kind of mistake and the information isn't correct?

In the cryptic conversation I overheard, it was obvious neither agent wanted to directly identify the disclosure issue that was causing such a problem. However, as I stood there listening (I guess they trusted me, at least up to a point), several things that might affect a prudent buyer's purchase decision came to mind:

What if the house across the street was a halfway house for teenage delinquents?

What if a convicted child molester lived there?

What if there was a past history of drug dealing from that house?

What if the present tenant, who might or might not have been the same one those two agents were so worried about, had a history of gun violence, poisoning household pets, or any other behavior that might frighten or endanger his neighbors or otherwise interfere with their right to "quiet enjoyment," to be safe and secure in their own property?

Some things also came to mind that explained why these two agents were being so careful about their words, and why the seller himself was not willing to make any disclosure.

What if the present tenant was a perfectly law-abiding citizen, who just happened to enjoy his privacy to the extent that he didn't want to know his neighbors?

What if the neighbors rarely saw him simply because he worked very odd hours?

What if the house was in fact a halfway house, but for some protected class of people—possibly making the seller or the agents risk some kind of discrimination charge if they made a disclosure?

What if that hypothetical halfway house was instead a shelter for abuse victims, making concealment of its true function and use necessary for the occupants' safety? But if it was a shelter, might there also be some risk to the neighbors and shouldn't they be informed?

So what, you ask, would be wrong with simply contacting the owner of that suspect house and asking him about his tenants?

Maybe nothing. In fact, probably nothing. He might not tell you, but at least then you'd know he was hiding something. Or maybe not. Maybe he'd think it was just none of your business. Or he might lie. That third-party owner has no obligation to tell the truth or to talk to you.

Then what, you further ask, would be wrong with checking with the police and/or the public record about criminal activity?

Definitely nothing. But they have rules and regulations about what they can and can't say. And, too, they may or may not have the information you need. But there's nothing wrong with asking.

So, what's the point here? Just to make people paranoid that they haven't been given all the facts? Not at all. Unfortunately, though, disclosure issues aren't always clear-cut. When thinking about gray areas, in your role as either buyer or seller, consider the following:

✓ Complete facts may be unavailable, even with everyone's best efforts.

✓ If you know as fact about activities in your neighborhood that a reasonable person might find objectionable and worry that disclosure might violate some statute, it might be wise to consult with an attorney about your liability if you do disclose—and if you don't. Even if there's a potential problem either way, you'll have a clearer picture and be able to make a better risk assessment.

✓ In Hawai'i, neighbors tend to know each other. It doesn't hurt to meet and talk to people who live near a home you're thinking of buying. But neighbors may report unsubstantiated rumor and gossip so, it's up to you how much weight to place on their comments.

✓ An agent who's familiar with the area you're considering, or who lives there herself, may know things an agent from outside the area doesn't. Do you and your agent have sufficient mutual trust to discuss sensitive issues without either one of you feeling at risk?

✓ Consider the source of information you receive. Is it authoritative? What are the supporting facts? Does the source have any obligation to tell you the truth?

Here's my bottom line opinion: It may not be politically correct, but as far as I know, there's no present legal requirement that statements of opinion, professional or otherwise, must meet that standard. We are all human beings. We all have prejudices of one kind or other. Having a prejudice in your mind can't be illegal, but taking action based on it may be. It is unreasonable—and, in my opinion, morally wrong—to expect anyone else to break the law to satisfy your prejudices.

However, it's also unreasonable—and, in my opinion, morally wrong—to allow someone else to go blindly into a situation that might put him at risk. Especially when he trusts and relies on your expertise to help him avoid making a bad decision.

Real estate professionals walk a thin line in this area.

15

Doing the Math

I know this is the scariest part of all, but for goodness' sake, don't skip it. The idea is to get over being scared now, so you can make good and successful choices when it comes to financing your new home and getting a mortgage. I am a real estate broker, not a loan officer or a banker. For the mortgage loan you want, you will have to work with an actual lender or mortgage broker. My job here (and part of your own agent's job, too) is to clarify jargon that may be confusing and to tell you about some of the tricks of the trade and how you can make them work for you (or if they never work).

But before we get into that, you have to take the first step.

Selecting a lender

Most banks and mortgage loan companies employ their own loan officers. These individuals deal only with loan programs offered by their companies. There are also mortgage brokers, who offer a wider variety of programs through many different lending companies. If the first lender you contact cannot offer you the program you need, he or she will undoubtedly recommend someone who can. Comparing programs and costs is discussed in detail later in the book.

A common mistake unknowing buyers make is shopping in the newspaper for the lowest advertised interest rate or the cheapest closing costs. Before deciding you've found the right loan, you need to know:

1. Do you qualify for it?

2. Does the property you're buying qualify for it?

3. Are the quoted closing costs true and complete, or are other charges hidden away under some other name?

(A Truth-in-Lending Statement (TIL) discloses the lender's all-inclusive charges. Ask for this and compare it with other lenders' charges for equivalent loan programs.)

And loan shopping for price alone isn't a good idea, anyway. When you're selecting a lender, treat the first meeting as an interview. If, for any reason, you don't care for the lender, don't commit—move on. If your questions aren't answered, if the lender brushes off your concerns, or if you sense he doesn't have time for you, you can be sure that will be the tone of your entire transaction. The lender should want your business.

 Red Flag: Searching for loan programs and lenders on the Internet has become very popular. It's easy, it's fun, it's embarrassment- and commitment-free. But unless you're on-line with a local lending institution, it's probably also useless, because, in general, no company without an office here will lend on Hawai'i property.

And you may not find that out right away. Very frequently, Hawai'i borrowers have obtained written credit approval and moved forward with an accepted offer only to find out at the eleventh hour (meaning a week or less before closing) that the lender does not do business in Hawai'i. So, when your agent tells you that you must deal with a local lender, there's a very good reason to listen and comply.

One final note before leaving the subject of selecting a lender. Reputable agents do not accept referral fees from lenders. Period. If you don't already have a lender, your agent will probably recommend one or more. These recommendations should be based on past successful transactions, good service and compatible working relationships, not on money changing hands. If you suspect your agent is accepting such fees, ask about it, find out for sure. If that is in fact the case, you may want to think twice about using that agent's services.

Some real estate companies are affiliated with certain lenders and/or have an in-house loan officer. This service is usually "on the up-and-up" and can make things easier for buyers. You may use this service, but you don't have to and should not feel compelled to.

Let's move on to some of the important things about mortgage loans and what it takes to get one.

Credit history and credit rating

Your credit history tells a banker or other interested party whether you pay your bills, whether you pay them on time, how much money you have borrowed and from whom. There are several nationwide credit reporting companies (private companies, not government agencies) that collect data from many sources, including credit card companies, stores, and banks. They sell that data to authorized persons. Whenever you apply for any kind of credit, including a mortgage loan, you usually sign something authorizing the lender or creditor to supply data to those agencies and to obtain any data they have on you.

Today's credit ratings are usually reduced to a number called a FICO score. The higher the score, the better the rating. (FYI, here's a rule of thumb: 500 is on the low side, 600 okay, 700 great, and 800+ nearly unheard of.) Much of the score has to do with timely payments and how much you owe. The number of your open accounts also comes into the picture. If you have, say, six open revolving credit card accounts and all or most of them are at your maximum allowed balance, this says you are an active credit seeker, which may negatively affect your score even if you always pay on time. Another factor has to do with the amounts you have borrowed from a single source. For example, people who have borrowed and repaid a million dollars from a single source will have a higher rating than people who have just as good a payment history, but have only borrowed, say, $100,000 from a single source.

What if there are errors on your credit report? If you are refused credit when you think you should have been approved, that's often the first clue that there's an error. When you apply for a mortgage, your lender should tell you if there is any problem that might affect your loan approval. He will also be able to tell you who to contact to get it corrected. You may also call the credit reporting agencies or go on line to get a copy.* There may be a small charge, but it's worthwhile if you suspect a mistake. If you have any doubts as to your creditworthiness, it's also a good idea to get a copy of your

* The three major credit reporting companies are Experian, Equifax and Trans-Union. They all have Internet sites through which you can obtain your credit report.

credit report before you apply for a mortgage loan. That way you can warn the lender ahead of time, let him know how you're taking care of the problem, and ask his advice on any further action you should be taking. Errors are fairly common, so don't panic if you find one—just get the record fixed. Then, when the reporting agency or creditor tells you they've fixed it, get written confirmation and keep it where you can find it.

If you have no credit or bad credit, this does not necessarily mean you cannot get a loan. However, you may have to accept a higher interest rate and less advantageous loan terms. (No credit isn't the same as good credit and will make it harder to obtain a mortgage. Some investors will accept paid utility accounts, such as phone, electricity, etc., that are or were in your name, but most want references such as installment or Visa card accounts, even if they have a zero balance.)

Tips to Take Seriously
If Your Credit Rating Isn't Good

1. This is the time to follow all the rules your mother taught you about honesty. Tell your lender up front if you know of any problems. They will be found anyway! Telling him in advance will allow him to find a loan program to approve you and also put him in a far better frame of mind when he's trying to help you. A lender who believes in your sincerity and honesty will go to far greater lengths to get your loan approved than one whom you have attempted to deceive.

2. Plan for the future. Your lender can give you specific ways and means of improving your credit rating. Talk to a reputable lender now, then follow his advice. If you want or need a home now, accept the less advantageous financing for which you can get approved. Once you've resolved the issues, you can refinance with a better loan. If you don't plan to buy immediately, fix the problem now. Then, by the time you actually apply, your rating may be much higher.

Getting your first mortgage loan approved will be more difficult than subsequent ones (assuming you make the payments, that is) because you've probably never borrowed such a large amount before. Don't get frustrated; learn the system, follow the steps. With a good real estate agent and a reputable lender in your corner, the job will get done.

Mortgage types and programs

In this section, there's lots of jargon you may not be familiar with. People in the real estate and mortgage businesses use short-cut language, because if we didn't, we'd never get to the end of a sentence!

There are many types of loans: Conventional, Jumbo, ARM, VA, FHA, HulaMae, and more. There are also second mortgages, equity loans, land loans, and construction loans. Additionally, there are developer loans (special financing offered by a developer to buyers in his specific project) and first-time-buyer loans (to assist first-time buyers who don't have equity to trade, meaning they haven't sold a property so they don't have any profit or gain to give them a large down payment).

What they're called doesn't matter. Their terms and conditions do.

Most Americans prefer "fully amortized, fixed 30-year conventional financing."

Fully amortized means the payments are calculated so that the interest and principal are fully paid off over the life of the loan in equal payments. (The term comes from a French word meaning "to kill"—once you've amortized the loan, it's dead!)

A fixed-rate loan has an interest rate that remains the same for its entire term.

Conventional financing means the loan amount is within a dollar figure established by FNMA or GNMA (large national mortgage clearinghouses) for ordinary or average single dwelling unit transactions. Conventional financing is not usually available for multiple dwellings of more than four units, whole apartment buildings, or luxurious mansions. Whether or not conventional financing is available for you depends on the loan amount you need and on whether you qualify for the payment.

What other choices are there?

VA and FHA loans can also be 30-year-fixed programs. These differ regarding eligibility, applicable property, closing costs and discount points, and other items. Ask your lender to detail these differences for you.

ARM (Adjustable Rate Mortgage) loans start out at a lower interest rate than conventional mortgages; that rate can change as often as monthly or as infrequently as every seven years. The interest rate changes based on a specific number of percentage points above some public guideline, such as the one-year treasury bond. There are usually maximum permitted adjustments on each occasion, as well as minimum and maximum rates over the life of the loan. You should be concerned with the up-side risk, a rising interest rate.

Most people don't want to deal with the insecurity inherent in an ARM, but there are times when it's helpful and appropriate. If you're going to own the property only for a short time and plan to sell it before the adjustment period arrives, you may want to consider the ARM option. If you're having trouble finding an affordable and acceptable home right now but expect substantial income increases fairly soon, an ARM may allow you to buy the home you want now and keep the payment affordable until you get that raise or promotion. Then you can either withstand an increase when it adjusts or refinance with a fixed-rate loan. In fact, any time you expect you'll keep the mortgage for a relatively brief amount of time, an ARM may save you substantial money.

I'll probably repeat this a hundred times before I'm done, but do have a frank conversation with your lender about your financing options and keep asking questions until you completely understand them. If your lender is unwilling to take the time to do this with you, find another lender!

HulaMae loans are available only in Hawai'i to first-time homebuyers whose income and debt fall within specific guidelines. The purchase price is also limited by those guidelines. Additionally, HulaMae funds are limited and not always available and the borrower must be an owner-occupant. However, if you and the property are eligible, HulaMae financing is extremely desirable. You can pick up the descriptive material at any of several local banks and lending institutions that offer the program.

A Jumbo loan is the other side of the coin and also a self-evident term. It's applicable when the loan requested is larger than permitted under conventional guidelines and usually involves a higher interest rate and higher points than conventional loans.

To Compare Loan Costs

Lenders are very competitive and often use banner ads saying things like "zero points" or "no closing costs" to entice buyers. To compare loans correctly, you need to put them all on equal footing.

Here's a hypothetical example:

Loan amount:	$300,000	$300,000
Interest rate	5.5%	6.0%
Points	2 ($6,000)	0 ($0)
Estimated monthly principal & interest	$1700	$1800

The monthly payment is approximately $100 more if you choose the zero point loan program that saves you $6,000 in up-front costs. If you divide the $100 savings into the $6,000 expense, you will find it takes about 60 months (five years) to defray the cost of the points. So, if you plan to keep that mortgage for more than five years, you are ahead of the game if you pay the points. If not, you're better off with the higher interest rate.

Sometimes lenders offer zero points, but include an origination fee. Make sure you check if that's the case.

Substitute accurate figures when your lender gives you your own Truth in Lending statement. Also, ask him for an amortization schedule, giving you principal and interest payments for different loan amounts, interest rates, and term—number of years—of loans.

Then you can make the same calculation for your own specific case, and make correct comparisons between different programs.

Other things you need to take into consideration in making any accurate comparison are whether or not you finance the points (if you have the cash, fine, but if you need to borrow it, you'll also be paying interest on the points), other lender closing costs (sometimes zero-point loans have higher fees in other areas), and the term of the loan.

Please note (with the usual caveat that I'm not a tax expert): Most points are tax deductible as interest paid in advance. If you pay them up front, you may deduct them in the year you make the loan. If you finance them, you may deduct them in equal proportions for every year of the loan term. Make sure you keep your closing statement for your tax preparer.

Jargonese and definitions

Whatever loan program you decide on, here are some other terms you'll probably encounter:

Points, Discount Points, or Origination Fee

These are the lender's charges for making the loan. A point is one percent of the amount of the loan. For example, if you borrow $300,000, each point will be $3,000. Zero-point loans do exist but usually involve a higher interest rate. (The lender will be paid somehow, no matter which program you select. See the box at the end of this section if you want to know how to compare loan programs accurately.) The most common number of points you will see is two, sometimes stated separately as one discount point plus one origination fee point.

First Mortgage

This is the primary financing. All liens are listed in order of who gets paid first should the bank or investor foreclose on the property: The first mortgage first, the second second, and so forth. Only property tax liens supercede this sequence.

Balloon Payment

You may hear a phrase like "fixed 30 with a 15-year balloon." This means the loan payment is calculated as if it were a 30-year fully amortized loan, but at the end of 15 years, you owe the entire remaining principal balance in a lump sum. (This is more common in second mortgages; unusual in primary financing.)

LTV (Loan to Value)

Usually expressed as a percentage, 80 percent LTV refers to a loan that is 80 percent of the property's appraised value or purchase price, whichever is less. (See Appraisal below.)

Equity

The percentage or dollar amount of the property's value that you don't owe to the lender.

Eighty-ten-ten, or Eighty-fifteen-five

This refers to loan programs with an 80 percent first mortgage, a 10 percent second mortgage, and a 10 percent down payment; or an 80 percent first, a 15 percent second, and a 5 percent down payment. These are common programs used when a buyer doesn't have at least 20 percent down payment, the amount usually needed to get the best available loan terms. It's a clever way to get a better first mortgage and to avoid paying mortgage insurance.

Mortgage Insurance

Not to be confused with mortgage *life* insurance, mortgage insurance does not pay off the loan if you die. It protects the lender against your default. It is commonly required when your down payment is not enough to convince the lender that your equity in the property will motivate you to make your payments.

Prepayment Penalty

Unusual in modern mortgages. Some B and C loans do have a clause that says if you pay them off early, you will be charged a penalty.

B and C (or even D) Loans

These lesser-quality mortgages have higher interest rates and higher costs and may also have other less desirable terms. They are used when the applicant is less qualified and lending the money involves higher risk to the lender.

TIL: Truth In Lending Statement

Required by law to be disclosed before you sign, this statement tells you the total cost of your financing if you retain the loan for the total number of years in its term. It also tells you the loan's APR.

APR (Annual Percentage Rate)

Do not panic when you see this figure! The APR is usually substantially higher than your note rate. That's because it is calculated based on the first year of the loan and includes all your discount points, fees, and other closing costs (which are called prepaid finance charges).

Note Rate

The actual interest rate of your mortgage.

HUD-1

The most common type of closing statement, the HUD-1 is prepared by escrow and itemizes all your costs and expenses in the transaction. You should be given a copy in advance of your signing appointment so you can review it and make sure all the charges and credits are correct. Your agent, your lender, and escrow will all be able to explain any items you don't understand.

Appraisal

An assessment of the fair market value of the property, detailed in its own section below.

The appraisal

The appraisal is prepared by an impartial professional who is hired by your lender—although you pay for it. Its purpose is to prove that the property is worth what you're paying for it. (Do not confuse the appraised value with the assessed valuation of your property done by the **State Tax Office**. The assessed valuation determines how much property tax you owe each year. The two are entirely different things and may not even be close to each other in dollar amounts.)

The lending institution will allow you to borrow the lesser of the percentage of the sale price you've qualified for or that same percentage of the appraised value. For example:

The purchase price you agree to is $300,000. You have 10 percent in cash, $30,000. Say you apply for a loan program for which the maximum allowable LTV is 90 percent, $270,000.

The appraisal is different than the assessed valuation of your property done by the State Tax Office.

If the appraisal comes in at $300,000 or more, the lender will lend you 90 percent of the sale price, the $270,000 you need. But if the appraisal only comes in at $275,000, the lender will only lend 90 percent of that amount, $247,500. In that instance, you'd have to come up with the difference between the $300,000 purchase price and the lender's maximum loan amount of $247,500—$52,500.

What if you only have the $30,000 you agreed to?

That is why there is a clause in your DROA that states your performance is contingent upon the specific financing described on that DROA. You can't be forced to come up with the extra $22,500. If you can't or choose not to, you may cancel the contract based on failure to get the loan you specified.

Don't, under any circumstances, sign a contract promising cash you don't have or aren't certain you can get.

The appraisal, while done primarily to protect the lender, also protects you. If, for any reason, the property's value can't be established at or near the price you've agreed to pay, you will at the very least be alerted to the fact before you close.

Appraisal contingencies

Strategy tip: Sometimes buyers who feel they're paying top dollar, or maybe even more, want to make their contract specifically contingent on the appraisal figure. Doing that is another type of judgment call—a strategic one. It can put one more roadblock in the path between offer and acceptance that may not be necessary. If you are already contingent upon financing, you probably don't need to plant additional fear in the seller's mind or call his attention to the idea that you think you're paying too much. However, there are exceptions. Sometimes, for instance, in heavy negotiations, a buyer may say, "All right, Mr. Seller, I'll give you what you want, but only if the appraisal comes in on the money. If not, I want to renegotiate our deal." Confer with your agent if you think this is a good strategy for you and think through the risks and rewards carefully.

Aren't appraisals just a game? Lots of people believe they are often simply boilerplate or made as instructed. Don't bet on that one. Here's what I believe, and I think common sense bears it out.

Appraisers are forced to write a single dollar figure on the paperwork despite the fact that no two properties are absolutely identical, there are many variables in the calculation, and there is no way anyone, professional or otherwise, can establish an accurate value of real property down to the penny. A range that is accurate can be established, though, and the appraiser knows what price you've agreed to pay. If that price falls within the acceptable range, chances are good the appraisal will come in at that figure. This saves many ridiculous arguments over petty differences.

However, if there is a wide divergence between the price and the appraiser's assessment, that will be an entirely different story. The bank or lender, after all, has hired the appraiser to tell them if the property—their security—is worth what they're lending. If they don't do that in a competent or honest manner, they won't have a job for very long.

There are certain circumstances when you can appeal appraisal results.

So what's considered a reasonable range? Good question. I believe three percent in either direction is acceptable ($9,000 in the above example), and experience tells me most appraisers are flexible up to that point, but I'm sure not everyone would agree. It's a judgment call.

Low appraisals do happen with fair regularity, especially in a rising market. Just as the comparables your agent prepares are based on past history, so are the numbers used by the appraiser when he makes his formal evaluation. Usually the discrepancy isn't great, but sometimes it is. And sometimes the buyer or the seller and/or one or both of the agents involved may feel the appraisal is too far out of range. Can anything be done? Maybe. It depends upon the facts.

It's possible to appeal the results and ask the lender to request a reevaluation, but you need to provide new information that changes the appraiser's calculation. That is usually in the form of a new comparable, a closed sale that he did not consider earlier and one that unquestionably meets the guidelines for similarity and proximity.

If the lender or the appraiser is unwilling to consider new material information, the buyer can always seek another lender. This means, though, that the transaction may be delayed and the buyer will have to pay another application and appraisal fee, which costs about $500 to $600 as I write this. Obviously, you'd have to know your new information is substantial.

As usual, forewarned is forearmed and information is one's best armament. If an appraisal problem is anticipated, it's far better to deal with that potential before the report is complete.

- ✔ The buyer or seller or their agents can supply comparable data—actual closed sales of similar properties—to the appraiser in advance; you should do this if there's any doubt that the report will be "on the money."

- ✔ Agents can also use the Multiple Listing database to research pending comparable transactions in escrow and find out when they're scheduled to close. If the closing date of a good comp is going to happen before the appraisal must be completed, the appraiser can be asked to wait for it to go on the record before submitting his report.

- ✔ Sellers can supply the appraiser with details about substantial remodeling or improvements to the property and their cost. This must be in writing, but most sellers who've done substantial work have records of their expenses.

- ✔ Finally, in a steeply rising market, comparable sales even three months old may not reflect current conditions. If there are no direct comparables recent enough to reflect

A Final Note on Appraisals

I've read in a couple of real estate manuals that sometimes lenders deliberately "sandbag" (sabotage) a transaction by asking for an artificially low appraisal. Supposedly this happens when the institution doesn't want to make the loan and wants to get out of their commitment.

Maybe that happens in some other places, but I've never heard of it in Hawai'i in all my 20+ years in business. I didn't believe it when I read it and I don't believe it now.

Why not? Because it doesn't make sense.

First of all, lending money is the lender's entire *raison d'etre*—the whole reason for the lender's existence. If they don't want to lend . . . You finish that sentence.

Secondly, if the buyer isn't qualified to make the payment, the loan won't be made no matter what the appraisal says. In fact, the application probably won't even get far enough for the appraisal to be ordered.

And third, if there's something wrong with the property that makes the lender not want to accept it as security, then either it doesn't qualify for the loan program at all, doesn't meet the guidelines in the first place, or there's a problem with its value. And if there's a legitimate problem with value, then the appraisal isn't artificially low.

When I read about this practice, it sounded to me as if the author believed some lending institutions do this to camouflage some kind of illegal discrimination. All I can do is repeat that I've never experienced anything like that here in Hawai'i, and I don't know anyone else who's experienced it either. I've run into some not-too-bright lenders over the years, but none who would shoot themselves in the foot quite so stupidly.

Your best strategy for trouble-free loan application, appraisal, processing, and closing is to select a knowledgeable and reputable loan officer or mortgage broker, who works with experienced allied professionals and wants your business.

the present market, an appraiser may sometimes make an adjustment using sales from outside the immediate area or that don't otherwise match up as well as is ordinarily required.

Strategies if a low appraisal can't be prevented

✔ Have some additional cash you can add to the down payment.

✔ Apply for a different loan program that requires a smaller percent down.

✔ Ask the seller to give you a small second mortgage to make up the difference.

✔ Renegotiate the sale price (very iffy unless no other buyer is on the horizon and the seller is highly motivated).

Loan processing

After you have made your loan application and the appraisal has been ordered, buyers usually sit back and wait for approval, frequently wondering what's taking so long!

Believe it or not, it takes between ten and twenty independent professionals and companies to make a closing happen. Here's a partial list: You, the other principal to your transaction, your agent, his agent, the home inspector, the escrow officer, the title search company, the loan officer, the loan underwriter, the appraiser, the surveyor, the termite inspector, the lawyer who drafts the deed, the lawyer who drafts the mortgage and note And there may be others.

Any glitch in the system can delay the process. That's what takes so long.

So go ahead and be nervous; everybody is. But try to be patient. If you're working with good people, all will ultimately be well.

> ## Loan Processing
>
> Your loan officer puts paperwork from all concerned into a loan package and submits it to the loan underwriter, a very important someone you'll probably never meet. That underwriter has all the power. He or she reviews the entire package and frequently requires a few more items ("conditions") before loan approval is granted. These will be listed on a conditional approval letter. They may simply be formalities, or they may be significant. They may be something you must take care of or they may be somebody else's responsibility. Regardless, you will not receive your loan unless and until all conditions have been met, and you should vigilantly make certain all concerned provide what's required.

Interest rates and your mortgage

Although most people either sell or refinance after about seven years, there's a rule of thumb that says if you have a 30-year mortgage and keep the house for the entire time, your payments will total two to three times the beginning principal balance of the mortgage by the time it's paid off. (The actual dollar figure appears at the top of your Truth In Lending statement.) Whether over seven years or thirty, those payments add up to a whole lot of money. How do you get the best value for your dollar?

A substantial part of the answer depends on your personal situation and financial plan, but here are a couple of ideas to think about.

If interest rates are high when you buy, refinance the house when rates drop substantially. To figure out when a refinance makes good sense, ask your lender for a written all-inclusive estimate of the costs involved. Then find out what your new monthly payment would be. Presumably, it will be less than your present payment. Divide that difference into the cost of the "re-fi" to come up with the number of months it will take to recoup your expense.

For example, say a re-fi will cost $7,000 but save $200 per month. If you do the refinance, you will have covered the cost in thirty-five

How Changing Interest Rates Affect You

Interest is the cost of borrowing money. Banks and other lenders make a profit in proportion to the interest rate they charge. From their point of view, the higher the better. From yours, the reverse. Interest is expressed as a percentage of the amount borrowed (the principal amount). On mortgage loans, it is calculated monthly on the declining principal balance, which is amortized (paid off) over the life (term) of the loan. You probably don't care about any of that. You want the bottom line. How do changing interest rates affect you?

If you borrow $100,000 (the principal) for thirty years (the term) at 6 percent interest, your payment of principal and interest is $599.55 monthly for 360 months.

If the rate goes down to 5.75 percent, the payment is $583.57—$15.98 less.

But if the rate goes up to 6.25 percent, the payment is $615.72—$16.17 more.

This doesn't appear to be a material difference, and it may not be.

However, if you're borrowing $500,000 instead of $100,000, you must multiply that difference by 5. It could start to eat into the budget or be a substantial savings, depending on which direction the interest rate has moved.

At 6 percent, your total of principal and interest on a $500,000 loan for 30 years will be approximately $1,079,191.00.

That same $500,000 at 6.25 percent will cost you approximately $1,108,291.00 if it's carried for the full life of the loan, a difference of $29,100.00 or about $1,000 per year.

Again, that may not be a material difference to you, BUT if rates jumped, say, from 6 percent to 7 percent, the monthly payment on that $500,000 loan would rise from $2,998.00 per month principal and interest to $3,327.00, an increase of $329.00. (The total cost over the life of a mortgage—360 months or 30 years—would be $118,440.00. And that makes a difference to just about everybody.)

So, if there's a general trend toward higher rates, you may want to purchase sooner rather than later.

months. After that, the monthly savings are real. Do you intend to hold the home for that amount of time or longer? If so, chances are the re-fi is a good idea.

To pay off your mortgage sooner than its full term, you normally can make additional principal payments at any time. Called "principal balance reduction," this usually does not decrease your monthly payment; it does accomplish a quicker payoff. You'll need to get instructions from your lender on how to make sure the additional money is applied against the principal.

There is one more thing to think about when initially arranging your mortgage: Many lenders offer a permanent buy-down of the interest rate in exchange for additional points. This strategy is more popular when rates are relatively high, but it can make sense in any market under the right circumstances. (One such occasion might be if you anticipate a reduced income in the future but have extra cash right now. The smaller monthly payment later on might be of tremendous benefit to both your wallet and your peace of mind.) To determine when your monthly payment savings becomes real, make the same calculation used above when comparing closing costs to monthly payments.

Bottom line: When you're applying for a mortgage loan, nothing is more important than working with a reputable, trustworthy loan officer who can offer a variety of programs customized to fit your requirements and qualifications. Often the property and the buyer must qualify. Do not deal with lenders who don't have offices in Hawai'i. There are many different types of loan programs, and terms and interest rates change frequently. A good loan officer will take the time to make sure you understand the terms of the financing you've applied for, will find the most favorable program for which you qualify, and will help you get your loan approved. Your real estate agent can give you valuable guidance in finding such a loan officer, but the final choice is yours.

Tips on refinancing and borrowing against your equity

People are frequently tempted to refinance or take out equity loans because the interest is tax-deductible whereas other types of interest are not. There can be limitations, though, and you should seek advice from a tax professional who understands your personal situation. People also take out equity loans because the interest rate can be a lot less for those loans than for other types of credit. That's true, too, but . . . **playing fast and loose with your equity is a losing strategy.**

In Hawai'i, a home's equity—that part of its value that doesn't belong to the bank—is frequently an owner's only savings account. Unfortunately, raiding that account—refinancing to pay off other debts—has become very popular, as has the indiscriminate use of equity lines of credit. It's unfortunate because the practice puts the homeowner's most valuable asset at risk and promotes the habit of living beyond your means. Over the last twenty or so years, almost every time I've worked with a seller who left closing with an empty wallet, he had already stripped his home of its equity.

I have one piece of advice: **Don't do that!**

Not ever? Well, almost never.
Here's a short list of times when it's okay:

1. Capital improvements, such as remodeling, building an addition, or maybe adding a swimming pool, add value to your home if done carefully and with adequate planning and thought. You are then not spending the loan proceeds, you are reinvesting them to make your home worth more money. Should you sell, you can then reasonably expect to recoup your investment.
    Note: Repairs don't count. They do not add value to your home; they only maintain its existing value. Of course, if you must borrow to make critical repairs, by all means do so.

2. When you'll still have at least 25 percent equity after you use the line of credit and other debts are so burdensome that your marriage, your peace of mind, or your ability to buy groceries is in jeopardy, you may want to borrow the money.

3. **And there's one time when it may be unavoidable:** A legitimate emergency when there's no other recourse. (If you think that's your situation, read the chapter "Strategies for Life Changes" for other possible options.)

If you're still not convinced that spending your equity is a bad idea, let's look at some more facts.

✔ You'll be making payments for a long time, as long as 30 years. Is taking 30 years to pay off a car or a refrigerator—much longer than the life of the vehicle or the appliance—good financial strategy? Even a very important investment, such as a child's college education, should be evaluated in terms of whether a student loan or other type of financing is a better idea than risking your family's home.

✔ Are there any closing costs? If yes, they must be added into the equation.

✔ How much extra are you paying each month for the additional cash? Multiply that by the number of months of the new loan's term and add the closing costs to the total. Then compare that against what you'd pay for the same amount of cash if it were obtained from another source, such as your credit union or bank. That will give you a true picture of the actual cost of the money you want to borrow.

What if an investment opportunity looks like it'll pay more than the interest you'll pay if you borrow against your house? It's your house, and it's your decision. I'm only advising you to think carefully and to take the time to figure out the real costs involved and the real consequences to you and your family if something doesn't work out.

The real danger of borrowing more than you owe on your present mortgage is if the market declines right after you pull out most of your equity, and then, for some reason, you have to sell. It is possible you'll then be in the position of owing more than the fair market sale price of your home. Bad.

Bad, bad, bad.

All of us in the business have seen cases where sellers were forced to bring money to the closing table, or worse, endure a foreclosure or a short sale (defined in the glossary), because they expected a rising market would keep on rising forever. In real life, that doesn't happen, so consider your options carefully when you borrow against your home!

When is refinancing a valid strategy?

To obtain a lower interest rate, so long as:

- ✔ You're only refinancing the existing present loan balance.

- ✔ The cost of the refinance (points, title insurance, and other closing costs) should be less than the reduction in monthly payment multiplied by the length of time you expect to own the home. (If you will save $100 per month and expect to own the home for five years (60 months) more, the strategy makes sense if it costs less than $6000.) Your lender must provide you with a **Truth-in-Lending** Statement that itemizes all of your costs.

Tips on Refinancing
and Borrowing Against Your Equity

Remember when you refinance, the term of the loan makes a difference as well. If you "re-fi" with a new 30-year mortgage, you're starting from scratch— 360 payments. If you've already made payments for ten years and plan to keep the home for the rest of your life, consider such things as whether the new loan term will extend beyond retirement and whether your income will then still be enough to cover the payment. Then calculate the new payment based on a 20-year term to make a true apples-and-apples comparison. If the new payment on a 20-year mortgage still saves you money, there's no question that it's a good idea. If not, then you must make a personal decision, balancing the monthly cash savings in the present tense against your ability to make future payments over the longer period of time.

Seller financing

You may have heard of real estate seminars where speakers—for a fee—will show you how to buy a home with no money, no income, and/or bad credit. I don't believe that's possible, at least not in Hawai'i, so that's not the subject of this section. Instead, this section will discuss legitimate ways buyers and sellers can work together to create a successful transaction when conventional mortgage financing won't work or is less desirable.

Agreement of sale
(sometimes called a contract for sale)

In Hawai'i, seller and buyer are called "vendor" and "vendee" in an agreement of sale, but I'll just use seller and buyer to keep things simple.

Agreements of sale are usually most popular when interest rates are high. A clever seller who doesn't need all his proceeds at closing can create a win-win scenario by, in essence, becoming the bank and lending what would have been first mortgage funds at a lower interest rate than conventional lenders. Also, a seller may occasionally prefer to transact this way for tax purposes or because a regular monthly income is appealing.

With this type of financing, the seller receives a down payment followed by regular monthly payments over a specific period of time at a specified interest rate, after which the buyer must pay him off in full or refinance the property. Agreements of sale for a full 30-year term are theoretically possible, but almost nonexistent. The most common terms are two to five years. The agreement of sale can be negotiated according to the personal needs of both parties without regard for bank or mortgage company guidelines or requirements and so can be a good vehicle for investor-buyers. The usual investor down payment required with conventional lenders is 30 percent; under an agreement of sale, the down payment is negotiable. You'll find details and particulars in a copy of the standard Hawaii Association of Realtors' Agreement of Sale Addendum that's included in the Appendix.

Here is some basic guidance about agreements of sale that both buyers and sellers should keep in mind:

Agreement of Sale

Benefits to the buyer:

- ✔ More favorable interest rate; lower monthly payments
- ✔ Down payment is negotiable
- ✔ No discount points; lower closing costs at initial purchase
- ✔ Tax position no different than with conventional financing
- ✔ Acquire property at today's price
- ✔ Buy time to allow interest rates to drop
- ✔ Sellers may consider exceptional circumstances when evaluating a buyer's qualifications and may be more accommodating than a bank or mortgage company

Benefits to the seller:

- ✔ May obtain a higher price because he can accept a lower interest rate than banks and mortgage companies offer
- ✔ May be able to sell more quickly in an unfavorable market
- ✔ Receives interest from the buyer in addition to the purchase price, ultimately increasing the total dollar amount of his proceeds
- ✔ Receives a down payment that may be sufficient for him to purchase a replacement property
- ✔ Receives a regular monthly income

- ✔ In Hawai'i the seller under an agreement of sale does not relinquish title to the property until he's been paid in full, but the agreement is recorded at the Bureau of Conveyances.

- ✔ The buyer, however, may convey the property to somebody else without the seller's permission, so long as the agreement of sale is paid off.

- ✔ The seller's own mortgage may be called fully due and payable if his lender finds out he's sold the property using an agreement of sale; the best seller is one who owns his property free and clear or who owes so little that the buyer's down payment can pay it off.

- ✔ The seller can (and should) require details about the buyer's employment and finances as a condition of the agreement, just as a bank would; should get authorization from the buyer to verify the information just as a bank would; and, if necessary, get assistance in interpreting such items as credit reports from his own bank, credit union, or other financial expert.

✔ The real estate commission is due upon the closing of the agreement of sale, so the down payment should be sufficient to cover that, in addition to other costs.

Seller secondary mortgage financing

A second mortgage is used when an otherwise qualified buyer doesn't have enough of a down payment for a first mortgage at favorable terms, or when that first mortgage would require mortgage insurance. Today, many conventional lenders also offer package loan programs to cover this situation. They are called "80-10-10's" or "80-15-5's"; the first number is the first mortgage's percentage of the price, the second number is the second mortgage's percentage of the price and the third number is the percentage of the buyer's down payment.

Seller second mortgages can also prove useful in a rising market, when the lender's appraisal (remember, that's based on past sales) might be lower than the sale price.

Seller Secondary Mortgage Financing

Red flag: Sometimes people are tempted to utilize an "under-the-table" second mortgage, one that is not recorded at the Bureau of Conveyances, to circumvent the primary lender's guidelines. This poses a great risk to the seller if his recordkeeping is not up to par or if for any reason in the future the property is sold without his knowledge—he may not be paid off. If he dies, his heirs may not know about or be able to prove the debt. There are also risks to the buyer and/or his heirs of lawsuits or liens being filed against other assets—though if he doesn't want to pay the debt in the first place, he may not care.

Sellers: Don't allow this.

Many of the benefits to both buyer and seller are similar to those of an agreement of sale; but there are significant differences.

- ✔ The second mortgage, by definition, is in second place to the primary financing. In the event of foreclosure, the seller will be paid off only after the first mortgage and other debts (such as tax liens) that may take priority are paid off. This raises the seller's risk.

- ✔ A second mortgage is usually for a relatively small amount (5 to 15 percent is common), so the seller gets most of his proceeds at closing thus reducing the seller's risk of loss.

- ✔ The buyer's qualifications will also be evaluated by a conventional financial institution, and the buyer may authorize that lender to share the information with the seller, perhaps giving the seller a higher level of confidence in his ability to make the payments.

- ✔ Conventional lenders generally require a minimum percentage of the down payment to be the buyer's own funds, so trying to purchase property this way with no down payment may sabotage the first mortgage financing.

Lease with option to purchase

Buyer and seller are called "optionee" and "optionor" in Hawai'i, but again I'll keep it simple and use buyer and seller.

A lease like this can be very useful when it's not possible or beneficial for one or both parties to close a sale immediately. A buyer may want to occupy and use the property right away but be unable to obtain financing now. Delaying receipt of sale proceeds or receiving monthly payments of rent instead of principal and interest may be beneficial to a seller, depending on his personal situation. Real estate speculators may use this vehicle to hedge their bets: it allows them to control property for a specific period of time and limits their financial risk.

A buyer makes a cash down payment, called an option fee, to a seller. This is nonrefundable; the seller can do whatever he wants with the money. (Logic will tell you this fee must be sufficient to persuade the seller not to market the property during the option period.)

The seller also gives the buyer a lease to the property for a mutually agreeable period of time and receives monthly rent. By the end of this period, the buyer must either pay off the property in cash, obtain financing to pay it off, or return the property to the seller.

A real estate attorney will formalize an option agreement according to the negotiated deal drafted by the parties or their agents. A sample form used by the Hawaii Association of Realtors is included in the Appendix.

What are some possible benefits and risks to buyers and sellers?

- ✔ In both agreements of sale and seller secondary financing, a seller lends money to a buyer to close a sale transaction. A lease with option does not close, thus foreclosure is not an issue.

- ✔ The seller does not have to return the option fee or any rent to the buyer if the buyer does not exercise the option unless he's specifically made a written agreement otherwise.

- ✔ The parties (buyer and seller) may agree that the buyer will pay more than fair-market rent every month, the excess to be applied to his down payment, thus allowing a buyer to gradually accumulate the lender-required down payment while he is occupying and using the property. This is generally acceptable to conventional lenders, *so long as the amount to be applied to the down payment is clearly spelled out in writing in the agreement as being in excess of fair-market rent.*

- ✔ The buyer's potential loss is limited to the option fee and possibly any excess monthly payments. He can walk away at the end of the option period with no further obligation. His credit rating will in no way be affected so long as he's made all his required monthly payments.

✔ The buyer may not transfer his option to a third party during the option period without specific written permission of the seller.

Borrowing from friends or family, or receiving a gift of the down payment

This practice is very common in Hawai'i given our high real estate values. Parents are frequently called upon to help their children obtain their first home.

There are explicit rules on how much of the down payment may be borrowed. Most lenders require a certain percentage to be the buyer's own funds. Check with your lender regarding the rules in your particular case.

The sudden appearance of an unexplained large sum of money in a buyer's bank account raises a red flag to the lender. It may appear the buyer has incurred a debt without telling his lender. If you receive a gift of the down payment, or part of it, the source of the funds must be disclosed, and the lender must be able to verify that source.

Many thanks to Barry Birdsall, president and owner of South Pacific Mortgage Corporation in Kailua, Hawai'i, who kindly consulted and advised on this chapter.

16

Closing Costs and Customer Trust Accounts

Closing costs are the buyer's purchase expenses and the seller's sale expenses. Many of them are listed on the DROA, which also designates which party pays what (unless otherwise specified). The DROA may not be comprehensive, however; each transaction may involve other expenses along the way. They must all be paid on or before closing.

For the buyer, the largest dollar amounts are usually discount points and origination fees for his new mortgage. For the seller, the largest single item after paying off his existing mortgage(s) will likely be the real estate commission. Both parties will be obligated for their share of escrow and title fees and other expenses. These can range from pest extermination (relatively expensive) to notary fees (relatively cheap).

Escrow prepares an estimated itemized statement, usually on a standard form called a HUD-1, before recordation. It's based upon the DROA, the escrow instructions issued by the agents, pay-off figures provided by lenders and invoices they receive from other involved parties. The estimate is provided to the buyer, the seller, and their agents before the formal signing of documents. This is the point where discrepancies should be caught. Review it carefully.

- ✔ All the seller's existing debts on the property and the transaction must be paid off upon transfer to a new owner.

- ✔ All of the buyer's obligations incurred for the transaction must be paid with the buyer's funds or covered by new financing.

- ✔ Escrow collects and holds all cash funds as well as the funds from the new lender.

✔ These funds must be sufficient to pay off all the buyer's and seller's obligations or the transaction cannot close.

✔ Once the HUD-1 has been reviewed, buyer and seller both sign their respective statements, agreeing that the funds should be distributed accordingly.

✔ An updated title search is done just prior to recording to be sure no new obligations have come into the picture.

✔ Upon recordation, escrow distributes the funds wherever they belong.

✔ The Bureau of Conveyances records the new transaction, as well as the new financing and releases for liens that the seller has paid off.

✔ Both the buyer's and the seller's closing statements may include items that affect their respective tax returns. Both will receive copies of their own final closing statements, signed by the escrow officer. It's important that you keep those statements for tax time. Oftentimes there are deductible items there that don't appear anywhere else!

The rules and procedures can be summarized this way:

Customer trust accounts are accounts set up by the lender to pay property taxes and insurance on your behalf when they're due. Here's how the accounts work. At closing, the escrow company collects from the buyer all prorated items, such as property taxes and homeowner's insurance, that were paid in advance by the seller and are due back to the seller. They also collect about two months' worth of those same items in advance from the buyer and give that money to the lender. The lender then puts the money into the customer trust account (also called an impound or an escrow account). Your regular monthly payment will also include one month's worth of those same items. Thus, the lender will always have enough money to pay the bills.

Title Insurance

Your closing statement will include a one-time charge for title insurance. It protects you—and your lender—against forgery, fraud, undiscovered owners, and many other hidden risks that could affect your ownership status. Title insurance is required by all lenders. The policy will be arranged by escrow; you don't have to initiate any action. In Hawai'i, the seller customarily pays 60 percent of the total premium for a standard policy; the buyer pays the other 40 percent. Extended coverage policies—which cover more eventualities—are also offered for an additional charge. If a buyer chooses one of these policies, he must pay the additional premium.

A comparison chart listing the possible situations that are or are not covered by the various types of policies may be found in the envelope you receive from the escrow company at the beginning of your transaction. If you don't receive a chart, ask for one.

Some real estate and escrow companies now routinely order an extended coverage policy unless they're instructed otherwise, and you may decide that the peace of mind that comes with the relatively small additional premium is well worth it.

You will receive an annual accounting of all principal, interest, and impounds from your lender. If the account grows larger than the lender is allowed to keep in your customer trust fund, it will refund the difference. If expenses such as insurance or taxes increase, your lender will increase your monthly payment accordingly. When a loan is paid off, the lender will reimburse any unused funds in the customer trust account. This, however, is usually by way of a separate check directly from the lender and it does not pass through escrow. Sellers, make sure your lender has your forwarding address!

Condominium maintenance fees are also collected by escrow at closing, but are given to the condo management company instead of to your lender. Ordinarily, you write a separate monthly check for maintenance fees.

If the property is leasehold, the lease rent is also collected in the same manner, by escrow at closing. The money may be sent directly to the lessor or to the management company or a condominium.

Mortgage Principal and Interest Paid at Closing

Interest is always paid in arrears. You don't owe interest on a debt until after the applicable accrual period has passed. This means, for example, that mortgage interest for January is paid in February.

When you obtain a new mortgage, your first interest payment will not be due until the following month. And if you close at any other time than the first day of a month, your first payment will not be even; it'll be for some portion of a month.

To avoid confusion and complications, as well as to circumvent paperwork delays and snafus with a new loan, escrow companies normally collect some funds at closing that actually constitute some part of a mortgage payment.

For example:

If you close on June 20, escrow will collect prorated principal and interest from June 20 through the 30, and principal for the month of July.

Your first payment will be due in August, and will include August's principal and July's interest.

What this means to you:

✔ You probably will need extra cash beyond down payment and closing costs at closing.

✔ You probably will not make a regular mortgage payment the first month after you close.

✔ The charge for mortgage interest on your closing statement (HUD-1) may not be reflected on the lender's year-end statement to you.

Important note: Other items on the HUD-1 may also affect your tax return, including prorated property taxes and discount points paid in cash at closing.

So you should:

✔ Keep that HUD-1 for your tax preparer.

Whatever the arrangement, you will be given complete instructions as to who must be paid and when.

These other expenses and fees affect your budget and are taken into account by the l en he's calculating your loan qualification. There are a couple of other things you need to know:

- ✔ Your mortgage will not be funded unless your homeowner's insurance policy is in place. You must pay a whole year's premium at or before closing. Don't forget to plan for it!

- ✔ Condominium maintenance fees affect the amount of the mortgage loan you qualify for; single family homes also require maintenance. Thus, if you're buying a property with no required maintenance fee, you will qualify for a larger mortgage.

- ✔ All items paid in advance or prorated are accounted for on your HUD-1.

How to Choose a Seller's Agent

Unless you inherited your property, you were probably represented by an agent when you bought it. If you received top service then, that is the best indication you will get such service again. If that experience was a good one, the first person to call when you're about to sell is the agent who sold it to you.

However, if rehiring your former agent is not an option, here's how to proceed:

✔ If you know a good real estate agent, call her. If you know several, call at least three—or everyone you feel might be hurt or offended if they're not given an opportunity to represent you. Ask them all for a formal appointment and listing presentation at the property you are selling (at different times, of course).

✔ Tell each of them that you are interviewing others. This disclosure makes the process objective and businesslike, allowing you to choose the best agent without hurting feelings or jeopardizing your personal relationships.

✔ An appointment at the property will allow you to assess the agent's marketing approach, enthusiasm, and professionalism. It will also allow you to discuss potential problem areas on the spot and evaluate suggested solutions.

✔ A formal listing interview should include a presentation of the agent's and company's services and marketing plan: a detailed strategy for exposing the property through open houses, showings, media, etc., as well as fees and itemized responsibilities of both agent and client.

Here are some things to consider when you're selecting a seller's agent that don't apply when you're selecting a buyer's agent.

The dual agency issue: You may be asked to sign a dual agency agreement at the time you list your home; or you will be asked to sign one if a buyer represented by your agent or her company makes an offer. There is only one question you need to ask yourself: If my agent (or a member of her company) has a buyer for my house, do I want to turn her away? Answer this for yourself and if the answer is "no," sign the agreement.

Taking care of your property: Your agent will have keys to your house and be there often when you are not there. You need to be comfortable with how your agent manages, among other things,

---

How to Choose an Agent
When You Are the Seller: Example 1

I once knew of a property that was coming on the market. I had represented the seller when the property was last on the market, so I was acquainted with the current owner but had never represented him. I called to ask for a listing interview and was told he'd decided with about 85 percent certainty to hire another agent. I'm fairly certain he only agreed to an appointment because he thought refusing my request would cause hard feelings, so I was fairly discouraged but decided to give the listing my best try. I made a formal presentation— including property analysis, marketing plan, services and fees, suggested list price, and estimated time for marketing. The seller asked to sign the listing agreement immediately after I finished the presentation. Astonishment must have shown on my face. He then explained he'd changed his mind when he saw I took nothing for granted. The other agent had assumed the listing would be hers and had not made any presentation at all.

There's a lesson there for both clients and agents. A presentation should show professionalism, enthusiasm, and product knowledge. If it does, put that agent on your list of finalists. If not, end of story. (Agents, if you need further explanation, you're probably in the wrong line of work.)

How to Choose an Agent When You Are the Seller: Example 2

Early in my own career, a rather scruffily dressed man (even for casual Hawai'i) rode up to my open house on a bicycle. He took my fact sheet, spoke politely, and proceeded to look at the home—for a very long time. I began to feel uncomfortable. I'd learned where people focus when they look at a house—not usually on the bedroom closets. A while later I noticed him carefully inspecting a glass sliding door that led out into the yard. Again, not normally a primary area of attention. When I said something, he muttered that the door appeared off the track. Not so, I knew very well. I trailed the man—if he was an honest buyer, he undoubtedly thought I was the most aggressive agent he'd ever met—and tried to make conversation. By then it was five o'clock, time to close up and go home. The man showed no signs of leaving—not normal for an unwilling victim of a hard sell. I left the front door standing open, the signs were still in the yard. The owners had told me to lock up and leave when the open house was over, they wouldn't be back until later that evening. I was alone there, feeling more and more insecure.

Fortunately, at that moment another car drove up. Its occupants were running late, they said, but really wanted to see the house, and would I mind waiting? Of course not, I said with great relief. The strange man faded back down the hallway toward the bedrooms and I followed the new visitors into the kitchen, quietly buttonholed the husband in the corner by the washing machine, explained my problem with great embarrassment, and asked if they would please stay with me until the other man left. Thankfully, he too had noticed the man's rather strange behavior. Of course, he said, and hustled off to whisper to his wife. It took about fifteen more minutes—an eternity under the circumstances—but the strange man finally left on his bicycle. All this happened in the days before cell phones—I didn't know where the owners were and had no way of reaching them. I thanked my presumed rescuers profusely and they went on their way. Maybe I should stay, wait for the owners, I thought, and made a quick call to my home. Not alone, my husband said. Leave the door open and the lights on, I'll be right up there. He came up and we waited together, fortunately not too long, for the owners to come home. I kept looking out the windows for a man on a bicycle, but he did not return.

The next day, at my company staff meeting, I mentioned the incident. Two of my associates jerked upright in their chairs and said they thought the same man had come to their open houses. His behavior with them had been odd as well. He hadn't done anything wrong, so there was no point in calling the police, but we decided to alert our competitors and made some calls to other companies. Eventually we discovered the man had alarmed several other agents. A couple of them felt he wasn't canvassing houses for burglaries, but rather trying to get them alone and vulnerable in empty houses. We never found out if our concerns were justified, but by the end of the day, there wasn't an agent in our town who hadn't been warned. The man was not seen either on the following Sunday or on any other Sunday afterward, to my knowledge.

That ending falls flat, doesn't it? Not very dramatic. But trust me, when you're marketing your home, drama is the very last thing you want!

I tried to think on my feet, use common sense, do the best I could to safeguard my client's property without causing an unjustified ruckus. Nothing bad happened. Maybe nothing bad would have happened. But after that, I always made sure I had at least two ways to get out of the house and that I knew how to lock everything. (In Hawai'i, we're in the habit of assuming we're safe. Many people still don't lock their houses.)

The point? When you're marketing a home, all kinds of people have access at one time or another. Keep that in mind when you hire an agent and make the showing arrangements together.

your lights, your locks, your pets, and, occasionally, your children. It's very important. Your agent will advise how you should take care of valuables and fragile items, etc., on a case-by-case basis, and you must tell your agent of any concerns of your own.

Handling questionable visitors: Your agent will probably hold an open house. There could be as many as fifty visitors. Problems with visitors are very rare in Hawai'i, but you still need to feel confident that your agent is capable of safeguarding your property.

> ## How to Choose an Agent
> ## When You Are the Seller: Example 3
>
> There are subtle as well as direct ways of interviewing agents. Here is a clever method that was used by one of my own eventual clients.
>
> *I had a lovely listing in a nice area of my hometown of Kailua. I particularly liked the family room in that house (it had a working fireplace, most unusual here, and wide sliding glass doors that opened onto a beautiful yard), so that's where I set up shop for my first open house. It was well-attended and several neighbors came by. I spent the afternoon greeting everyone, telling them how nice the neighborhood was and how pleasant it was to sit in that terrific family room. The following week I got a call from one of the open house guests. At first I thought they wanted to buy my listing, but soon learned they already lived across the street, were moving to the mainland, and getting ready to put their own house on the market. They had attended several open houses to find out how various agents showed the properties and how they handled potential buyers.*
>
> I thought this was a very clever idea, and not just because they liked my approach and asked me to be their agent. And Jean Wade smiled quietly when I told her the story. She had taught me never to ignore the neighbors—or to assume they're simply snoopy.

However, while security is important, it's not the primary focus of an open house or any property showing.

Personality and manner: Your agent must be able to gain rapport, quickly, with different kinds of people, not just you. She must have an enthusiastic attitude, a courteous and friendly manner and be able to talk-talk-talk to many, many people. In a word: She must be a communicator.

A positive attitude is crucial. Your agent *must* have a positive attitude toward your home. Are there any negative features to your property? Yes, there always are, no matter how desirable your property may be. Talk to your agent about those features and satisfy yourself that she will put them in the most positive light without being deceptive. Is there a lot of street noise? Maybe it's offset by the home's convenient proximity to bus stops and shopping. Is the yard small? There's not a lot of maintenance. Is the carpet stained or damaged? Perhaps there could be a credit for the buyer to select his own floor covering.

There's a buyer for every house. Make sure your agent's mission is to reach out and find the buyer for yours. Some find it valuable to have a highly critical, fault-finding agent when they're buying, but when you're the seller? No way.

How do you know if an agent really likes your property?

Here's how:

She will express enthusiasm for the property even when she's dealing with its negative factors. She will have an idea how to handle potential buyer objections.

My mentor, Jean Wade, who I believe is perhaps the best realtor who ever lived, had a simple piece of advice for dealing with valid buyer objections: "Just look the client in the eye, tell him he's right, and call him by name." It took me a while to figure out what that meant and why it worked. What it meant was, argument is useless so acknowledge and validate him. He will let you know if the objection is a deal-breaker. If it is, you need another buyer. If it's not, don't shoot yourself in the foot belaboring the issue.

(A question for those thinking of representing themselves: Can you be that cool-headed and diplomatic when a buyer makes negative or tactless remarks about your home?)

A good agent welcomes objections and takes time to handle them carefully and well. What sounds like an objection often is, to an agent's experienced ears, really a question that indicates interest in the property. Would a person spend valuable time discussing a property he's not interested in? A good agent can tell the difference between an objection that's really a question and one that says the buyer is not interested.

A good seller's agent will find something unique about every property, even a condominium that has 100 identical units, and will be quick to recognize your home's special features.

A good agent will also advise you frankly about negative features you can fix or change before marketing (for example, the above-mentioned carpet). The chapter on seller's strategies discusses how to show a home to its best advantage; for now, just keep in mind that it's your agent's job to obtain the best possible price and terms for you, so it's a good idea to listen to her constructive suggestions.

A good seller's agent will find something unique about every property.

I'm often asked about neighborhood specialists. Those are agents who have a great deal of specialized knowledge and experience about a relatively small area. They may live there themselves and therefore be very enthusiastic about it. Many of them know everything that's going on, have many contacts in the area and may have buyer clients interested in the area. They probably can predict the actual sale price of your property within one to two percent.

Product knowledge is as important in our business as in any other, and a neighborhood specialist may impress you with how much she knows about your property and those of your neighbors. She also will undoubtedly impress potential buyers the same way, and they are likely to feel confident it's a good area if she lives there herself.

Hiring such an agent can be a good strategy if:

- ✔ The agent is just as experienced and qualified as others you've interviewed.

- ✔ The agent has an excellent personal reputation and works for a reputable company.

- ✔ You trust her and feel comfortable with her.

- ✔ You don't owe your loyalty to somebody else.

The first three items should be obvious. What about that last one? Isn't it better to get the best agent than offend your last agent?

Yes, it is. But I wrote, "If you *owe* your loyalty to somebody else." A good experience with a good agent should earn your loyalty and override and supercede anyone else's listing presentation because your previous agent has already proved herself worthy of your business! And if that agent represented you when you bought the property, you know how she will present it to potential buyers now—you bought it, didn't you?

However, listen to the neighborhood specialist's presentation. If she tells you she can get a higher price for you, that's where you should see a large red flag because all agents who are members of their local Board of Realtors have access to the identical database, whether or not they specialize in a particular neighborhood. Any reasonably competent agent can find out all the pertinent facts about an area in a couple of hours' research on the computer. No agent, competent or otherwise, can guarantee to get you more money than any other. That should never be your sole reason for hiring anyone.

Bottom lines:

- ✔ Enthusiasm and a positive attitude are critical attributes in a listing agent.

- ✔ Personal trust is also important, as your agent must represent your views, carry out your instructions, and deal with people in your property when you are not there.

- ✔ If the agent who represented you when you bought the property did a good job, you should consider that agent first when selling it.

- ✔ If you're considering more than one agent, a formal listing presentation will demonstrate the candidates' relative expertise and communication skills.

- ✔ Intelligence, common sense, professionalism, and a willingness to follow through are the agent qualities most likely to bring you the highest and best offer.

✔ Do not select an agent based only on which one suggested the highest asking price. Asking prices do not necessarily result in a sale at, or even near, that figure. It's far smarter to select the agent whose suggested asking price most closely matches the actual supporting data. Don't hire an agent who doesn't provide that data.

✔ Make sure the agent you hire will be working personally with you. (If a licensed assistant is going to be your actual agent for all practical purposes, then you need to interview the assistant.)

Strategies For Selling Your Home Successfully

To fix or not to fix

Everything you'll consider doing to your home to get it ready to put on the market falls into one of three categories:

Major repairs

Major defects must be disclosed, and buyers usually estimate repair costs much higher than they actually will be and then factor those estimates into their offer price. So selling your home as a fixer-upper is a losing strategy unless you have no other choice.

Having no choice comes down to one of two things: Either the problem can't be fixed, or you can't afford to fix it. In the latter case, you will almost always be better off if you can find a way to afford the repairs. If you do repair, make sure you do the following:

- ✔ Use licensed professionals. Poorly done repairs are often worse than none and will be spotted by buyers. Undoing a bad repair job later often costs more than doing it properly in the first place. In addition, many kinds of work are required by law to be done by licensed contractors.

- ✔ Get permits if they are required. Your buyer will probably ask for them, and getting retroactive permits is more expensive than getting them before the work is done.

- ✔ Keep all paperwork. You can show a buyer exactly what you did and what it cost. Also, you may be able to deduct the cost if it meets IRS requirements.

If you decide against a major repair or if one can't be done, then you must disclose the problem (as advised exhaustively elsewhere) and give even more emphasis to the next two categories.

Minor repairs and maintenance

Pay particular attention to anything that leaks and anything that's electrical. Fix torn screens, broken hinges and handles, sliding doors that are off-track, cracked glass, etc. Repair and repaint any exterior areas that are damaged or showing signs of rot. On the inside, repaint any surfaces that don't come clean or where the paint is worn or chipped. Repair damaged drywall. Recaulk sinks, tubs, toilets, and wherever necessary. Regrout ceramic tile if the grout is stained or cracked. Reattach loose floor coverings or wallpaper (so long as they aren't damaged).

Do anything else you can think of to put everything in working order. Then move on to:

Cosmetics

Generally the term cosmetics refers to things that make the house look nice, but don't affect its usability. Certainly, major repairs that affect value should be done first, as should maintenance items and minor fixes. Cosmetic items can range from a major remodel of a kitchen or bath to a complete interior and exterior paint job to all new appliances or floor coverings. Your changes will depend on your budget and your time, as well as an assessment of how much will likely be recouped in a higher sale price.

Make your home look and show its best

Once you list your home for sale, it's a piece of merchandise like any other, and it will be viewed judgmentally by home shoppers with a multiplicity of different needs and desires. There's not much you can do about that. You can't change your home's location; you undoubtedly don't want to add a bathroom or a swimming pool to a house you're going to sell. But anything you do to make that house appeal to the emotions of home shoppers, make them feel welcome, let them visualize themselves living there, being happy there, will undoubtedly pay very well in the end.

Cleanliness is job one. I have seen sale prices drop as much as $10,000 because the sellers didn't take cleaning seriously.

Cleanliness is job one. If you can afford it, get a professional cleaning job (including windows, screens, and carpet shampooing) before showing the home to anyone but your agent. Get the yard done also. Beautiful landscaping is a major plus that adds dollar value. But even if the yard is filled with weeds, cut and trim everything.

If you don't have the money to hire cleaners, use elbow grease and enlist the aid of family and friends. Make a party out of it. Make the place sparkle.

Nothing should smell. While you're in cleaning mode, make sure nothing—absolutely nothing—creates an unpleasant odor or any kind of strong odor. Other people may not like the aroma of your favorite garlic spaghetti sauce—or air freshener, for that matter. Get rid of the smells that make the air freshener necessary. Smoke outside. Hold off on odoriferous cooking. Dump that litter box daily, if not more often. And for goodness' sake, let there be no doggie poop anywhere!

Get rid of the clutter. I know you need your stuff, but keep your eye on the goal. While you're on the market, that's not your home you're living in. It's an extremely expensive investment you're asking someone to pay top dollar for.

Beautiful decorative objects and paintings are one thing; 382 videotapes and that extra chair that doesn't fit in the living room are quite another. Clean up, pack away, rent a storage locker if you have to. Put everything away and clean off those countertops—though family photos are an exception. It makes people feel closer to the house to see nice pictures of your family or a wedding or other happy occasion. Many agents have a wonderful talent for staging a home beautifully for showing. Use your agent shamelessly! Follow her advice.

Get all trash, junk and discarded objects off the property. That means gone, not out on the curb or stashed in the garage. It also emphatically includes cars that don't run. (Unless it's in the garage, in its parking space, and covered neatly with a tarp.) It also includes things you intend to keep but that other people might see as junk—for instance, that TV that you're going to fix someday or that rusty boat trailer your brother-in-law asked you to keep for him.

Discontinue all activities that make the house or property unsightly. If your home includes a separate workshop, that's a big plus. It should be put into meticulous order—an inspiration to buyers!

For most homeowners, though, the workshop is the patio, lānai, garage, or even a bedroom. Leaving tools or work-in-progress lying around makes the house appear cramped and messy. (It should go without saying that any dangerous or potentially dangerous tools or materials must be put away—preferably, locked up—during open houses and showings.)

Deal intelligently with your pets. Remove dangerous or potentially dangerous pets at any time the property is being shown, even if you are present. If a buyer thinks he's being threatened by an animal, even if the threat is imaginary, he will run—not walk—away. Your potential liability should also be obvious, along with the fact that all dogs can be unpredictable when confronted by a stranger.

In addition, if a seller keeps a vicious dog, a potential buyer might get the idea that the seller has a very good reason for doing so. A vicious dog can have the same psychological effect as bars on the windows or triple-locked doors—raises concerns about neighborhood safety, even if the concern is totally unwarranted.

And then, some people are simply afraid of some animals. Cats, for instance. Or even Jackson chameleons. Finally, don't forget to consider the safety of the pets. Make appropriate provisions with your agent for your animals' safety. If removing the animals isn't practical, at least tell everyone ahead of time that the animals are there. Cage any that the average person would expect to see confined.

Provide as much access as possible to as many people as possible

You can't sell what you can't show. Maximize exposure through open houses and make private showing appointments with as little advance notice as possible. Allow your agent to install a lockbox. If you feel your agent should be present for all showings, then make sure you hire one who's willing and able to make that extra effort.

Try to be away from home for showings

During open houses, leave. If you have to be there, step outside. If you can't do that, at least don't follow people and don't say a single word except hello, goodbye and other meaningless courtesies, unless asked a direct question. If asked a direct question, look to your agent for guidance. More sales are lost by a seller trying to be "helpful" than by any other single factor. It's true, so don't bother being sensitive or thinking you're the exception. You're not.

Control your tenants

Tenants have rights, and you must respect them. However, tenants seldom help a landlord with the sale effort. If at all possible, don't market a house until they have moved out. Failing that, don't be penny-wise and pound-foolish: Offer a free month's rent if tenants cooperate with showing appointments and open houses, and make themselves scarce when the property is being shown. Emphasize that part of their cooperation includes keeping the place spotless, and tell them if your agent complains about cleanliness, the deal is off.

Price it right

Your property is not going to sell for more than it's worth in the marketplace you are in at the time you are in it. Period.

Follow the instructions above to maximize value. Then, when your property looks its very best, price it correctly—not too high and not too low.

But don't buyers spend all their time trying to figure ways to get sellers to accept less than the asking price? So isn't it a good idea to build in a buffer?

No. Read on.

Consider the psychology of buyers

Let's assume your property is a nice one in a nice neighborhood. You like it, you've been happy there, there's no reason somebody else won't be equally content. Your agent has given you the comparable data, so you know what similar homes have sold for and you know the asking prices for similar homes on the market now. The data tells you how a buyer and the bank's appraiser will evaluate your property; the current listings tell you what your competition is.

In a rising market, you'll probably see that the asking prices for current listings are higher than the sale prices over the past six months (the only sales that matter when it comes to impartial appraisals). In a level market, you'll see the sale prices are about the same as asking prices now, and in a declining market, you'll probably see the same thing! Why? Because in a declining market, agents usually advise clients to price their property close to recent past sales. They're often afraid they'll antagonize sellers and lose listings if they tell them they probably won't get the same price as they would have six months ago.

In a rising market, it may be all right to ask a little more. If, however, you are perceived as trying to take unreasonable advantage, prospective buyers will indeed spend all their time finding reasons why your house isn't worth what you think it is, and if they make an offer at all, it's likely to be the dreaded lowball!

In a level or declining market, pricing your property higher than the competition means only one thing: *Your house will sell last!* And you definitely don't want that. Here's why:

- ✔ The longer a property is on the market, the more likely it is to be perceived as a problem property, or for the seller to be perceived as unmotivated or gouging. When that happens, it's too late to make up for lost time by reducing the price. Buyers are already thinking you've got a problem and are trying to figure out the lowest possible price you'll take.

✔ The best time to find a buyer who will pay the most money for your property is in the first three weeks of marketing. That is when people who've been out looking for a home such as yours will find out about it; if they're sincere buyers (the only kind you care about), that's when they'll come. If those buyers believe your house is priced fairly, they will make their offers in a timely manner, knowing that if they don't, somebody else will.

✔ For every month your home is on the market and unsold, you are carrying that mortgage and other expenses.

✔ For every day your home is on the market and unsold, you and your family (or your tenant) are living with the considerable stress of keeping the place ready to show, vacating the premises during open houses, and having groups of strangers trooping through at inconvenient times.

So take an objective step back before you tell your agent to price your house above your closest competition. Are you in a rising market? Is your house nicer? Really, truly nicer? What are the specific features that make it nicer, and what are they worth in dollars?

If you still can't bring yourself to price your property competitively, at the very least agree to reduce the price if you don't have any offers or seriously interested prospects in the first three weeks. That allows your agent to have at least one broker's open house and two Sunday open houses, as well as however many private showings are requested during that time. If you don't have many private showings and the open houses are poorly attended, there is a problem!

✔ *Every house will sell in a reasonable time if it is priced correctly for the current market.* You can figure out how long a reasonable time is by looking at how long it is currently taking competitive homes to sell.

Strategies for evaluating offers

Getting an offer is very exciting. It's the first indication your hard work is paying off. But your ultimate goal isn't getting offers, it's closing, and it can be a long road from one to the other. It's critical to consider all offers carefully and with a clear mind, to analyze everything that's in the fine print, and to evaluate as best as you can whether an offer is viable and the buyer sincere.

- ✔ No offer is binding on the buyer until he's completed his due diligence period, so knowing his motivation is critical.

- ✔ Give heavier weight to offers that are accompanied by mortgage preapproval letters. These are different from, and superior to, prequalification letters and contain "credit approval," or words to that effect.

- ✔ Pay attention to "weasel clauses," contract elements, other than standard terms, that allow a buyer to back out or demonstrate he's only marginally qualified for the purchase. A common one found in the financing section of the DROA calls out a specific interest rate and/or specific points. A weasel clause says something like, "a new mortgage loan at no more than six percent interest with no more than two discount points," whereas a non-weasel clause will say, "a new mortgage loan at prevailing rates and points."

- ✔ Look for excessive time frames for due diligence issues or loan approval, or for an extended closing date. Once you have accepted an offer, you are bound and your property is tied up until that buyer's due diligence period is over. Seven to fourteen days is normal. Don't allow any longer than that unless there's a really good reason. Your agent can tell you what's reasonable for loan approval. A prolonged closing period works against you in at least three ways:

1. You can't accept any other offer;

2. If interest rates rise during that time, the buyer's loan may be jeopardized; and

3. You must make all your mortgage payments and carry all other expenses until closing.

✔ Read the cover letter the buyer's agent sent with the offer. It may give you facts about the buyers that indicate their sincerity, their mindset, whether there's a good fit between the buyer and the property—any number of things that may give you subliminal clues as to how much that buyer wants your house. (I've had sellers accept offers ostensibly because cover letters said the buyer was a dog lover, had a child by the same name or of the same age, had gone to the same high school—for any number of reasons you wouldn't think were relevant. They weren't relevant, and they weren't the real reasons the offers were accepted, either. The real reason was that something in the cover letters made the seller feel secure about the buyer's desire to close.) Those letters are important. The buyer's agent knows more about his or her client than you do, and clues to that knowledge may be found between the lines of that letter. The simple fact that the agent took the time and trouble to sit down and write it is an indication of professionalism, and it also tells you how much she believes in the client's sincerity.

✔ All these factors, and others your agent may point out, can be very important in judging a buyer's ability and desire to fulfill his offer.

If you are fortunate enough to receive multiple offers, you may be faced with a highly desirable dilemma: Choosing between two or more equally good ones. It's nerve-racking because you don't want to accept one that falls through and reject one that, in hindsight, would have succeeded. There's no way to hold onto all the offers indefinitely, but there are ways to minimize your risk and maximize the likelihood of success.

- ✔ Review all your offers, weed out the ones that are out of the question, then go back through the ones that have merit.

- ✔ If you note gray areas, room for misinterpretation, or unclear statements, you'll need to clarify.

- ✔ If any item in the offer raises a question or a red flag, you may need to make a counteroffer. You may even decide to counter more than one offer simultaneously. In that case, state that you're countering more than one offer and specify how you will ultimately make your selection. A sentence like, "Seller has countered more than one offer equally. If more than one buyer agrees to the counteroffer terms, seller reserves the right to choose, at his sole discretion, which contract to accept" informs everyone and levels the playing field.

After acceptance

It's a very good idea to continue showing your property for backup offers until your buyer has completed and approved his due diligence inspections and research and has final written loan approval. It's hard work and it's inconvenient, but nothing's over until it's over, and your marketing job isn't done until the check is in your hands.

Bottom line: While agents advise and facilitate, sellers control the marketing of their property. While your property is on the market, view it as merchandise and display and treat it accordingly. Cleanliness and good order are critical. Make showing easy. Price the property correctly. Gain cooperation from tenants (pay for it if you have to). Let your agent handle all contact with potential buyers and remain out of sight throughout the process. When considering offers, factors other than price may clue you in to the buyer's ability to purchase and also to the strength of his motivation to close.

Foreclosures and Distressed Properties

Many books and classes offer to teach people how to make serious profit buying and reselling foreclosed properties. Most agents, myself included, are frequently approached by people who want help finding and buying foreclosed properties. My objective in this chapter is to explain a bit about how foreclosure sales fit into the overall picture of real estate here in the Islands.

First, a little perspective: Most owners who allow foreclosure to occur don't care what happens to their property. Many such owners are angry about being foreclosed and sometimes vandalize the property or strip it down to bare floors and walls, thinking they'll prevent anyone taking advantage of what they perceive as their personal hard luck. Many owners refuse to move out and remain in residence until forcibly evicted.

Most owners will sell on their own before they allow foreclosure to occur. This is partly cultural: There is shame involved in not paying your bills or in being foreclosed. Almost everyone in Hawai'i who comes upon hard times will let go of their real estate last, after they've relinquished other less valuable assets, but before they lose all hope of saving their reputation and/or recapturing at least some of their equity. Hence, some of the very best opportunities for buyers happen before a property goes into foreclosure, not afterwards.

There are several different circumstances, though, under which people can lose their real property and several very different ways those circumstances are handled.

Judicial foreclosure

If an owner fails to make required payments—mortgage, property tax, lease rent, and sometimes even condominium maintenance fees—they may be foreclosed. If the matter goes to court, a judge may issue an order for judicial foreclosure.

In that instance, the court assigns a Commissioner of Foreclosure, an intermediary who is responsible for handling an auction sale in accordance with the law (and who, by the way, need not be a real estate agent). The commissioner then places the legally required advertisements, supervises the auction, and attends the confirmation hearing afterwards, in which the judge approves (confirms) the new ownership.

The process of locating and purchasing a judicial foreclosure property is very different than finding a property in the general marketplace. These differences include and are not limited to the following:

- ✔ Properties to be auctioned are advertised in a public newspaper a minimum of three times in three weeks.

- ✔ It may not be possible to get inside the property to do an inspection.

- ✔ If access is possible, all inspections must be done before the auction.

- ✔ The property is sold absolutely as-is. There is no seller's disclosure, no contingency on a later inspection, no guarantee that the property will be in the same condition when the new owner takes possession as it was when he saw it or when the auction took place. The new owner will have no recourse against anyone if he has a problem after the fact.

- ✔ There's usually no upset price, but the lending institution that holds the mortgage may start the bidding at the amount of indebtedness plus their expenses; or, if the indebtedness exceeds fair market value, at some realistic amount that minimizes their loss. (If their bid succeeds, the property then becomes bank-owned property, which we discuss a little later on.)

- ✔ The bids are open, so everyone knows what everyone else is bidding.

- ✔ Bidders must have 10 percent of their bid price in cash or certified funds at the auction.

- ✔ There is no contingency regarding financing. If the successful bidder cannot obtain a mortgage, he may lose his 10 percent deposit.

Buying foreclosed property is not for the faint of heart.

- ✔ If the successful bidder fails to perform any other aspect of the contract, he may also lose his deposit.

- ✔ The high bidder may not end up with the property. At the confirmation hearing, which is open to the public, anyone who offers at least five percent more than the successful bid may reopen the bidding.

- ✔ The buyer pays all closing costs in addition to the purchase price.

- ✔ If the buyer uses the services of a real estate agent, he must also pay his agent.

- ✔ If the property is occupied at the time title is transferred, eviction is the buyer's sole responsibility.

As you can see, buying foreclosed property is not for the faint of heart. Nor probably for a newcomer to the Islands or any inexperienced buyer. For the average person, getting a great deal through this method is unlikely. Competing bidders are usually highly experienced pros—banks and contractors—who know exactly what they're doing and how much the property is really worth—and who don't stop bidding until that point is reached. (My consultant for this chapter said she's seen a member of the general public successfully bid substantially less than market value only two or three times in her ten years as a commissioner.)

Strategy tip if you're still interested: Investigate several foreclosure properties as thoroughly as possible, question the commissioners of those properties to the fullest extent they will allow (technically they're not supposed to volunteer information) and attend several auctions as an observer only before actually becoming involved.

There are a couple of other conditions under which property may be auctioned. The state may hold an auction when an owner has died without a will and no heirs can be found. Occasionally, real property that has been seized by law enforcement may also be auctioned. These auctions will be advertised in a public paper, along with instructions for finding out the terms and conditions under which the property will be sold.

Bank- and HUD-owned property:

These properties are frequently (also carelessly and incorrectly) referred to as foreclosure properties. However, these properties have already been foreclosed and are now owned by the lending institution or the Department of Housing and Urban Development (a federal agency that guarantees certain mortgage loans).

The risks involved here are not as great as with judicial foreclosure property. Among other things, the new buyer will not have to evict occupants, and the property will be accessible for inspections; it is usually vacant. However, determining the property's condition is the sole responsibility of the buyer; there will be no seller's disclosure and the seller makes no guarantees of any kind.

Bank-owned property most often is listed with a real estate agency. Thus, it usually appears in the Multiple Listing database. It may also be advertised in the paper.

- ✔ Bank-ownership will be disclosed.

- ✔ The property may or may not have been cleaned up or fixed up.

- ✔ The property will probably be sold absolutely as-is but the buyer will have the right to inspect and to cancel if his inspection isn't acceptable.

- ✔ This is a "cold-blooded" situation. Strategies involving personalities, personal situations, or personal needs don't enter in.

✔ The property will probably be priced realistically for the market, based either on an official appraisal or an agent's written opinion of value. There will likely be very little wiggle room.

✔ A loan preapproval letter is generally required for any offer to be considered, but the contingency upon financing still exists. (If you lose your job during the escrow period, your deposit is probably not at risk.)

✔ The initial deposit doesn't have to be 10 percent of the purchase price. If a specific amount is required, it will be stated in the listing information.

✔ Offers are usually made on the standard DROA form. There will probably be an addendum that stipulates and emphasizes any differences from a standard transaction. You or your agent may obtain a copy of this addendum before making an offer. Its terms are usually nonnegotiable.

✔ Offers are generally presented as they are received, but there may also be a statement such as "no offers will be reviewed prior to [a certain date]."

✔ The bank-owner is not required to accept the highest offer or any offer. It may accept, counter, or reject at its sole discretion.

✔ Commission and seller's closing costs are usually paid by the bank or institution in the same manner as if an individual were selling.

Properties that have been foreclosed and are owned by HUD are also slightly different.

✔ HUD properties will be advertised in the newspaper, and also online along with a number to call for more information and the deadline for bids and inspections.

✔ Many real estate agencies receive property facts and information about newly available HUD-owned properties on a regular basis.

- ✔ Real estate agents can obtain permission to show the properties to buyers.

- ✔ As in bank-owned properties, the purchase is as-is, with no seller's disclosure and no liability accruing to HUD.

- ✔ HUD will pay many, but not all, closing costs normally accruing to a seller and will pay a commission to a buyer's agent.

- ✔ Offers are submitted on a special HUD contract form that is identical nationwide. Blank copies can be obtained from HUD, from your agent, and also on the Internet, along with detailed instructions for filling out and submitting it.

- ✔ Your bid is confidential; nobody knows what you've bid unless you tell them. You don't know what the competition is bidding either.

Successful buyers of auctioned properties are experienced in the real estate market. They have done their homework and their math. They know when to stop. Inexperienced bidders may get caught up in "auction fever" and bid more than fair value.

Since most foreclosure properties sell at or near market value, restricting your search to these properties is a losing strategy, because you eliminate other properties that you can purchase for approximately the same price, but also with all the protections of the normal marketplace.

A far better strategy involves searching out distressed properties. This is an area where some of the very best buys in real estate can be found.

Actually, though the property may be in distress, more likely it's the owner who is. Homes in need of serious repair, or even homes that have a lot of delayed maintenance often graphically demonstrate that the owner is in financial difficulties or otherwise cannot take care of his property. But owners who are in financial distress by no means always sell property that is in bad condition. And owners whose mortgage payments are current may have other critical reasons they need an immediate sale.

Often the listing or advertising will provide the first clue by such statements as: "owner transferred, must sell"; "priced right for immediate sale"; "lowest price in building since last year"; or even "$5,000 credit to the buyer who can close by [a specific date]." It might even say "pre-foreclosure." You or your agent may also find out a seller is under duress by reading between the lines of more subtle statements or by picking up on casual remarks in conversation.

But regardless of the reason for the seller's need, or how you find out about it, buyers who are alert, patient, and prepared to act immediately find distressed properties offer a far wider and more fertile field than the strictly foreclosure market.

Here time is usually an extremely critical factor for the seller. Very often—almost always—the faster the buyer can close, the better price he's likely to obtain.

Sometimes a seller's "upset price" (the amount needed to pay off the mortgage and cover closing costs) is the asking price. It may be on the low side in the hope of saving time in negotiation. It may be on the high side in the hope of a miracle. Regardless, a smart offer is based on fair market value, not asking price.

You don't have to buy property below current value in order to make a serious profit.

You may not need to buy property below current value in order to make a serious profit. Time offers a winning strategy to Hawai'i buyers. History tells us that no matter where a previous market topped out, the next cycle, or the one after that, surpassed the previous high point. Given our stable demand and limited supply, there's no reason to believe this trend will not continue. Property owners who can hold on and hold out will come out ahead in the long term. Those who lose, generally speaking, are those who are forced to sell under unfavorable conditions.

"Duress" can be emotional as well as financial. Be alert and sensitive to other issues that may be mentioned or hinted at. The specific reason a seller is selling may provide you with a strategy to obtain a terrific buy for yourself and simultaneously give the seller what he needs—the win-win that marks true success.

Strategy tip: The very best way to get the very best deal is to find out about the property before anyone else does and take immediate action by writing a reasonable offer that meets the seller's needs in terms of both money and time, accompanied by verification that you are a qualified buyer. And require an immediate response to your offer.

Finding out about a property ahead of everyone else requires a certain amount of luck and a diligent agent. (Agents often get advance scoop on properties.) Eliminating competition is key; any advantage will be totally wiped out if you don't act quickly. The offer must meet the seller's critical needs (and also sometimes requirements of the seller's present lender) and be sufficiently enticing that he will not want to risk losing it by failing to respond quickly.

This strategy requires decisiveness, a well-grounded education in real estate values, good instincts, the desire to achieve a win-win transaction—and courage. When it works, it's a beautiful thing.

Bottom line: For foreclosures, bank-owned, HUD-owned, or distressed properties, fair market values rule.

- ✔ The involvement of professional investors, contractors, and financial institutions in foreclosure auctions makes it unlikely that successful bidders will pay much less than fair market value.

- ✔ An apparent lower-than-market price usually involves far greater-than-usual risks to the buyer.

- ✔ Inexperienced and/or uneducated buyers are at even greater risk.

- ✔ The ability to buy low so you can resell for quick profits is not the only key to success. The ability to hold property long term and wait for the right seller's market is just as important.

- ✔ Distressed properties offer more frequent opportunities for smart and well-educated buyers, with fewer of the risks involved in auction or foreclosure.

20

Spotting the Predators

Through years of watching every word and checking every written statement three times, I've developed the habit of avoiding topics that make people focus on the negative or rile their sensitivities. But there's something I feel must be addressed: The public perception that real estate agents are aggressive, pushy wheeler-dealers, untrustworthy and slippery people whose only goal is to get a big commission as quickly as possible. This perception is simply untrue.

Below, I'll examine why people tend to view agents this way and why their conclusions are wrong.

Appearances are a double-edged sword

As agents we are trained to dress for success and to drive nice cars. If we don't look successful, people will think we don't know what we're doing. It's also important for our clients to be comfortable while we're driving them around for hours and hours. The flip side is that clients may believe we've got a lot more money than we do—or more money than they do, which is probably worse—and feel removed from their comfort zone or even envious. Of course, these folks don't think about the fact that often clients have a lot more money than we do.

> *Several years ago, times were very tough in real estate here. My car was serviceable but eight years old. The broken air-conditioning was unfixable and the windows didn't always work, but I couldn't afford a new car. I have some wonderful clients, including, in particular, a tactful, lovely couple with whom I spent many hours on the road searching for property. Although I knew they must have longed for air-conditioning and a smoother ride, they never uttered a single complaint about my old faithful minivan. After we ultimately located and closed on their new property, I was*

invited to a celebration lūʻau. Afterward, as we were saying our goodbyes, the husband took me aside. "Fran," he said, "I know you made a decent commission on this sale. Please, please, please, do yourself a favor and go spend it on a new car. It'll make the world of difference in your business." Smiling, I gave him a big hug and a thank you. Then I walked him over to the new car I'd bought within two days of the closing and showed him I'd already taken his advice.

The point? While it's fine for you to go out looking at houses in shorts and sandals, your agent is working. He or she is supposed to look professional and as good as he or she can and is neither showing off nor trying to show you up!

Reason, logic, and a positive attitude are easily confused with a "pitch"

Another perception the general public often has is that an agent's only objective is to sell you something. Well, what other objective would an agent have? Here's what I point out to people who are brave enough to openly express their fear of being sold:

I couldn't care less which house you buy. I don't own the houses I show you. I will get paid regardless of which one you choose, so long as you choose one, and I want to be your agent for the rest of your life and mine. Therefore, it's in both of our best interests that I find homes that suit your needs and your budget. If I do that, we will both end up with what we need: you with the right house and me with a paycheck.

And if that isn't enough to satisfy you, here's what Jean Wade used to tell us: "Be careful what you sell people. You'll have to list it one day, and you'll want to be proud of it."

But isn't it the agent's job to sell their listing? Yes, if I'm the seller's broker. I've been trained to teach people how to make their house look its best. I've also been trained to know what's important to most buyers, and to show a property in its most positive light, as well as to suggest how negative features might be modified or corrected.

It's in the agent's best interest to find a house that suits your needs and your budget.

A sales pitch is entirely different. A sales pitch tries to persuade someone they need something in the first place, whether they do or whether they don't! Any good agent quickly determines whether a particular property meets a potential buyer's needs, and if it doesn't, will be more than glad to hunt for homes that do.

Forget about worrying that you'll have to deflect pitches from aggressive brokers, and forget about somebody selling you something you don't want. Be upfront with all the agents you meet and judge them by their responses to you and your statements. If the house doesn't suit you, tell them. If you don't want them to call you, tell them. And if you instinctively like the agent but not the house, say that as well. Honesty in both directions marks the start of every successful business relationship.

But, you say, you know very well agents exist who make their living fooling innocent victims with a smooth line. True. I won't argue. In every industry, there are those who take unfair advantage of others. But most agents who last in this business learn that honesty is truly the best policy. It's better for us if we match up the client with the right house than if we try to make a bad fit work, and it's better for us if we lose a transaction by telling the truth but keep the client's good faith.

Seller's concerns about listing agents tend to go like this:

Can't they take unfair advantage of sellers by pricing properties too low to get a quick sale; or can't they promise a high price to get the listing and then pressure the seller to accept a lower offer? Remember: Sellers control sale prices; agents don't. Period. You sign the listing, the sales contract, and the closing documents. And if you sign off on a listing price without knowing the facts of your present market, who's responsible for that? You or your agent?

Today most agents back our local trade associations (the Honolulu Board of Realtors and the Hawai'i Association of Realtors) in publicizing the code of ethics all of us agree to abide by. These associations also give the public a vehicle for reporting anyone who violates that code and possibly for getting satisfaction of their grievance without the stress and expense of filing a lawsuit.

The purpose of this book, though, is to teach you to conduct the business of real estate as an honest person dealing with honest people. Hopefully, along the way, it'll also teach you how to recognize and avoid the few bad apples, and, through experience, you'll learn that the negative public perception about real estate agents is highly exaggerated.

Okay, you argue, but why do ordinary real estate transactions sometimes turn into nightmares that make clients hate real estate agents forevermore?

- ✔ **Incompetence.** There are incompetent agents and there are also agents who really aren't interested in following through with all the details that make a transaction flow smoothly. But if you've selected your agent carefully, that's not going to be a problem for you.

- ✔ **Fear.** Simply stated, buyers and sellers alike are scared to death of being used. People who are usually honest, considerate, and courteous can, when they become involved in a real estate transaction, suddenly turn into evil beasts with criminal intentions or irrational crazies whose only goal is to be as unreasonable and obstructive as possible.

They may have been influenced—through the media and sometimes unfortunate personal experiences—to trust no one. They often look for the thorns instead of the roses. In so doing, they may not notice the rose at all, much less ever get the courage to pick it. And that fear may turn them into the type of person they never thought they'd become.

- ✔ **Pride or ego.** People don't always look at events with an objective viewpoint, and they don't always tell other people the truth either, especially if doing that would reveal that they used bad judgment or made a bad decision. If a person has made a bad decision, it's human nature to look for some one else to blame. When it comes to real estate, the target is obvious.

Frankly, most of us agents know that almost everyone will blame us long before they will blame a spouse, a family member, or themselves if something doesn't work out right. Speaking only for myself, I completely understand. Nobody with half a brain will allow their marriage to be destroyed over a bad real estate decision when the agent is conveniently standing between them and that very undesirable result. And sometimes people would rather create a tale to save their pride than take responsibility for their own decisions. (I'm less understanding of that.)

Taking a balanced look at both the thorns and the roses before you become involved in buying or selling a home should allow you to proceed confidently so neither you nor anyone else involved with your transaction becomes an evil beast or an irrational crazy, and your agent doesn't become so frustrated and discouraged that she goes back to whatever business she was in before she lost her mind and went into real estate.

Thorns:

- ✔ Unethical or unintelligent agents.

- ✔ Disclosure errors or outright misstatements of fact (lies).

- ✔ Pressure and manipulation.

- ✔ Lack of perfection. Yes, it's true that a used house, or even a new one, probably won't be perfect, and after you move in, you probably will find things you didn't know about.

- ✔ Risk of loss. It's possible to lose money in a real estate transaction. Even the wealthiest and most successful real estate investors occasionally have a losing transaction. They stay in the market, however, because most of the time, their intelligent decisions let them end up as winners.

Roses:

- ✔ Escrow. In Hawai'i, we use escrow companies to hold all money and documents until both parties have performed all their obligations and nothing remains to be done except disbursing the funds and handing over the keys. Escrow companies are licensed, bonded, insured, and absolutely guaranteed to treat all parties honestly. Do not engage in any real estate transaction with anybody—anybody at all—without using escrow services. Pay the fee gladly.

✔ Title search. You will receive a complete title report and both lenders and buyers receive a title insurance policy prepared by an impartial, licensed, and bonded title company before any transaction is recorded. The report discloses anything in the public record that affects the seller's right to sell, the buyer's ability to buy, and anything on the record about the property itself, including liens, easements, or other restrictions.

✔ Inspections, documents, and public records. In Hawai'i, real estate buyers have the right to have property inspected by any professional, or many professionals, of their choice before any contract is binding, so long as they pay for the inspection and it is done within the time frame stated in the agreement. Buyers may also obtain copies of any and all documents, such as building permits and tax office records, that may not be mentioned in the title report but which are on record at the Bureau of Conveyances, the Department of Land Utilization, the Department of Planning and Permitting of the appropriate county, or any other government agency dealing with real estate matters. Do not engage in any real estate transaction with anybody—anybody at all—without taking advantage of this right to your complete satisfaction.

✔ Disclosures. In Hawai'i, real property sellers have a legal obligation to disclose any and all facts they know about their property that affect its value in the eyes of a reasonable person. That means everything. Buyers, read the disclosure statement and independently confirm any statement you doubt. Sellers, tell all the truth, knowing that if you don't, you can be sued and lose everything you may have gained and more. The smart seller is the truthful seller. The smart buyer believes but confirms. In

Hawai'i, agents who know a detrimental fact about a property are also required by law to disclose it.

✔ Consumer protection laws. In Hawai'i we have some of the strongest laws in the country. The laws apply to both consumers of real estate services as well as consumers of real property, buyers and sellers. This vigilance is reflected in the listing agreement and purchase agreement (DROA) as well as in all the related paperwork. These documents spell out the obligations of all parties clearly.

Compromising is not the same as losing

As agents, we look for ways to satisfy all concerned. Often this involves compromise. What we do—and what we're supposed to do—is find ways to make everything work for both parties. That can mean working things out so you give up something you don't care about in exchange for something that does matter to you. In win-win situations, everybody cuts everyone else a little slack and everybody gives everyone else a point or two. And that leads me to the true subject of this chapter's title:

Con men and sharp dealers: the predators

They exist anywhere there's money to be made. Deception is their stock in trade and they are expert at it. And, knowing smart and aware people are likely to catch on to them, predators look for victims who are emotionally vulnerable, who are financially on the edge or who are simply greedy. They look for victims who do not have expert knowledge. And they are opportunists who will use any and every ploy that presents itself.

Scared yet? Don't worry too much. Fortunately, predators are rare in real life. Most people in my profession, as in every other, do their best to do a good job in good faith. Whether they succeed or fail has to do with talent and intelligence and not with cheating. But it can happen.

> *My own parents were nearly taken to the cleaners by a contractor who looked like my son, their dearly beloved grandson. The resemblance was so strong that they trusted everything he said, as they would have if my son had been doing the talking. He looked honest. (First mistake.*

Appearances tell you exactly nothing.) And after my parents remarked on the likeness, the scammer used that to talk them into contracting for a new roof. Their roof was in terrible shape, he said, after going up on it. If they didn't replace it now, it was likely to cost a fortune in structural repairs later. And as a final enticement, if they hired him, he said, he'd also make some repairs to their screened porch as a goodwill gesture—for $1,000 cash right now.

Fortunately, before he could start on the roof, a neighbor who had been victimized earlier by the same man took it upon herself to warn my parents that the "contractor" was not only unlicensed, his workmanship was so poor that it usually had to be redone at a far greater expense than doing it properly in the first place would have involved. My parents got a second opinion, which revealed they didn't need a new roof at all. My husband and I personally redid the shoddy work on the screened porch on our next visit—and it didn't cost anywhere near $1,000. My parents lost what they'd already paid, and the deposit they'd made, but thanks to their alert neighbor, saved the bulk of what would have been a very expensive mistake.

What were the clues that might have warned my parents in the first place; the clues you should look for yourself?

Playing on emotions

In addition to his resemblance to their grandson, the scammer mentioned several personal tragedies to soften them up. A true professional never discusses his or her personal problems with total strangers in order to induce sympathy. It's simply not done.

Subtle threats

They had to do something now, or the problem would be far worse later. This con man knew that most people my parents' age are on fixed incomes and anxious to save a few dollars if they can. He counted on the idea that they'd be worried about the expense of further deterioration. Of course, his statements might have been true. To check this out, get a second opinion, preferably before you hand over any money.

Offering something for nothing or for less than it's worth

A true professional expects fair pay for his or her work and could not be in business if he incurred a loss with every transaction. A discount is sometimes offered by honest professionals, though, and it's not always easy to determine if a discount is a legitimate business tool or a scammer's ploy. Check other factors, such as licensing and references, and whether a similar discount is common practice. If every other aspect of the transaction is on the up-and-up, it's likely the discount is straightforward.

Making statements and claims that are difficult or expensive to check out

The scammer knew my 85-year-old father was not able to walk around on a steeply pitched second-story roof to verify the facts. He'd hoped to take the money and run.

Let's talk about real estate scammers specifically

What constitutes a scam? Persuading you to enter into a real estate contract if the person doing the persuading knows your loss will be his gain and hides this fact from you. This could mean selling your property for less than fair value, buying property for more than fair value, selling your property today when the scammer knows it's going to be worth a lot more tomorrow and doesn't tell you, persuading you to buy property today when he knows it's going to be worth less tomorrow and doesn't tell you.

How does the ordinary person recognize and avoid scammers?

Trust but verify.

Check on anyone you don't know before you do business with them. Real estate agents in Hawai'i are licensed by the state. Their activities are under general scrutiny by the Department of Commerce and Consumer Affairs. Also, the Hawai'i Association of Realtors and the Boards of Realtors of the various Islands keep records on their members. It's actually pretty easy to check an agent's credentials. Don't skip that step if you don't already know the agent who's asking to represent you.

- ✔ Educate yourself. Even general, very basic information about the real estate business and property values is enough to protect you against most obvious scams.

- ✔ Don't sign what you don't understand or haven't read. Be particularly on guard if someone wants you to sign any agreement whatsoever without giving you time to read it carefully and understand the fine print. Look out if someone doesn't answer your questions in a forthright manner.

Con men and cheaters prefer victims who are hard up or simply greedy. Therefore watch out if:

- ✔ Anyone asks you to circumvent your real estate agent to "save the commission" or for any other reason. It's more likely they don't want you to consult a professional who can educate you about facts. If your property is already listed with an agent, they are asking you to cheat. This is a fair indication that cheating is their way of life. Beware.

- ✔ Anyone asks you to enter into a real estate transaction that will not be recorded at the Bureau of Conveyances. This is very dangerous. Later on, it may be difficult to prove that the transaction ever took place.

- ✔ Anyone asks you to enter into a real estate transaction without using an escrow company's services. The definition of escrow—a neutral third party that holds all funds and documents until all conditions of the contract have been met—should tell you their services are for the protection of all parties. (As a sidebar to that last, don't write earnest money or deposit checks to anyone but an escrow company or a licensed real estate firm. Specifically, don't make an earnest money check payable to a seller or to a real estate agent personally.)

- ✔ Any stranger who approaches you shortly after a death in your family or some other traumatic event in your life.

This is when con men know people are at their most vulnerable.

- ✔ Any stranger offers to "do you a favor."

- ✔ Anyone offers you a deal that seems like it's too good to be true.

- ✔ Anyone asks you to trust them without clearly and satisfactorily demonstrating why you should.

- ✔ Someone can't show you why their proposal is a win-win for all concerned.

- ✔ Anyone tries to manipulate you by playing on your emotions.

- ✔ An agent fails to tell you up front that he/she is an agent. It is the law in Hawai'i that agents must disclose that they are agents whenever they enter into a personal transaction, before anyone signs anything.

- ✔ Don't do business with any agent who refuses to identify her client.

Con artists in real estate, licensed agents or not, are usually acting as principals. Scamming just for a commission is too penny ante.

In my first real estate training class, my teacher said, "You can make a good living listing property and working with buyers, but where you make the real money is through your own transactions."

- ✔ The people you really have to look out for are those who want you to get into a transaction with them, personally, without full disclosure and without representation.

- ✔ Unless you really know what you're doing and are highly experienced in Hawai'i real estate, your best protection is a licensed agent whose reputation and credentials you've verified.

- ✔ If you suspect something is wrong, get a second opinion from another licensed agent.

What to do if you're not sure if you're smelling a rat

Real estate agents in Hawai'i are very competitive. Sometimes agents (particularly newer ones) will use unethical tactics to take someone else's client. You shouldn't trust an agent who uses these tactics to get your business, and you can get a second opinion if you need one without causing discontent in the ranks of agents.

How? Tell the truth.

Call the principal broker at a second reputable company in the same geographic area. Why the same area? Because good advice for one area may be very bad advice for another. Why the principal broker? The principal broker is in a slightly different position than an agent who works on commission. She is usually either a company owner or a salaried person and is more generally knowledgeable than most. Tell her up front that you already have an agent and you won't change agents if it's not warranted, but you need a second opinion. Ask if there's a charge for that opinion. (There won't be.) Either ask for an appointment or explain the problem on the phone. Make sure the broker you're speaking with has all the facts.

If the second opinion is slightly different than your agent's, ask your agent to explain her position. It'll probably come down to a difference in viewpoint, and you can then discuss it until you're satisfied. If the second opinion is *drastically different*, you may want a third opinion. If, however, it's caused you to see the light, you need to take appropriate action: Change agents or give your agent appropriate instructions and insist that they be followed. Remember, your agent has a fiduciary duty to act according to your instructions, and in your best interests. It's the law.

What if someone offers you a private real estate transaction without using any agents, and you find it tempting but aren't sure whether it's really a good idea? *Tell the other party you want representation. Period. If he doesn't, that's up to him.* Tell him you want your agent's commission included in the price. Sophisticated investors will jump at that proposal—they know your agent will be doing all the work for half the fee. Honest people who just think that's a good way to save money can save half of it and are usually satisfied. If the numbers simply don't work with a commission figured in, tell the other party you're going to pay your own agent—and have her review the paperwork before you sign anything. Follow through on this. You'll find it's worth every dime. If you're dealing with a con artist, he'll head for the hills.

What about consulting with an attorney if you suspect a scam? Make sure you go to one who specializes in real estate. Here in Hawai'i, most attorneys are not involved in the day-to-day practice of real estate. Most lawyers here use real estate agents to facilitate their personal transactions and consult with them regarding complex situations.

Bottom line: If you're worried about being victimized, don't go into any transaction alone and defenseless or do anything under the table. Conduct your business in the open. Consult with reputable professionals before committing yourself on paper and be willing to pay the going rate for services. Do not ask for, or expect, something for nothing.

Most of all make sure any contract you sign gives you time to do the appropriate research and investigation before it becomes legally binding. Any legitimate person will understand, and all legitimate real estate agents respect that attitude.

21

Strategies for Life Changes

Decisions on real estate often arise when there's a life change. These can be commonplace (changing family size or a transfer for work) or traumatic (divorce or death).

We all usually try to avoid even thinking about the latter two unless and until we are forced to. However, when you are under a great deal of stress or faced with a situation you've never had to cope with before is probably the worst time to make permanent decisions about important issues. You may not be thinking clearly. And, too, you may have options you're not immediately aware of, or you may later wish to consider choices you hadn't thought about before.

Therefore, first and foremost, do not buy or sell real estate when you are traumatized, grieving, or even seriously upset, if there's any way to avoid it!

Just don't. It's a bad idea.

But life changes are inevitable, and reading this may give you some ideas to consider, even if only hypothetically.

When an owner dies

Death is an inescapable fact, which is why so many people make wills and establish trusts. Estate planning is beyond my scope in general, but I do know this much: If you don't make a formal advance decision about how you want your property to be distributed after your death, the state will do it for you. If you don't want to leave things up to the state, seek out a reputable estate planner or lawyer who specializes in wills and trusts to help you make sure your wishes will be followed after your passing.

Beyond that:

Tenancy by the entirety

In Hawai'i, this is a type of property ownership reserved for married couples or "reciprocal beneficiaries." (Talk to escrow about the definition of reciprocal beneficiaries if you aren't legally married to a co-buyer of property.) Briefly, under Tenancy by the Entirety, if one spouse or co-owner dies, the other automatically owns the entire property, regardless of what arrangements were made about other assets. When you initially purchase your home, it's a good idea to consider this option. If you should die, your spouse can then make an independent decision about how to handle it.

Briefly, under Tenancy by the Entirety, if one spouse or co-owner dies, the other automatically owns the entire property, regardless of what arrangements were made about other assets.

Mortagage life insurance

Sadly, though, if one of you dies and adequate provisions, such as life insurance, haven't been made in advance, it may be simply unaffordable for a widowed spouse to keep up payments and maintenance on a home. One of the best things you and your spouse or partner can do for each other is to plan for the "worst case scenario" to the very best of your ability.

During your younger years, when you may have a growing family and your income hasn't reached its peak, consider a mortgage life insurance policy. This is very economical, starts out with the same amount as your mortgage balance and gradually decreases to match it, so that if you die at any time during the life of that mortgage it will be paid off. Your spouse will not have to worry about making that monthly payment. There are many other plans that you can consider and should discuss with a reputable life insurance agent and/or other financial planner.

If you are recently widowed

I can't emphasize this advice enough: *Given a choice, if you are recently widowed, do nothing, take no action whatsoever* until you have had time to thoughtfully evaluate all the relevant factors that enter into a good, constructive decision. Don't sell, don't buy, for at least a year, preferably two. Period.

During my time in real estate, I've met more people than I can count who have said to me, "I wish I'd never sold my home; I wish I had it back today. I thought moving out would make it hurt less, but it didn't. Now, instead of losing just my spouse, I have lost my home as well." Hopefully, I don't need to say anything more to make this point hit home for you.

There are some circumstances where postponing action is the worst thing to do. When is immediate action appropriate?

- ✔ If selling the home was part of a carefully considered financial plan made before the death of the spouse or partner, then following through may not be impulsive or precipitous. However, if acting now is contrary to your intuition, if you think you want to change your mind, if it's just to "get it over with," or because "the kids are pressuring me," or if market conditions aren't good for sellers, think twice. And consider whether you are emotionally up to handling the stress of marketing the property. If there's nothing to lose by waiting awhile, that may be the best idea.

- ✔ If, after exhausting all your options, you know you cannot maintain or take care of the property, then it's better to sell right away, simply because it will be worth less after months or years of neglect. (And, no matter how sentimental you may be, you won't even enjoy living there if you are upset and angry over its deteriorating condition and know your future financial well-being is draining away.)

- ✔ If you cannot make the payments, call your real estate agent right away. Ideally, that agent should be someone you know well. (This is one case where it's really good to have a friend in the business.) Ask him or her to put you in touch with a reputable lender or financial advisor, if you don't already have one, and ask their help rearranging your finances so you can keep up the payments, at least until you have had time to think your situation through. If those efforts fail, then you should market the property as quickly as possible.

Unfortunately, some people do take advantage of inexperienced people in vulnerable positions. There are even agents who send solicitations to people named as survivors in obituary reports. In general, be skeptical about the motives of any stranger who approaches you. In order for anyone to help you, you'll have to disclose financial details that you might otherwise keep confidential. Use extreme caution in discussing them with anyone you don't know, at least by reputation. It's far better to pay for objective, impartial advice than to get free advice from someone who will benefit by influencing your decision one way or the other.

Once you've located reputable people willing to help you, try to get a second opinion. If you get the same advice from at least two, preferably three, different individuals, you can be reasonably certain their recommendations make sense.

- ✔ If your payments are already delinquent. First, follow the above steps. Immediately. Every month the payment is not made drains more of your equity away through accruing interest and penalties. You will make more money now if you sell than you will if you wait until you're about to be foreclosed and have to accept the first viable offer, or the bank takes over your home. Foreclosure is a very bad thing that may haunt you for years to come. Ask your agent to go to your lender with you, and ask for assistance in preventing foreclosure and harassment while you are marketing the property.

- ✔ **Very Important:** If you know you'll be able to make the payment eventually, but funds are tied up due to pending estate matters or a life insurance settlement, do not wait until you are already behind to contact your lender. It may be difficult to find someone at a major lender who is available to discuss payment issues with you, but be persistent and insistent. Explain the situation and ask for guidance until the funds become available. If you don't get satisfactory answers, ask your real estate agent or your lawyer to intercede for you. If you still don't get satisfactory answers, ask your agent or lender to research interim means, such as taking out an equity line, that will allow you to keep the payments current until your funds are available.

✔ *If you know you'll eventually have to sell and it looks like a strong seller's market is "topping out" and that values may decline substantially in a year or two.* This is a difficult dilemma. How do you know the market has really topped out? Basically, you don't, unless it's already started to go down. Next question: Will selling the home at today's value bring you enough money that you'll live in reasonable comfort for the foreseeable future? Will you be content with the proceeds at today's value, even if you later discover you'd have been able to sell for more if you waited? Conversely, if values decline, and you end up selling for less later, will your ability to live in reasonable comfort be jeopardized? If all the answers are "yes," and a strong seller's market has been ongoing for a while, it may be wise to sell now.

This is a very cold-blooded analysis. If you are not capable of being cold-blooded about your own home—and almost nobody is—get professional advice from one or more real estate experts, who are personally acquainted with you, your property, and your complete financial picture.

It is very important to get second opinions and to carefully select financial or real estate advisors. The following scary but true story explains why.

A woman's husband passed away, leaving her the sole owner of their home. The couple had started a renovation prior to his death. The interior of the house had been substantially demolished with the expectation of installing new bathrooms, a new kitchen, and relocating many interior walls. The widow didn't have enough money to complete the renovation and, in fact, had difficulty making the mortgage payment, but she loved the home and did not want to sell it. A year later, she was in arrears on her mortgage payment by several months, and the bank was threatening to take over the property. At the same time, Hawai'i was in a cycle of escalating prices. An agent associate of mine, an acquaintance of that woman, thought he could help her sell the property for enough that she could "start over" with a smaller home. That would certainly be better than losing it to the bank, which would then keep all the profit on resale. The owner refused to formally list the property, but said she'd look at offers. Eventually, my associate brought her an offer from a potential buyer who specialized in "fixer-uppers." The offer's fairness was substantiated by contractors' estimates of the cost of completion of the renovation, and comparable sales in the area. She accepted the offer, but three days later wanted to cancel the transaction.

Why?

Because a "friend of a friend," who had discovered her situation, had approached her to say that he could arrange refinancing for her, that he could get her a new mortgage with an affordable payment. She didn't really have to sell, he told her. All she had to do was give him $5,000 to cover his "expenses," and he would "make it happen."

Desperate to keep the home she loved, the lady had scraped some cash together, borrowed the rest from relatives, and was about to hand it over.

When my associate told her that she had signed a binding contract and that she was committed to the sale, she was furious. She threatened to refuse to close and to sue all concerned. She did not understand that she was the one who could be sued for breach of contract. Fortunately, my associate is a caring person who understood her feelings and her anger. He begged her to hold off on giving over the $5,000 until he could investigate the new financing she had been promised, and asked her to show him the paperwork she'd been given. Sure enough, as we all had expected, no new loan was guaranteed. All that was promised was that the individual would make his best effort to secure a new loan for her, for a fee of $5,000 for professional services. When he was asked where he was going to get this loan, he refused to disclose the information. However, when he learned a licensed and experienced real estate agent was aware of his involvement, he backed off very quickly and, so far as I know, did not contact her again.

> *Eventually, and with great reluctance, the lady saw the reality of her position and allowed the sale to go forward without further incident. Hopefully by now she has realized that her real friend was her agent. He was the one who cared about her best interests and helped her to the best of his ability.*

Notes for friends and family members

Quite often, in my experience, sincere and entirely well-intentioned relatives or friends insistently, even aggressively, pressure a bereaved person to make immediate decisions. Vulnerable and knowing it, the widow or widower may not trust his or her own judgment and may bow to suggestions that would have been rejected out of hand only a short time previously—and will be deeply regretted later on.

Many times the script goes like this:

"Mom, I don't know how you're going to cope with this big old place now that Dad is gone. I think you should sell and move to a condo where you don't have to worry." Having everything taken care of is a very tempting idea for someone who is already overwhelmed.

Assuming that the bereaved person is not mentally or physically disabled and that it is financially feasible for them to maintain the property, discourage any irrevocable decisions until a year or two has passed. (And if you yourself are grieving, know that you, too, need to recover.)

Why?

- ✔ That's the shortest amount of time it takes a person to get back on a stable mental and emotional track after a trauma. (If you don't believe me, ask your doctor, your minister, or any mental health professional of your choice.)
- ✔ Decisions made under extreme stress aren't necessarily the same that would be made once conditions normalize, and what you would choose in the same circumstances might be very different from what the bereaved person might choose.

✔ Decisions instigated by someone else may be resented after the fact.

Finally, if you believe someone else is exerting undue pressure, especially if you think your relative or friend may be being victimized by an opportunist, do not sit quietly by.

✔ Use your influence to persuade him or her to get a second opinion.

Help him or her check the references and reputation of any stranger who has approached them.

If you find yourself unexpectedly divorced or abandoned by your partner

All of the advice that applies to the recently bereaved also applies to the recently divorced. However, very few people realize that the breakup of a marriage or a family involves many of the same emotional issues as a death, and many people are far too angry to listen to advice anyway, no matter how sensible it may be. Lots of times, though, people will curtail their anger and resentment if they clearly understand it will directly affect their financial and material well-being. So, in that spirit, read on.

Assuming you control what happens to the real estate you used to own together (although many times divorce decrees take that control away from one or both parties), you may be tempted to just get rid of it, so you can move on. You may be having difficulty making the mortgage payment without the assistance formerly provided by your partner. You may feel frightened at the prospect and threatened by doom and gloom predictions of foreclosure. You might want to keep the home but believe that selling is your only option. Or, conversely, perhaps you'd rather sell but, on your income alone, can't purchase an equivalent home.

✔ This is when you really need a knowledgeable agent, preferably one who specializes in financing.

✔ You also need an agent with whom you feel comfortable up close and personal, somebody objective, whom you trust with your true financial picture, and who understands your personal needs.

✔ If, after exploring all options, keeping the home is too financially burdensome, then sell. Have a detailed conversation with your agent about market trends, probable sale price, time it will take to sell, and other factors.

✔ If you want to sell, determine whether you can afford to indulge your emotions if the market is poor. Consult with your agent and do research to determine if this is a good time for sellers. If not, remember that, in Hawai'i, patience in real estate generally means profit.

✔ If you will buy another home when you sell the one you now own, the timing is probably less critical. In a strong buyer's market, your home may sell for less or take longer to sell, but when you buy, you'll have the advantages of buying for less and being able to pick and choose among properties. In a seller's market, you may sell for more than you expected, but you, too, will have to pay more. Either way, it's a wash.

✔ If you hate downsizing or downgrading, but there seems to be no other option, here's the best strategy: Sell the present property and follow the steps necessary to obtain the highest possible price.

While you are doing everything necessary to obtain the highest possible price, instruct your agent to find you an affordable replacement property in the best possible neighborhood. You are looking for a property that will appreciate, so that eventually you can trade up to something equivalent to the home you're selling.

✔ This advice also applies to divorcing couples who have the good sense to work together on marketing the joint property so they can both buy smaller homes independently.

As an example of creative and constructive thinking, here's the story of a woman I'm well-acquainted with.

> *Sarah and her husband had a three-year-old child and owned a home when they divorced. In the divorce decree, Sarah received custody of the child and title to the home. However, the decree also said she had to pay off the couple's joint debts and make the mortgage payments. She had a good job, but making that mortgage payment on her income alone was going to be difficult. She had to pay for all those debts. And then her ex-husband failed to make his required child-support payments.*
>
> *For a while, she struggled along. She didn't want to sell the home she loved and felt it was important to give her son the security of a permanent home, but things didn't look good. Then an opportunity arose.*
>
> *Sarah met a woman, another recent divorcee with a child, who had been forced to move into her mother's small rented home. Things were very cramped, and all concerned were beginning to resent the lack of privacy. The two women soon realized they could help each other solve their problems. Sarah rented two bedrooms and a bath in her home to her new friend. This allowed her to continue to make timely mortgage payments and turned out well in other ways. The two children became friends, and the two women provided each other with moral support during difficult emotional times.*
>
> *However, Sarah knew the arrangement was only a financial stop-gap. The minimal rent she received wasn't sufficient to keep up the maintenance on the house, and it was slowly deteriorating. She was a stubborn woman, though, and refused to quit. Another opportunity would come along, she was sure.*
>
> *About a year after her divorce, she met Charlie and fell in love. Once burned, twice shy, she proceeded slowly. After they'd been going together several months, Charlie's rental lease ended, and he was told his new rent would be double what it had been—a real problem. He asked to*

move into Sarah's home. It would be a win-win situation, he said, providing a further relief from the financial burden on her and allowing him to pay an affordable rent. Sarah was hesitant. She wouldn't give her son a series of unstable surrogate fathers, she told him, and she needed to know he had a serious commitment to their relationship. He did, he insisted.

Eventually, Sarah was convinced, and Charlie joined the hobbled-together "family." This turned out to be a fortunate happenstance, as Sarah's female housemate decided to take a job on the mainland and moved out shortly thereafter. A year later, Charlie told Sarah he thought her large home was simply too expensive to maintain; they needed to sell and move to something more affordable. She would make a decent profit, if she sold, and they would have a substantial down payment for the new home. Reluctantly, Sarah was forced to agree with his reasoning, but she worried that owning something together wasn't a good idea. What if they broke up and he decided he wanted her to move out? But she loved him, she didn't want to discuss things that might offend him or make him feel she was pushing marriage on him for the wrong reasons.

Now here's the part where Charlie really proved himself.

While Sarah was still struggling to find the right way to bring up the subject herself, Charlie told her, "This house is yours. You're the one who worked hard to make the payments all this time. I didn't take any risk and I don't have any responsibility. You earned the equity. It's all yours. I'm just a tenant, really. We're not even married. So you should choose the new house, and it should be in your name only."

And that's when Sarah realized she'd found the right man.

They sold the big house, bought a smaller one in her name only. A year later, they married. Five years after that, when they refinanced the home, Sarah gladly added Charlie's name to the title. "He earned it," she told me. "It's only right to include him now."

As I write this, Sarah and Charlie have been married for nearly thirty years. He adopted Sarah's son, and they have two other children, all adults now. They live in yet another home, one that is worth, in today's dollars, substantially more than the one Sarah was so sad to sell. But, in addition to its higher value, the home they own now truly belongs to both of them. It's a happy family home.

What did Sarah do right? Wasn't she just lucky? Yes, she most certainly was. However, she didn't rely on luck alone.

- ✔ She was open to opportunities that would allow her to hold onto her primary asset, her home.

- ✔ She was willing to give fair exchange of value—housing at an affordable rent to her friend and her boyfriend—to keep it.

- ✔ She protected her asset; she didn't allow anyone who hadn't earned her trust through time and experience to take financial advantage of her.

- ✔ When she decided to sell, it was neither under financial nor emotional pressure. She'd had time to make a sensible plan and timed the sale to maximize her gain.

- ✔ She also didn't make the mistake of believing that she could buy a stable relationship and purchased a replacement property on her own with a payment she could readily afford if she found herself alone again. She didn't mix love with money until she knew it was safe to do so.

And as she told me recently, she proved to herself along the way that she could manage on her own if she had to. She did not have to be a victim of divorce court economics.

If you're selling your home as the result of a divorce, keep the future in mind, don't dwell on the past, and don't make decisions based on wishful thinking or unproven relationships.

As the process moves along, you may be rightfully proud of how you're handling the sale of your present home so that your hard work maximizes its potential. You may also find yourself very excited at the prospect of selecting a new home for yourself, by yourself, looking forward to fixing up and customizing it, anticipating it will be a successful investment, and eventually a happy home. That is a good thing! A healthy thing! Feel good, not guilty.

What if you have suddenly lost your job or your source of income?

It's often most difficult to be objective when it's most important.

If you've lost your job and you're holding onto unaffordable house payments, waiting for things to get better, you could lose everything—the home and all its equity. This is the time when the old saying, "Pride goeth before a fall," really enters in.

The common sense wisdom is this: If your loss of employment is more than a temporary layoff; if you are having difficulty finding a comparable new job; if the economic forecast is generally not good in your industry or in your area; and, particularly, if you have put even one house payment on a credit card, it's time to think about an immediate sale.

In Hawai'i, though, unlike some other places, your real estate is probably more valuable than your other assets. People do (and for very good reasons) dance through many hoops and withstand many hassles just to hold onto their property through hard times.

And it's also true that if the employment situation isn't good here, the real estate market probably isn't good for sellers either.

Finally, it's historically true that Hawai'i real estate rebounds, generally to even greater heights than before, after every downturn.

So, should you really sell your property if you lose your job?

Well, you may have no choice. It's usually better to sell than to be foreclosed on, unless you owe more than the sale will bring. In that case, you should hold on if you can, because selling will gain you nothing. Also, in that case, you may be able to work with a lender to restructure your payments.

It's not necessarily a bad idea to liquidate other assets, such as stocks or pension plans, before selling a home you love. There are usually alternatives and options if you take time to think things through.

- ✔ For people who own property with a lot of equity, remember that if you both sell and buy at the same time, market conditions are far less relevant. You could sell your current home for enough money to allow you to buy something smaller for cash, or at least a much smaller mortgage.

- ✔ Parents or other relatives may be able to help with the payment. (Notice, I don't include friends here.) Whether this is an option is very personal, of course, and based on your relationships, but don't write it off without checking it out.

- ✔ You could put your parents on the title to the property.

- ✔ You could get a second mortgage from your parents with deferred interest and payments.

- ✔ You could share equity when the market improves and the property can be sold at a gain. People have used lots of creative ideas to retain their homes during difficult times.

- ✔ Again, you need an experienced real estate agent who is a financial specialist to consult with you, explore choices and possibilities with you, and help you plan your future.

A job or military transfer

This is a very commonplace circumstance in Hawai'i. If it happens to you, what do you do about your home? There are only three choices: 1) Sell the home, 2) rent the home, or 3) leave it vacant until your return.

1) Selling seems simplest, but it may not be clear-cut, and your decision may need to be partially based on whether you plan to return. Answer these questions before you act:

   Can you sell at a gain or at least break even?

   If you sell now, and later return to the islands, should you expect to be priced out of the market, or will you be able to buy another similar home at that time?

2) If you can't sell at a gain now, what about renting the house until the cycle moves into a more favorable seller's market? You may need advice from your real estate agent. Even if you think you know the answers, it's a good idea to confirm the facts and run the numbers with a professional by your side.

   If selling now seems inadvisable, or if you just don't want to part with your home, renting may be a better choice.

   Can you afford to do that?

   Do you want to do that?

Renting is often a very viable option, as rentals in Hawai'i are hard to find and expensive compared to most mainland locations. You may be surprised to find you can rent with few or no out-of-pocket expenses each month. There may be favorable tax ramifications for landlords, too. Absentee landlords are required by law to have a local rental manager, though, so don't think you can just find a tenant and leave town. Your agent can refer you to someone trustworthy if he or she doesn't do rental management. The usual fee is ten percent of the monthly rent, plus whatever out-of-pocket expenses the manager incurs—repairs, advertising, etc. It's money well-spent.

Renting is a viable option, but absentee landlords are required by law to have a local rental manager.

What's the upside of this choice for the average person who isn't a millionaire or a professional investor? Even if the monthly cash flow is negative, you may more than compensate for that if you'll have tax advantages now, while waiting for a favorable seller's market that will allow you to make a profit later. If you're leaving the

Islands only temporarily, your equity will keep pace with the long-term upward trend of Hawai'i's prices, you'll have a home when you return and won't have to buy down to something less desirable.

3) Leaving a house vacant is the third option. Here's why it's not so desirable:

It can be an invitation to burglars and vandals.

There can be delayed maintenance. If there's a problem, a lot of damage can happen before anyone finds out about it, or alerts you to the problem.

It's expensive. You'll need to keep the mortgage current while simultaneously paying for housing in your new location.

If selling doesn't make sense and you don't want to be a landlord, consider getting a house sitter or hiring a caretaker to come in periodically. I know several professional house sitters who take care of people's homes in exchange for a discounted rent. These are trustworthy people who can provide numerous references. They care for and protect your property in exchange for a quality of life they couldn't otherwise afford—a win-win for all concerned.

What if you are getting along in years and your children or other relatives are urging you to sell your home?

Here are at least some of the questions you need to answer for yourself before you decide if you're going to listen to them:

Why are people advising you to sell your home?

- ✔ Is it because you're having a hard time maintaining it or paying for it?

- ✔ Is it because you're not in good health and they think you no longer should live alone?

- ✔ Is it because their inheritance is tied up in your home, and they'd like to see some of it now?

Ask yourself:

- ✔ Do you want to sell your home?

- ✔ Is that what you'd choose to do if nobody was pressuring you in any way?

- ✔ Where would you like to live after you sell?

- ✔ If you sell, will you be able to afford to live where you'd like to?

- ✔ Is the present market good for sellers?

If you want to move, have a good new home in mind and market conditions seem favorable, then call your agent. If you don't have an agent, follow the steps for selecting a good one.

But if you love your home, have no desire to move, and are in good health physically and mentally, remember: you are the only person who can know when the time has come for you to sell.

If you think you'll be selling in the next few years, then find a wonderful real estate agent now, when there isn't any urgency. Keep tabs on the economy and the real estate market.

Then tell your children what you've decided to do. And while you're at it, if you haven't already arranged for the disposition of your property it's a good idea to do so and to let your children know where to find the paperwork.

What if your last child has just moved out, your home feels very large and empty, and you're wondering why you need such a big place any more?

If you've been waiting with bated breath for that last college graduation so you can downsize and spend your extra money on cruises, then call your agent and rock and roll!

But in truth most people don't want to leave the home they raised their kids in. And here in Hawai'i, long-term real estate equity only grows, so deciding to keep your home after your children have moved out is probably a good financial decision, unless the payments are eating you alive and preventing your enjoyment of other aspects of life.

Before you decide if a change is in order, think about what you'd be giving up.

Would you also be leaving your community, your friends, and the activities that make your life fun and worthwhile?

What about your garden? And your pets? If you move to a smaller home, you will probably still be able to enjoy those things. But if you move into a condominium or a townhouse, maybe not.

And there are other things to think about that apply here in Hawai'i but may not be pertinent elsewhere. Will your home only be a temporary empty nest? Is it likely one or more of those grown children will need to return? Or that one or more of them will need help buying their own home? Is it a good idea to sell now, move into a smaller place, and save the equity so the kids will have down payment money later? Or would it be better to hold onto your home and let your equity continue to grow until it's needed?

How do your children feel about the home? Would one of them want to raise his or her own family there? Is it a good idea, or even possible, to make an addition, or otherwise convert the property into something suitable for an extended family?

All these questions are personal and individual. Only you can answer them, and only you can know what other questions you should be asking before you decide to sell your family home.

There's an alternative plan that has served many people well here in Hawai'i. Some people never sell real estate; they only buy.

I have good friends who have acquired four properties over the years—one for each child. When a mutual friend commented that they were being very nice to their children, the wife replied that she knew by the time the children were old enough to own their homes, prices here would probably have gone so high, they couldn't afford to stay in Hawai'i. Her plan, she stated, was a win-win for all concerned. She and her husband have investments and income and tax breaks from the real estate now. When the children become independent, they can start out as tenants, paying rent to the parents. Later, they can buy the homes, either to live in or to sell to buy something else of their own choice, for far less than they anticipate the future value will be. Since the children will eventually become the beneficiaries of the parents' estate anyway, my friend said, they weren't doing their children any extreme favors, but rather using good financial planning to benefit all concerned.

In addition, if time brings changes, the couple can move out of their big house and into a smaller one. They can rent their properties at fair market value. They can sell, if they ever choose to do so, when the time is right—for them.

In short, they have great flexibility and independence because they realized at the beginning of their marriage that owning real estate in Hawai'i was better than owning gold. Their plan was thought out and executed over years, not overnight.

Even if you're already at the point where retirement is near and your kids are grown, it's not too late to modify my friends' idea to suit your own needs.

If you want to move into something smaller, but market conditions aren't optimum for selling, investigate all your options. Do the math. If numbers aren't your thing, ask your real estate agent and tax expert to help you.

- ✔ Can you rent your big home for enough to cover the payment and maintenance?

- ✔ What are the tax consequences of renting out your home versus selling and buying something smaller?

- ✔ Can you purchase the smaller home you have in mind without selling the one you own?

A note for concerned children

Please note: If you now, or may soon, have to take care of parents who are very elderly, in poor health, or not mentally competent, you rightfully have a lot to say about housing arrangements and finances. In that case, this commentary is not intended for you.

I'm a real estate agent, not a family counselor. Oh, but wait! Real estate agents usually are family counselors; they just don't get paid for that part of the job. And if mistakes are made, I, or some other agent, will have to deal with the fallout.

Most kids love their parents and really do think their advice is for the best. They just give it much too freely. I know that because I'm the parent of three adult children. Do my kids think they know better than I do? Of course they do! Do they think they need to tell me how to manage my money? Yes, indeed-y! Do they ever overlook the fact that my husband and I provided them with a secure home throughout their youthful years, and we might know what we're doing? Absolutely!

Fortunately, my kids know better than to push me too far or the wrath of Mom will fall on them.

However, if something devastating happened, or I were somehow disabled, where would I turn? To my children. Of course. Yes, indeed-y. Absolutely!

I would depend upon them to be fair-minded, smart, and selfless. I'd trust them to have my best interests foremost in their minds. I'd rely on their decisions.

Depend. Trust. Rely.

Powerful words and a powerful responsibility. One that you should not take upon yourself because you can, but only because you must.

Bottom line: When there's been a death or other traumatic event, do not make any permanent decisions, and most particularly, do not sign any contracts or binding agreements when you are distraught. If at all possible, avoid making any new or permanent decisions for at least a year or two. Don't make any decision just because friends and family members think it would be best for you.

If you cannot make payments, or are in doubt about your ability to carry them for the immediate future, consult with at least two independent, impartial, and expert professionals who can help you to explore all possible options. (Many times people are totally unaware of how many options they really have and are often far better off than they think they are. Don't assume anything.)

If you have a sudden loss of income, other choices than selling may be available. In Hawai'i, your real estate is usually more valuable than other assets such as stocks or bonds, and selling those things to keep your house may make more sense.

The same advice goes for those who are unexpectedly transferred. Consider all your options before selling property. Especially during unfavorable market conditions or if you'll eventually return, renting the property may prove a better choice.

For empty nesters: Your home is probably your own most valuable asset and chances are your children don't have any assets that are remotely comparable. If your children are just starting out, it may be a long time before they do. Before you sell or tradedown that asset, be sure that doing so will leave all of you better off than you are now.

Whatever your circumstances: Don't feel you have to figure things out all alone. Good professional financial advice is available from many sources, among them real estate agents, lenders, financial planners, tax advisors, and attorneys.

Footnote to the Bottom Line: Life changes aren't always sad, bad, or even difficult! Getting married, having a baby, getting a raise or a promotion or a great new job are all life changes, too.

And those are times when people are most likely to think about a new house. Whether it fills your needs, is a lifelong dream, or a symbol of your success, or all three, it's a celebration, a happy and wonderful experience. House shopping is fun. Moving into your new home, settling in, filling it with your things, decorating it the way you like, are all even more fun. With a little education, proper planning and the use of common sense, you'll maximize your enjoyment and your investment.

22

Strategies for Buyer's and Seller's Markets

Buyer's or seller's markets occur when one or the other has an advantage in the market, as opposed to a balanced situation. Supply and demand, interest rates, and other economic factors determine which type is currently prevailing.

There are various theories about predicting them in advance. People may say, "Hawai'i's market follows the mainland's by six months," or "Hawai'i's market follows the Japanese market," or some other supposed indicator. In fact, Hawai'i's real estate market is influenced by both, and sometimes by the economies of other countries as well. People also talk about a "seven-year cycle." None of those theories work all the time. There are simply too many unknowns that can change the equation. Wars, disasters, high unemployment, recession, all affect the housing market one way or another, as they do the entire economy. And so do positive things, such as new businesses coming into an area, or widespread publicity that a town has the best beach in the world, the cleanest water, or whatever.

While bankers, statisticians, and economists are expected to make accurate predictions, except for the ubiquitous success of 20–20 hindsight, all of them have failed at one time or another.

In short, the crystal ball is cracked.

And, too, Hawai'i's market is unique in several ways. Those ways lead us to an easier, more common-sense way to get an idea about what happens here, what constitutes buyer's and seller's markets here, and how what's happening may affect you. It's oversimplified, but makes the point.

One of the most significant unique factors is limited land. The Pacific Ocean provides a very finite border that prevents developers from just moving out of town another five miles and building a new subdivision. It also limits "infrastructure"—roads, water supply, sewage disposal, garbage disposal, all kinds of things people need to live comfortably. Another is our isolation from the rest of the world. That makes many kinds of businesses unfeasible here, thus limiting jobs, and also making our cost of living more expensive because of the need for importing many materials and goods from other places.

Countering those factors (that both limit *supply*) is our desirability —more people would like to live here than our Islands can support. Many people want to move here from other places; a very high percentage of existing permanent residents wouldn't leave if you beat them with a stick. This creates ongoing *demand*.

And also a constant tug-of-war between those who see a potential solution to one problem and those who see that same solution as creating yet another problem.

Some of the results (again, oversimplified) are these:

- ✔ Relatively high housing prices in both the sales and rental areas.

- ✔ Very high prices for buildable land, especially when that land is convenient to workplaces and essential services.

- ✔ Overcrowding and stress on existing infrastructure (frequent road and sewer repairs, traffic problems, to name just a couple) in some key older areas.

- ✔ Expensive new infrastructure that must be included in the prices of new developments.

- ✔ New housing, of physical necessity, being built in areas generally considered less desirable—a long drive to work, school, shopping, or the beach, etc.

- ✔ New housing being built of economic necessity to squeeze every possible allowable housing unit into the available land.

Given these and many other factors that make Hawai'i different from most other places, here's how the mechanics that create buyer's and seller's markets take place.

Every year many families are ready to enter the housing market for the first time. Most of them are on a strict budget. Affordability is Priority One. They are waiting for a "good buy," a "window of opportunity," or for that new job or raise to come through. When prices have remained stable for a while, or even declined, or when interest rates drop, these folks jump in to buy up the inventory of entry-level homes. This allows the sellers of these homes to "move up" to the next level, and so forth. Gradually this activity permeates the entire market place. Home shortages at the entry level then cause prices to begin to rise. However, that can't go on forever. Sooner or later the pent-up demand has been satisfied and prices have reached the point where buyers begin to resist further increases. Agents start hearing things like, "That's ridiculous. I won't pay that price for that house," on a regular basis. That's the first indication a period of stability is approaching.

In Hawai'i, we also have a large market of "high end," or luxury homes that responds to somewhat different stimuli. That market is comprised largely of people who buy for other reasons than simply to own a home—they often already own one or several. Interest rates may not be as important as tax advantages. Sometimes the high-end market has been very active while the entry level stagnates, and vice versa.

If you want to make a down-and-dirty analysis for yourself at any given point in time, *determine what the supply and demand situation is like.*

- ✔ Are open houses busy and agents working 16-hour days?

- ✔ Are desirable properties sold in a week or staying on the market for several months?

- ✔ How many ads are in the Sunday paper?

- ✔ Are there lots of yard signs in your area or just a few?

- ✔ Are interest rates changing dramatically in either direction?

- ✔ Have prices been rising for several years? If so, a turning point may be coming. The same goes if prices have been relatively stable for some time, or if interest rates show signs of increasing.

If you're thinking of selling and want to know if it's a "good time" for you, your agent can blend knowledge about your particular home and personal situation with understanding of overall market conditions to help you make an informed decision.

We often say it's always a good time to buy here, though, and that's generally true because over many, many years, despite temporary fluctuations, prices have trended upward because as explained above, there's a constant demand and a limited supply. However, there are still times when it's more advantageous to buy and times when sellers do relatively better.

If interest rates have "shot for the moon," as happened in the early 1980s, many buyers are discouraged. (Fact to keep in mind: It's not the purchase price that makes a property affordable or not; it's the monthly payment. Even if the price is a million dollars, you can afford that property if you can make the payment.) When buyers drop out of the marketplace because they can't afford the high interest rates, properties don't sell as quickly, the inventory grows. Sellers have more competition and may start offering some of the extra incentives described below. It's a buyer's market.

When there's a lot of demand, shortage of available properties, but interest rates and the economy are still favorable, sellers have an edge. They don't have to make concessions to sell their property, and prices rise. Then we have a seller's market.

Experienced investors time their own plans to take advantage of favorable conditions when and as they occur. But what if you aren't able to time your transaction according to the market and are forced to buck the current?

My friend and client Tom began looking for a home during a buyer's market, two years before I met him. His agent tried hard, but for one reason or another, nothing was exactly right and his interest cooled. Then, when he suddenly discovered he had to vacate his rental house within forty-five days and called his agent again, the market had turned. Prices had risen sharply. We were dealing with the strongest seller's market we'd had in years. His agent was about to leave on vacation, so she asked me to help him while she was away. We both had our doubts about finding something before he had to move, but she set up a lender's appointment for him, and I promised to give it my best.

I called Tom. He'd seen the error of his ways, he said and would now be more flexible and less choosy than he'd been two years ago, but he still had some pretty specific needs. It was going to be difficult and frustrating, I told him, but with luck, we'd find something that would work.

At this point, Tom had done several things right: He was meticulous in paying his bills—his credit was solid gold. The lender gave him a credit preapproved mortgage commitment. And he'd told me exactly what he did and didn't want in terms of neighborhood, size of home, and other things that were important to him—a garage, a yard big enough for his Labrador retriever, proximity to a public park, etc. He'd also told me what didn't matter to him—one story or two, swimming pool or not, whether or not it was a fixer-upper. Our town, Kailua, would be best, he said, but he knew it was too pricey, so we had to go further afield. I started hunting.

Tom and I scoured the Island, traveling at least a hundred miles on each outing—not easy to do here. Tom had never owned a home and wanted to understand the process from beginning to end. He was very smart and a fast learner. My car became a mobile classroom, but as you will see, I missed explaining a critical matter that almost cost us both dearly.

After three weeks of finding interesting homes that had just been sold to someone else, having offers rejected just by a hair, and visiting at least twelve totally unsuitable and seriously terrible houses, he was ready to give up. He was praying, he told me, for a landlord who'd allow his dog. The chances of that happening, I knew, were slim to none.

"If we find something this weekend, we can still close before you have to move," I told him. He was reluctant and discouraged. I twisted his arm. He agreed to look one more time. I didn't know what in the world I could show him, but by now I was too invested in that dog's welfare to quit.

His agent returned from vacation. Ordinarily, she would have taken over then, but instead she told me to keep on working with Tom. "By now you know him better than I do, and you've got a better handle on what's right for him."

I was sure her confidence was misplaced. But then came the miracle. The first one, actually.

As I turned back to my futile search on the computer, she mentioned she was getting a new listing, right in Kailua. My ears pricked up as she described it. It was Tom's house! I knew it! But, like everything else in Kailua, it was $100,000 above his budget.

I don't show people property that exceeds their ability to purchase. I just don't. But maybe because I knew Tom was inexperienced, something told me to call his lender directly. "Is that budget written in blood?"

"No," she said. "His credit's so good he can borrow just about anything he wants, but he has an affordable payment in mind and doesn't want to exceed it." Oh. Or maybe, aha!

I begged my associate, Tom's original agent, to let me preview the house before it was ready for the market. We were running out of time. I couldn't afford to waste it on anything that wouldn't work for him, but I also couldn't afford to miss an opportunity. Because of her own good nature, and maybe a little bit because I made her feel guilty about handing me Tom's problems, she agreed.

It was his house. My heart soared when I saw it, and then sank immediately: We still had a major budget problem. He can afford it if he wants to, I reminded myself. The decision's his, not mine. I called Tom, afraid he'd bite my head off, but my search had netted zero other options. We were at the end of the road.

"I'd love to stay in Kailua," he said rather longingly. "But I can't afford it, Fran." At that point, for the first time, he told

me his actual paycheck amount. "After taxes and everything, I don't have enough left to live on."

Taxes. Taxes . . . . The light dawned—a little late. But maybe not too late.

"Tom," I said, feeling both negligent and stupid, "Your net pay will be a lot different after you buy a home and take the interest and property tax deductions."

"What? What are you talking about?" Not knowing that his payroll tax withholdings would change radically after his purchase, Tom had been figuring his budget on incorrect take-home pay all along! I hadn't talked to him about that, even though I knew he was inexperienced and neither had the lender. And this was the rather backhanded second miracle. Belatedly, I explained.

"Call your tax guy right now," I urged him. "And meet me at the house at five o'clock. It can't hurt," I encouraged. "We've got nothing to lose."

Tom's courage—and love for his dog—overcame his reluctance to be disappointed again, and he agreed. While he called his tax preparer, I talked with my associate. "What do we have to do to get an offer accepted before that listing gets into the computer?" I felt nervy asking, but Tom and I had nothing to lose.

"Bring me full price," she told me, "and clean. You know the drill. They need to move by the end of the month, they can't afford a transaction to fall out of escrow."

"You know he's qualified," I replied. "I can have a pre-approval letter faxed over in five minutes and the lender's already told us we can close on time . . . . Are the sellers going to wait for multiples?" Multiple offers are the bane of a buyer's broker's existence. I held my breath.

"I don't think so," she said. "They've told me they'll work with the first offer that meets their price as long as the buyer's qualified and they sense he's sincere."

"You know Tom's sincere," I pressed. "If he likes the house enough to make an offer, he's going to close unless something really wrong shows up on the inspection."

"I do know that," she acknowledged. "I'll cross my fingers and see you at five."

> *So, the upshot: Tom's tax man told him his increased net pay would cover the larger monthly payment. He loved the house and so did his dog. He made a clean, full-price offer, and I wrote an accompanying letter to the sellers about his dog, his urgent need to find a home, and his delight in finding one in a town he'd previously thought he couldn't afford. The sellers kept their word, the inspections didn't reveal any problems, and we closed on time. And that's the end of the story. Almost.*
>
> *Tom gave me a Christmas present to commemorate our work together. The little pig with wings will hang in my office always. And I will never again assume a first-time buyer knows about withholding taxes!*

Buying in a seller's market

Say there aren't many affordable houses out there, there's heavy competition for those that are, but you need a home now. Things can still work out well for you, although you're more than likely to be frustrated along the way. This is when self-discipline, patience, and smart offer strategies pay off the most.

Most of Tom's story has nothing to do with miracles and everything to do with the correct strategies for buying in a seller's market. A little recap is in order.

First: *Get a realistic fix on your budget.*
Read the chapter on financing and go to a reputable and knowledgeable lender. Know exactly how much cash you have, and how much may be available to you if you need help. Get an estimate of your closing costs, and don't forget them when calculating your available down payment.

And *remember to recalculate your withholding taxes* in case your agent forgets.

Second: *Get a reliable and dedicated real estate agent on your team.*
She needs to know you will buy only through her. Share your budget information frankly and completely. Communicate your needs clearly and in detail. Why? Because agents sometimes find out in advance when a property is going to become available. And you want the first number your agent dials to be yours.

Third: *Be prepared to act fast.*
You don't have time to cogitate or meditate. In a seller's market, a "good buy" is often gone in less than twenty-four hours—this is a fact, not a sales ploy. (Remember you'll have time to do a detailed property inspection after your offer is accepted.)

Fourth: *As a corollary to the above, make your highest and best offer immediately.*
Expecting to negotiate price in a seller's market is a losing strategy. Your offer should be for a figure that, if it's one dollar higher, you don't want the property or you know your loan application will be rejected!

And last: *Be an honorable person!*
When you're trying to buy in a strong seller's market, your agent often must guarantee your sincerity to associates who trust her. Don't make irresponsible offers, don't promise what you don't intend to perform, don't try to tie up property for days or weeks while you make up your mind whether you want it. It's not fair. Besides, if you do, your agent is likely to dump you and the word will get out that you're playing games. Then no one will trust you, and you may well end up with nothing.

Selling in a seller's market

If the timing of a seller's market coincides with your plans to sell your property, excellent! It's a good time for sellers to make money. But beyond just listing your property and waiting for those multiple offers to pour in, there are strategies that will help you make the most of your opportunity.

If you've been planning to sell your property, but waiting until "the time is right," how do you decide if that time is now?
Partly, that's determined by personal urgency. If you have a very large mortgage debt and have been simply waiting until you can break even on a sale, determine your bottom line—how much your actual sale price must be in order to pay off that debt, cover your closing costs and expenses, and recoup any down payment you have invested. Your agent can figure this for you, but you can get a ballpark idea right now if you do the following:

Add your mortgage principal balance(s)—include any second mortgage or equity loans—to the down payment you made. If you've spent significant money on upgrades, add those amounts as well. Divide the grand total by 93. Then multiply that total by 100.

This is a pretty reliable estimate of the minimum sale price you can accept with no loss.

If your need to sell is urgent, give your agent the facts and ask her to let you know when the market has reached the point where you'll accomplish the goal.

But most people want to do more than break even. Perhaps you want to "move up," or "move down" and use your gain for living expenses or retirement. It's in your best interests to make as much money as possible, so we'll assume that's what you want to do. But don't let greed run away with common sense. It's smartest to plan for a reasonable gain, and leave some money on the table for the next guy.

Why not wait until the market has topped out?
Partly because hitting that mark, if you do, is blind, dumb luck. The only sure way to know that's happened is when it's already turned down again. But a better reason is because even in a very frenzied seller's market, buyers need to see a potential upside for themselves. If they don't, they may decide to wait for the cycle to turn back in their direction.

So ask your agent for weekly updates on what's happening. Read the real estate section of the paper. Watch for the frequency of "For Sale" signs going up and coming down in your area. And don't push your luck. Look for an "optimum" time instead of a "maximum time." (Note: Most people don't see significant gains for a while after they buy.)

Several items figure into your net gain.

✔ Remember closing costs. If you're going to buy another property, you'll have closing costs there, too.

✔ And if you're not selling your personal residence, you may have tax consequences. If you've owned for less than three years and will come out way ahead upon sale, you're extremely fortunate.

✔ On the other hand, if you've owned your home for a long time, perhaps through one or more complete cycles, you're probably stunned by the asking price your agent is suggesting. But before you take all that money to the bank (or worse, to Vegas), take a realistic look at replacement properties, what your new monthly payment will be, and what your tax position will be after you sell.

✔ Even in the hottest seller's market, following the guidelines to successful marketing will net a significantly higher sale price and faster sale than arrogantly dumping your property on the market any which way or inhibiting market exposure.

✔ Remember the key to making serious money in Hawai'i real estate and moving up to your dream home is realistic planning and repeating a successful strategy over and over.

Okay, you've decided the time is right and you've put your property on the market. Fifty agents came to the broker's open house, and more than thirty visitors showed up on Sunday afternoon. Your agent is delighted, you are stoked. It looks like you'll shortly have several offers. *What fly could there possibly be in the ointment?*

Oops! You may have missed a step in the planning.

✔ The time to decide how to handle multiple offers is before the property is listed.

Failing to do so, allowing the cards to fall in a haphazard manner, can lead to serious misunderstandings and the loss of offers you might have found ideal. You may decide to consider all offers in the order received; this rewards the buyer who acts fast, and may, in your mind, seem the fairest. Alternately, you may decide to look at all offers on a specific date—the Tuesday following the first Sunday open house, for example, or maybe one week after the listing is entered into the MLS. Whatever you do, informing all concerned in advance is one important key. Another is giving yourself enough time to review all offers carefully. Under no circumstances should you rush through that process. If you, as one client did, receive thirteen offers, you'll need time to read them all. If your pre-established deadline turns out to be too short, you can ask your agent to request extensions for response, but you may lose offers that way. It's better to plan ahead realistically and stick to it.

The initial review process with multiple offers is even more important than if you are working with only one. Why? Because if you accept the "wrong offer," and it falls through, it may be too late to recapture one of the other buyers. You and your agent may have to start marketing again from scratch.

Negotiating simultaneously with more than one buyer is difficult at best. Without careful planning, correct notification to all concerned, and meticulous adherence to the rules and the law, a seller can find he's contracted with more than one buyer (oops, you can only sell the house once!), or lost them all (trust me, buyers who feel they've been abused or that fair play has been violated become very hostile very fast).

One way to minimize the risk is to accept what appears to be the best offer, but try to put one or more others in "backup" position immediately. Your first-place buyer will know there is someone waiting to jump in if he "weasels," or fails to meet a deadline. This will inspire him to perform all aspects of his contract in a timely manner. It will also allow you and your agent to keep track of the alternate buyer(s) and save a lot of time should something go wrong with your first-place contract. (You'll find more about backup offers in the chapter on seller's strategies.)

Selling in a buyer's market

Buyer's markets are a normal part of the economic cycles—they won't last forever. What matters to you, as a seller, is that in a buyer's market, prices have peaked or are trending downward, and there are many homes for each buyer to choose from. Hence, you should avoid selling if you can. But if, for one reason or another, you must market your property now, how can you minimize the competition and maximize your gain?

✔ **Get realistic.** Get a detailed and comprehensive market analysis from your real estate agent—and heed what it tells you.

If prices are declining, it's likely you won't get as much for your property in six months, or even three, as you will now. Correct pricing in the first place yields not only a quicker sale but more money in your pocket. (Don't forget to factor in the expenses you must meet every month that it remains unsold!) If the market isn't clearly in a downward spiral, but there are many available properties comparable to yours, you still need to price your property correctly, or your home will be the last to sell. Remember this basic fact: The most interested buyers will show up during the first three weeks of marketing.

If your home is not competitive, buyers will forget about it and move on. By the time you lower the price to where it belongs, you'll have lost your best opportunity. If you then end up frustrated and hoping for any offer at all, you'll have only one person blame—yourself.

✔ *Make your home as attractive as possible.* Pay attention to little details that appeal to buyers' emotions. (Particularly in condominiums, townhouse projects, or subdivisions, where there may be several units with identical floor plans, giving yours that extra "oomph" can be critical.) It's simple common sense: When buyers can choose between several affordable and comparable homes, they will buy the one that feels most comfortable and needs the least work.

✔ *Hire an agent* who will actively and aggressively market your property. This means an agent who will hold at least one open house every two weeks and advertise them in the Sunday paper, put the listing in Multiple Listing Service and on the Internet, host broker's open houses at least monthly, and send postcards or make phone calls to other agents in the area to call attention to the listing.

✔ *Don't restrict showings or make appointments difficult.* Keep the house ready to show at all times and available with the shortest possible notice. Make arrangements for your pets and children. (If the children are old enough, enlist their help. Let them know their efforts are important and appreciated.)

Going into sale mode in a buyer's market is hard work for everyone. You may get appointment requests at nine o'clock at night. Answer them. Politely. (Ten o'clock's too late to call anybody; that's when you can turn off the phone. But return that call first thing in the morning!) Your Saturdays may be spent cleaning, and your Sunday afternoons will no longer be your own. Don't complain to your agent; she's working then, too.

- ✔ ***Be patient*** when the house is shown to unqualified buyers, or to people who are clearly not interested, or when somebody makes an appointment and then doesn't show up. Your agent is turning over every stone and making a concerted effort to get anyone and everyone to take a look. Cooperate as fully as possible.

- ✔ ***Be creative.*** Think of anything you can offer a buyer that might turn him in your direction. If interest rates are high, perhaps you can offer a seller's second mortgage or an agreement of sale to a qualified buyer. (Often this is a win-win because you get interest income to compensate you for delayed receipt of your proceeds. It sometimes also can give you tax benefits.) If you have an interested party who's short on cash, perhaps you can inspire them to act by paying some of the buyer's closing costs. If your house is in need of a fixup, perhaps you can offer a credit to the buyer at closing, so they will have the cash to do what's necessary right away.

- ✔ ***Discuss and analyze*** what's going on in the market and the economy with your agent and what options might provide good buyer incentives.

- ✔ ***Don't be penny-wise and pound-foolish.*** I'm not recommending you give away the store. You need to know exactly where, dollar-wise, you must draw the line, but it's also true that when competition is heavy you have to spend money to make money. It may be tempting to market your property on your own, but it's a losing strategy. During tough times, your property needs maximum exposure—everyone needs to know it's available. In a downturning market, if that listing does not appear in the Multiple Listing Service, you are giving up the single most important sales tool available to sellers. Even if you offer "courtesy to brokers," without a listing agent to provide that necessary exposure and other aggressive marketing strategies, your property may not sell until prices drop even further. Then you'll have done all that work for less than nothing, especially after you consider your carrying costs for the marketing time.

✔ *You need professional advice and service* during a difficult economy. All the other sellers out there will be utilizing all their resources. You can't afford to fall short. Even if you find a prospective buyer on your own, turning it into a closed sale is the hardest part of the job. It's time-consuming and exacting. Avoiding the many pitfalls that lie between accepting an offer, closing escrow, and getting the proceeds into your pocket requires expert and full-time attention.

Nevertheless, at times like this it's important to save whenever possible.

✔ *Ask your agent to provide a home buyer protection plan* at no cost to you. (Some companies routinely do that.) That's a buyer incentive, covers repairs to electrical, plumbing, and appliances for only a minimal deductible (around $50) for a year after closing. It also covers you during the marketing period.

✔ *Ask for a discount on the commission.* However, be prepared to offer something in return. Like what? Maybe like pricing your property realistically in exchange for a discount on the commission if it sells in thirty days or less. Or maybe, if you're going to both sell and buy, guaranteeing you'll use your agent for both transactions. If your agent knows you well, sometimes all it takes is a reminder of how loyal, cooperative, and wonderful you are to work with! (That always gets my favorable attention.) During difficult times, though, agents have to work harder than ever to get the job done, so don't be surprised if it's an uphill battle to get that discount, or if your attempts are unsuccessful.

✔ ***Other ways to save:*** Escrow companies often give discounts to senior citizens and sometimes to military. It doesn't hurt to ask. You or your agent can also comparison-shop for services such as the survey or termite treatment.

✔ ***Price the property correctly to sell quickly.*** This is the single most important factor when you must sell during a buyer's market. Nothing else will make up for your failure to do that.

Buying in a buyer's market

If you're in a buyer's market, your offer may be the only one a seller has seen in a while, and he may be strongly motivated to make it work. You may have time to negotiate back and forth several times until you come to a meeting of the minds.

✔ This is prime time for a buyer to squeeze into something that's just a little more expensive than he can afford by negotiating for extras, such as those mentioned above.

✔ It's also the time when it doesn't hurt to try an offer that's a little on the low side. The seller may not accept it, but you'll likely get a realistic counteroffer instead of a rejection. And if you don't succeed in a particular negotiation, there's a good chance you'll find another seller who can work with you.

✔ In a buyer's market, don't be turned off or discouraged from making an offer if asking prices are higher than comparable data indicates they should be. Sellers often overprice their properties in this market—not because they're trying to gouge but because prices have fallen below a certain benchmark they rely on, such as what they paid.

Note to sellers: What you paid for a property matters to you. It does not matter to a buyer nor does it have anything to do with the current market value of your home. In the late 1980s and early 1990s, foreign investors saw Hawai'i as ripe territory, bought homes and residential land heavily, and drove prices to record highs. Those people who live here all the time and need housing here—who make up the foundation of our economy—could not pay those inflated prices. And then those foreign investors experienced downturns in their own economies and left town, often selling for far less than they'd paid, sometimes abandoning their properties altogether. Our market dropped. Hard. Sellers had trouble getting offers that covered their mortgage debt and closing costs, much less recouping their down payment. I, along with many other agents, advised clients not to sell at all unless they had no choice. Waiting it out was the only winning strategy I could see for my seller-clients at the time. Those who were forced to sell often couldn't bear to list their homes for what the market would actually bring, and no one could blame any of them for trying to salvage as much of their investment as they could.

Buying and selling simultaneously

If you're buying and selling in the same economy—in the same place or in two places that are experiencing similar market conditions—your gain or loss on one side may be "washed" on the other; you'll come out even overall. Whether it's a buyer's or a seller's market then matters less, but there are still some strategies to think about.

Many people sell their homes in order to move up, hoping to eventually afford their dream home. But often such a homeowner isn't sufficiently motivated to put his present property on the market until he sees a For Sale sign in front of that dream home.

If that happens to you in a seller's market, you may be competing with several other buyers. You must sell your present home before someone else buys the one you want or find some other way to tie up your desired purchase until you complete your sale. You need a smart and creative agent, and you must be smart and creative yourself—as well as brave. Even then, you may not succeed—but if you don't try, you certainly won't. Here's what to do:

- ✔ First, with your agent and mortgage lender, analyze your resources. Go through your finances in detail, and think of anyone, such as a family member or an equity lender, who could give you a short-term loan or any other help. This is not the time to be too proud to ask, and it's not the time to keep financial details to yourself!

  Find out if there's any way you can buy the new home before closing the sale of the old one. If you can, that's your best option. If you can't, you've got a difficult road ahead. Have a frank discussion with your agent.

- ✔ What price should you ask for your present home to generate an immediate sale?

- ✔ What's a realistic sale price for your dream home. In a strong seller's market, it could be substantially more than the asking price.

Don't forget to figure in all of the expenses and closing costs of both transactions. If the figures don't work out, be willing to accept the fact that the timing's not right for you and stop there. You may have to go through more steps to reach your goal. Don't give up. Delay is not the same as defeat.

If it looks like there's a chance to make it work, you'll have to try a contingency offer. Now you've got to be brave.

Your most likely winning strategy is to offer something the seller wants that other buyers may not be able to offer. It could be something like delayed occupancy. Or it might be a strongly phrased as-is clause. Ask your agent to find out what might help. It may not be specified in the listing, and it won't necessarily have anything to do with money. I've seen many unlikely contracts succeed because the buyer was aware of the seller's special circumstances and gave him what he wanted.

Be entirely straightforward about the contingency, give details about your present home, and have your agent write a strong cover letter about the likelihood of an immediate sale.

Put your present home on the market right now. Otherwise, no seller will consider your offer.

If you will only sell your present home if you're able to purchase the one you want, make your listing subject to the purchase of that home. This condition must be written on the listing agreement, in the Multiple Listing Service, and on any offer you accept. And then pray.

While you are doing that, realize you've chosen the most difficult way to achieve your goal. You may want to rethink your position. Would it be to your advantage to sell now, even if you don't get that particular home? It might, if you suspect the seller's market may be nearing its end.

What if you list your present home subject to the purchase of any home of your choice within, say, fourteen days after accepting an offer? Then you would have two weeks to search for a house, and any offer you make would be contingent only upon a close of escrow—far stronger than "contingent upon sale," although still not optimum.

You could also sell the house and move into a rental until you find one to buy. That option presents its own set of challenges, but at least you wouldn't have to make contingency offers in a seller's market.

I'm not telling you what to do; just advising you to think everything through with a clear head.

It may be tempting, in the heat of competition, to forget to mention your contingency at all.

Bad. Bad, bad, bad.

But enough people think it's a legitimate strategy that sellers have learned to be wary of what should be a self-evident no-no. Honesty and fair play aside, you will probably be found out almost immediately because the standard contract authorizes a seller's broker to check on your loan progress. Your lender can't lie for you;

that's fraud. And if you lie to your lender, that's fraud, too. Breach of contract may be the least of your worries then. If a seller finds out you've contracted with him in bad faith, he may have grounds to cancel. You will then net exactly nothing except a bad reputation and may also lose any deposits you've made. Don't do it. Period.

The only exception is if you have a backup plan in place. Say, for instance, if your house doesn't sell in time, your mother will buy it for the interim period, and she doesn't have any contingency. If that's the case, write your offer that way. Period. Don't listen to an agent who suggests any less-than-honest strategy. Get rid of her immediately. Competent agents don't need to use such tactics.

If you find your dream home during a buyer's market, you may be able to negotiate a great contract. The seller may be willing to accept a contingency offer or make other concessions to help the transaction along. However, no seller will wait forever and that contingency offer will have an expiration date. If you haven't sold your home in time, you may lose the one you want, or, if interest rates or other factors have changed, you may no longer be able to purchase it. Selling your present home in a timely fashion and for enough to close your new purchase is your greatest challenge.

Once again, the key to success is pricing your home realistically for immediate sale and putting it on the market right away. Your buyer, in turn, may want concessions such as you received from your seller. Be prepared for that. Know what you can concede, and what you can't.

✔ *Now is not the time to play your cards close to your vest.* A better strategy is open communications on several levels. It's perfectly acceptable, and sometimes advisable, for your agent to tell potential buyers, "My client has an accepted offer on another home. He will make every effort to work with a realistic, sincere offer right now. But if he doesn't sell in time to buy the home he wants, he may become less motivated." That statement has the virtue of being both true and able to inspire fast action.

What other details you disclose depends upon the situation. You and your agent must decide, keeping in mind that most people will help others out if it doesn't hurt them to do so, or if they see a simultaneous advantage to themselves.

It's also very important to communicate openly with the owner of the home you want to buy. If you receive an offer and have negotiated to the best of your ability, but the offer is still just a little short, tell your seller. If he's highly motivated and has no other buyer, he may negotiate further or come up with another idea that will work. At the very least, knowing you're making every effort will make him inclined to cut you any slack he can!

Bottom line: Be aware of the market you're in and strategize accordingly. Try to buy when competition among sellers is the heaviest, and sell when competition among buyers is the heaviest. If you can't avoid swimming against the current, know that you'll have to make concessions and make them immediately. Wasting weeks or months trying to force your will on a contrary market will only cost you heartache, frustration, and lots of money.

23

Getting into
Real Estate for Money

For those who dream of getting rich quick through real estate speculation in Hawai'i, here's my advice: Forget it.

Because quick doesn't work. Those classes and seminars that promise you a way to make a fortune without any substantial investment of your own? Truly, they don't tell you what you need to know to do real estate successfully in Hawai'i. Save your money and your time.

And speculation means gambling. Here in Hawai'i, real estate is not a gamble unless you've done something extremely foolish. In Hawai'i, real estate is an investment, most often a long-term one. It takes money of your own no matter what. And, as with any other investment, for it to pay off, you need to make it knowledgeably and carefully and look after it that way, too.

Let's rephrase the first sentence, leaving out "quick" and "speculation": If you dream of getting rich through real estate, as other people have done, and if you use good judgment, common sense, and careful planning, you can.

- ✔ You must be willing to learn and willing to follow expert advice.

- ✔ If you want to take a class, there are many good choices, including a real estate program at the University of Hawai'i. Classes in business and finance might be worthwhile, too. And the real estate schools for agents offer great information and are worth every dollar, even if you don't intend to become an agent yourself.

- ✔ You'll need lots of self-discipline, patience, and really good analytical skills.

- ✓ If you are a born negotiator, have an unerring sense of timing, and an intuitive grasp of how little details add up in the big picture, great—those are the characteristics most successful investors have.

- ✓ You'll need money, disposable funds above and beyond the money your family eats on.

- ✓ And lots and lots and lots of luck.

It's not easy. Novices should start small. So . . . since everyone has to be a novice at least once, how do you start?

A very popular choice for many people, that's been dealt with extensively throughout this book, is **purchasing a fixer-upper for resale**. You must accurately calculate all costs to find out if the property in question is right for your purposes. A bare-bones outline of how to make that calculation bears repeating:

- ✓ Add about three percent for closing costs to your offer price to arrive at your true purchase price.

- ✓ Take the average neighborhood resale price for a home in good condition and subtract about seven percent for closing costs upon sale to arrive at a probable net resale price.

- ✓ The difference between those two figures is the amount you can spend on repairs and improvements just to come out even on resale.

But you're looking for a property you can sell at a profit.

It's very important to calculate accurately before purchasing the property. There are computer programs that can help you make an analysis, but the figures you insert have to be realistic or the exercise is useless. Getting contractors' estimates is helpful for a smaller job, essential for a big one. You should also add a substantial amount—at least 10 percent—for contingencies, because unexpected things crop up in all remodeling jobs.

After you've figured out how much the entire package will cost, you need to estimate how long it will take you to turn it over and how much profit will make the project worth your while. Arrive at your final figure—your net profit—without adding in appreciation over time. That's gravy if you get it but cannot be relied on.

If you are going to live in the house, its shelter value is also important to your calculation. That can make the difference between fixing up for fun and profit and losing your shirt.

Another way to get your feet wet is to **purchase an investment home or apartment for rental purposes**. Investigate keeping your first home as a rental unit instead of selling it when you're ready to move up. This has been a very successful long-term strategy for many investors who started with one rental unit and now own many.

Another idea: Perhaps you can't afford to buy a home in the area where you need to live. Purchase an affordable unit elsewhere and rent it out while you continue to live in your own rented home. Rental units in Hawai'i offer both income now and appreciation for the future.

Careful analysis is the key to both those options. Your agent and your lender can offer invaluable assistance.

Finally, **if you think you've got what it takes to become a real estate agent**, who's to say you shouldn't? On O'ahu alone there are several thousand of us, and many make a very good living. There are three basic specialties: Residential real estate sales, commercial real estate, and rental real estate. I will deal only with residential sales—it is what I know. For information on the other specialties, you should consult with experienced—and successful—agents in those areas.

But just as you need a list of requirements and desires to look for a home, you need such a list if you're thinking of going into this business—and also a serious and objective analysis of your personal aptitudes and capabilities. First and foremost:

> ✔ You must be financially able to go without an income for as long as two years.

I know you don't think that'll happen to you. But it can. It's happened to others. Many others. Even after you've established yourself, it's possible to go several months without a paycheck. If your family's finances can't withstand that, don't become a real estate agent. (And forget about that part-time idea. No good. Nobody will give you any credibility.)

> *I was recently watching one of those daytime advice shows. A woman asked how to get her husband to stop free-loading off his parents. It had been going on for over a year, she said, and it was humiliating and degrading to her. He'd used excuse after excuse to avoid taking financial responsibility. She wanted him to get a job and support their family, which included two toddlers. "Doesn't he work?" the astonished host asked.*
>
> *Turned out, this husband had decided he was more of an entrepreneur-type than an employee-type and could succeed at a business in which he had no experience and no education, while maintaining their present lifestyle, which included a nice house with a big mortgage, two cars, and a stay-at-home wife. So he simply up and quit his job and went into—you guessed it—real estate. He knew it would take a while to "break into the business," so he persuaded his parents to take care of his family—pay all their bills, including credit cards, etc. Nice work if you can get it, but that's not the point. At the time the show aired, he'd been in the business for ten months and had yet to pick up a commission check.*

Why, one wonders, had he not successfully closed a single transaction in all that time? The market was good in the state where he lived. He was properly licensed and worked for a large company, presumably a reputable one.

Well, it's pretty obvious if you've ever been there and I have.

Two reasons: Unrealistic expectations, followed by total inaptitude for the work. Okay, somebody should have warned him the way I'm warning you, but as adults we are responsible for our choices. I don't know if anyone warned him, but if they did, he wasn't listening.

He didn't consider possible financial pitfalls and he also didn't pay any attention to whether he was suited to real estate sales as a career! He didn't realize he was going to have to work very hard to be successful and didn't realize his job was to satisfy other people's needs before worrying about his own. He only wanted to get rich and was an abysmal failure.

I spent the balance of the hour shaking my head at the poor man's foolishness, feeling very sorry for his wife, and even sorrier for his parents. After all, they raised him.

Enough said about the money. Let's say you can handle the dry spells and want to try real estate.

What about the aptitude? (It sounds like "attitude," and in lots of ways the two can be synonymous.)

What does it take to be a good real estate agent?

- ✔ If you're experienced in other types of sales work, real estate will be completely different.

- ✔ Good agents are service oriented. Your goal is not to sell anybody anything, but rather to find what your clients want and help them acquire it. (If you've got great customer service skills, those will come in very handy. If you don't, learn them.)

- ✔ Good agents tend to be sociable types, too. You'll need to be able to talk to anybody any time, establish rapport in a hurry, and remember lots of little details about people you meet very briefly and usually when others are simultaneously demanding your attention.

- ✔ A background in accounting is really helpful, as is banking or lending experience. Basically, you need to learn a lot about mortgages as well as other types of financing, and a mathematical brain helps. But it does not do the job alone. People with this type of focus must be careful not to stress the financial aspect to the exclusion of the critically important emotional and practical needs of the client.

- ✔ If you're a hands-on person, from the building trades or the like, you'll be great at explaining the ins and outs of a home's construction, but the job is making a good match between house and client. It's just as important to understand your client's thinking and abilities.

✔ You must be interested in houses/apartments/townhouses: physical appearance, utility and practicality, construction, floor plan, amenities, landscaping . . . everything about houses.

✔ You must be interested in people, enough to listen to and heed their wishes and to pick up on their unspoken thoughts.

✔ You must listen to the clients' needs without judging them according to your own standards.

✔ You must care enough about those people to want to help them—not yourself—be successful.

✔ You must be willing and able to learn about financing and to think creatively about how your clients may be able to attain their goals.

✔ You must be able to say "I don't know" when you don't. You must also be able to say "I don't know," when you do know but cannot be officially described as an expert on the subject. If you can't do that, you'll be in trouble.

✔ And you must be willing to go find out the answers when you don't know them.

Where to hang that shingle

Once you've made the decision to become an agent, gathered your courage and gone to real estate school and have a brand new license you're itching to hang proudly, you still have one more decision to make: Where?

That depends on many personal factors such as:

✔ Where you live

✔ What area you're interested in working in

✔ If you want to work with a friend who's already in the business

✔ Whether a small company or a large one fits your personality

✔ Whether you have lots of business experience or need lots of training

Agents are usually independent contractors, not employees

In practice, agents interview companies, not the reverse. Here's my suggested strategy:

- ✔ Make a preliminary list of all the reputable real estate companies that, on the face of things, appear to meet your basic requirements. Reputation's a nebulous thing, especially if you're new to an area, but we live on islands—the word gets around. You'll have learned lots of relevant information during your training. If you're in doubt, though, follow the steps suggested in selecting a real estate agency to represent you. That will give you the picture very quickly.

- ✔ Make appointments to interview the principal broker or broker-in-charge of several of these companies.

After the interview:

- ✔ Delete all that don't fit your needs.

- ✔ Delete all those for which you don't feel personally compatible with the office atmosphere or the broker-in-charge, personally.

- ✔ Delete all those for which you can't live with the office policies.

- ✔ If more than one company still remains in consideration after that, choose the one that has the best reputation among other agents. Don't be bashful about asking agents, even if you don't know them well. Listen carefully to their reasons and make your selection according to how those reasons match up with what's important to you.

Note: You may have noticed commission splits or pay didn't come into the strategy. That's because those are negotiated (within the guidelines of company policy, of course) and subject to change with experience, credentials, and performance.

If you sign on with a reputable and successful company, you will receive fair and honest compensation. Once you've paid your dues, both literally and figuratively, there's just about no limit to your potential income.

The Gender Question: Why Are Most Real Estate Agents Women?

There are many successful men in this business. In fact, it's one of the few fields where there is no discrimination on any basis other than competence. One of the most successful agents I know is a man who just celebrated his 90th birthday. But, it's true that most agents are women. In my opinion, it's because residential real estate sales started way back in the Dark Ages with ladies talking to each other over tea:

"I really want a house with nanny quarters, but I just can't find one."

"I know exactly what you mean, dear. Come to think of it, I was just talking to Mrs. Detweiler. She told me they're moving to Virginia. *Her* house has nanny quarters. Let me introduce you."

Women generally are highly interested in homes, in décor, and in neighborhoods. They are family managers and decision makers. They usually write the checks and have a very practical awareness of the family's budget. And, trust me, any woman with a husband and at least one child knows how to negotiate. Women also talk to each other. A lot. They feel comfortable having very personal conversations with each other. They usually want to help their friends and family attain success and are more into cooperation than competition. Match those facts up with the characteristics of a good agent and you'll have the answer to the question. Additionally, women tend to be the ones who have the final say on buying a home. Do you know a man who'd buy without his wife's okay? If you do, the marriage is doomed, so don't bother trying to sell them anything. And women clients tend to like talking to women agents— it's a sisterhood thing.

Certainly not all women fit that description, and certainly some men do. My point is that the above-mentioned traits are typically female, and many women make fine real estate agents simply because they learned at their mother's knee. That's my opinion. You don't have to agree.

The second reason most agents are women is that up until a generation or two ago, men were almost always the primary breadwinners and couldn't risk going into such an unpredictable business. I certainly couldn't have done real estate if my husband hadn't had a regular income.

There are many successful husband-wife partnerships, too. My mentor Jean Wade and her husband, Bob, were a great team. Bob had originally been in an unrelated business, but when Jean became successful and decided to open her own firm, Bob agreed to join her, having first made sure the family finances could withstand any dry spells. They divided the work along their lines of expertise. Bob ran the office, took care of the books, did all the hundred-million things needed to keep 30-plus agents happy and successful. Jean supervised the transactions, dotted the I's and crossed the T's and lent her tremendous common sense and intelligence to making all of us the best we could be.

When I joined Wade, Ltd., in 1983, there were five other married couples on the staff, who also worked as partners. My present broker, Jack Ainlay, is partners with his wife, Carky, in a very similar arrangement to the one Jean and Bob Wade had. Serendipitously, Jack also started his career with Wade, Ltd. When you learn from the best, you just can't go wrong.

If you're thinking of doing real estate with your spouse, income questions aside, just make sure you can tolerate being around each other all the time, and that you have complementary, not competitive, skills.

Bottom line: Whether becoming a real estate agent or buying and selling for yourself, doing it right requires the right aptitude (or attitude) and the same kinds of expertise and experience. In the latter case, you'll use your skills in your own transactions; in the former, you'll use them to help others succeed. Valuable skills and past experience include sales, public relations, law, accounting, construction, interior design, and psychology. Personal aptitudes include such things as great negotiating skills, a nose for what's going to make or break a deal, an instinct for matching up people's needs and desires with a physical home, and a sincere desire to be of service.

Appendix: The Transaction —Who Does What

In addition to the agents, whose roles are detailed exhaustively elsewhere, your transaction will require some ten to fifteen other professionals to close. It's your agent's job to coordinate with these companies and individuals and to make sure that nobody drops the ball. As a principal (buyer or seller) in a transaction, you may have little direct contact with some of these professionals, but it's good to have an idea of their various roles and functions nonetheless.

The following is a list of the companies and individuals that commonly participate in a real estate transaction. There may be others, depending on circumstances. As you will see, most of these people are task-oriented and not allied to either buyer or seller. The specific advocates of the principals are their agents, home inspectors, and professionals such as lawyers or accountants hired directly by the buyer or seller to advise or protect their interests.

Escrow officer: (neutral party) Employee of a licensed and bonded company that holds all money and documents until everyone has performed their duties and is ready to close. When a purchase contract has been executed by all concerned, both agents submit copies and instructions, and the buyer's agent submits the earnest money (deposit) check to the escrow company/officer specified in the contract. An Escrow Coordinator (or Assistant) may also be assigned to keep track of timing and details. When all contractually required actions have been completed, the officer arranges a signing appointment for the buyer and another for the seller, makes certain all necessary documents are properly executed and notarized when necessary, and then sends those documents (called a closing packet) to the Bureau of Conveyances for recording.

Bureau of Conveyances: (neutral party; duty is to the state and the public) The state agency responsible for keeping records of property ownership current.

Title Officer: (neutral party) An employee of a licensed and bonded title company (often the same company as escrow) who searches the public record to determine all pertinent facts about the property and its ownership and states whether or not title insurance (protection for the buyer in case of error) will be provided. This process may be quite involved and requires specialized knowledge and training. The title officer will issue a preliminary title report (prelim), stating, among other things, the identities of all legal owners of the property, any recorded liens (debts for which the property might be seized if not paid) against either the property or the owners, and the exact legal description of the property itself. (It's called a prelim because it is issued before the proposed sale is consummated.) The buyer must sign his approval of the prelim; the seller may need to take care of discrepancies or errors appearing there; and there must be sufficient funds to pay off all existing liens prior to recordation.

Home Inspector: (responsible to the buyer) An independent expert who inspects the property before the buyer is committed to the purchase. Home inspectors in Hawai'i are not required to be licensed. However, many of them do carry errors-and-omissions insurance and/or are franchisees trained by nationwide inspection companies. The home inspector may also be a contractor or any other individual the buyer chooses to hire. There may be more than one inspector, too. During the due diligence period following execution of the purchase contract, the buyer normally may have any inspections he wants by as many people as he wants so long as he pays for them. Home inspectors are employed directly by the buyer and are responsible directly to the buyer, although many agents provide a list of reputable inspectors to their clients.

Termite Inspector: (neutral party) Termite inspection is normally provided and paid for by the seller. It must be made by a licensed pest control inspector, either an extermination company or an entymologist. The inspection report is provided to all parties as well as to escrow and to the buyer's lender. A "clear" termite report is usually required as a condition of the buyer's mortgage, and the buyer must approve the results prior to the transaction being recorded. If live termites are discovered, the seller normally orders and pays for the recommended extermination treatment before closing. In Hawai'i, unlike some other places, repair of termite damage is not normally required, although damaged areas the inspector sees will be noted on the report. The inspector may also note conducive conditions, areas where termites might gain easy access, and/or areas where dry or wet rot are seen. Notations like this on the report may not be comprehensive and also do not create any requirement for the seller to make repairs. However, previously undisclosed termite damage may provide the buyer with the means to cancel his purchase contract, to renegotiate the sale price, or to demand repairs as a condition of his purchase.

Surveyor: (neutral party) Normally required as a condition of purchase for single family residences and certain attached dwellings, the survey defines the property boundaries and specifies any violations. The seller normally orders and pays for the survey before closing. The drawing or survey map does not normally include placement of the house footprint unless the buyer requests it and pays the extra charge. Minor deviations are very common in Hawai'i. There is a law (referred to as the de miniumus rule) under which these deviations may be ignored. Your agent and/or escrow or title officer can explain the exact number of inches by which an improvement may encroach. If there are boundary issues that exceed the de minimus standard, the seller may need to obtain encroachment agreements with neighbors, relocate the offending improvements, or find other solutions as may be appropriate in the individual case. (Together with a seller-client and some friends, I once spent a Saturday night that ran into a Sunday morning physically moving a hollow tile wall that was encroaching into a neighbor's yard an inch more than the de minimus allowed. And a long time ago, prior to the passage of that handy rule, recording of a transaction was nearly canceled because an overzealous surveyor saw fit to note the "encroachment" of a large nail sticking out of a fence into a neighboring property. Fortunately, the seller saved the day by removing it with his claw hammer.)

Loan Officer: (responsible to the buyer, but normally also required to keep the seller accurately informed of loan progress) Either an employee of a bank or mortgage company or an independent mortgage broker, this very-important-person holds the key to approval of the mortgage and is the expert relied upon to obtain the best possible financing for the buyer and to tell the seller whether or not that buyer's application can be approved. In addition to the loan officer, a loan processor and a loan underwriter may also be involved.

Real Estate Attorney: (responsible to whichever party she represents) The escrow company will hire an attorney to draft the deed or other conveyance document; the loan officer hires or employs an attorney to draft the mortgage and note documents. If the property is leasehold, the required plain language disclosure of the lease terms is frequently prepared by yet another attorney. The buyer or seller, or both, may also employ their own attorneys to give them legal, financial, tax, or other advice. Ordinarily, these will all be different individuals.

Management Company: (responsible to the owner's association of a condominium) Most condominium boards of directors employ a management company to keep records and take care of day-to-day business. One of that company's duties is to provide all current disclosures and documentation ("condo docs") to prospective buyers. A list of required documents will be specified in the purchase contract, to be read and approved prior to the buyer's final commitment to purchase a condominium unit.

Lessor: (usually neutral) If the property is leasehold, sometimes the actual land owner or his representative must approve transfers of the leasehold interest. This is usually a routine operation, but extra time to close may be necessary.

Appraiser: (responsible to the lender) Not to be confused with the home inspector, the appraiser's duty is to report on the fair market value of the property in accordance with specific standard guidelines and procedures. Employed by the mortgage lender, his role is to protect the lender's interest. Based on the appraisal, the lender will determine how much money is appropriate to lend on the property.

Insurance Agent: (ensures the homeowner has adequate coverage and protects the insurance company from undue risk) Homeowner's insurance is a requirement of mortgage lenders and a common-sense investment for everyone. Condominiums normally carry insurance on the buildings and common areas, but individuals need to insure the contents of their specific apartments. It is a condominium purchaser's responsibility to find out exactly what is covered by the condominium association's policy and to purchase additional coverage when and if that's appropriate. Hurricane insurance and flood insurance may also be either required or desired, and neither of these may cover tsunami (tidal wave) damage. Certain properties regarded as high risk (such as those near lava flows, for instance) may be difficult or expensive to insure. It is the purchaser's responsibility to obtain the required policies and to decide what other coverage he may desire. Normally the seller's insurance coverage is canceled simultaneously with the sale.

Appendix of Standard and Frequently-Used Forms

The forms here are provided as samples, for general information only, as revisions are frequently made and those printed here may be out of date by the time you see this book. Most of them are standard to the Hawaii Association of Realtors® and are reprinted here with HAR's permission. Those entitled "Dual Agency Addendum" and "Standard Addendum" are in use at this time (either as they appear here or in slightly different format but with generally similar contents) by many different real estate companies in Hawai'i.

AGREEMENT OF SALE ADDENDUM TO THE DROA
Hawaii Association of Realtors® Standard Form
Revised 9/03 (NC) For Release 11/04

COPYRIGHT AND TRADEMARK NOTICE: This copyrighted Hawaii Association of REALTORS® Standard Form is licensed for use by the entire real estate industry on condition that there shall be no alteration of the printed portions, pagination, or paragraph numbers or breaks. The use of this form is not intended to identify the real estate licensee as a REALTOR®. REALTOR® is a registered collective membership mark which may be used only by real estate licensees who are members of the National Association of REALTORS® and who subscribe to its Code of Ethics.

AGREEMENT OF SALE ADDENDUM is made a part of DROA:

Reference Date: _____

Property Reference: _____
                                                    Address

Tax Map Key: Div. _____/Zone _____/Sec. _____/Plat _____/Parcel _____/CPR _____ (if applicable).

Buyer and Seller agree as follows:

1. **Credit Check and Information:** Seller requires the following information from Buyer within_____days from acceptance of DROA.
   [   ] Credit Report   [   ] Tax return(s) prior:_____ year(s)
   [   ] Current financial statement   [   ] Other _____

   • If Buyer fails to provide Seller the Credit Report and/or other information within the time required, Seller may elect to terminate DROA, pursuant to Paragraphs C-20 and C-21.

   • Within _____ days after receipt and after review of all financial information provided, Seller may deem the credit worthiness of Buyer unacceptable and may terminate the DROA pursuant to Paragraphs C-20 and C-21 of DROA.

   • In the event DROA is terminated, Seller agrees to return all documents to Buyer.

2. **Payment Terms:** Agreement of Sale principal balance of $_____ together with simple interest on the outstanding principal accruing from recordation at _____percent (%) per annum, shall be payable in _____(monthly, quarterly, etc.) installments beginning one month following recordation or _____, with final satisfaction payment due on _____ or _____.
                     (months, years)
   A. Monthly installments (based on current estimates; exact figures to be determined and adjusted at closing)
   [   ] Buyer Collection Fee: $_____   [   ] Lease Rent: $_____
   [   ] Real Property Taxes: $_____   [   ] Other: _____ $_____
                                                                            Specify
   [   ] Insurance premiums: $_____
   [   ] Sewer Fee & Assessments: $_____   [   ] Interest Only: $_____

                                                                         or

   [   ] Association Fee: $_____
   [   ] Maintenance Fee: $_____   [   ] Principal and Interest: $_____
                                                ESTIMATED TOTAL MONTHLY PAYMENT: $_____

   Buyer agrees to pay all expenses relating to Property.

   B. **Special Payment Terms:** _____
   _____
   _____

   C. **Interest Rate Adjustment:** Buyer and Seller understand that the interest rate(s) on the existing mortgage(s) outlined in Paragraph 3 may increase or decrease during the term of the Agreement of Sale. The parties agree as follows:
   [   ] Payment Terms will remain unchanged as noted above.
   [   ] Other_____

3. **Existing Mortgages:** At time of recordation, the Agreement of Sale shall be subject to the following mortgage(s):
   _____
   _____
   Seller agrees to provide Buyer written consent to the Agreement of Sale from Mortgagee(s) prior to closing.

   _____
   BUYER'S INITIALS & DATE   Page 1 of 3   _____
                                                                           SELLER'S INITIALS & DATE
©Hawaii Association of REALTORS®
Agreement of Sale Addendum To The DROA
RR203 Rev. 9/03

4. **Further Mortgaging:** Seller may [   ]   may not [   ] further encumber Property. If Seller may further mortgage, then Standard Provision Paragraph D shall apply, or: _____

5. **Late Payment and Fees:** Any payment not received within _____ days after it is due will be a "Late Payment" and shall constitute a Default. For each Late Payment, Buyer shall promptly pay Seller a late fee of $_____ or _____% of payment then due.

6. **Prepayment Penalty:** [   ] Yes   [   ] No or as follows: _____
[   ] Buyer   [   ] Seller agrees to pay any prepayment charges incurred due to Buyer's prepayment of this Agreement of Sale prior to the satisfaction date set forth in Paragraph 2.

7. **Collection Agency:** A collection account shall be established on or before closing and thereafter maintained with a neutral Collection Agency. The costs of the collection account are to be shared equally or as follows: _____
Name of Collection Agency: _____

8. **Satisfaction Escrow:** Prior to final satisfaction, an escrow shall be opened with escrow fees to be shared equally. Buyer shall pay for costs of title update and recordation of the satisfaction and conveyance document. Seller shall pay for costs of drafting the conveyance document.

9. **Document:** Agreement of Sale document to be drafted by _____.

10. **STANDARD PROVISIONS:** BUYER AND SELLER HAVE READ AND AGREED TO ALL PROVISIONS IN THIS ADDENDUM. INSERTED PROVISIONS SHALL PREVAIL OVER STANDARD PROVISIONS

BUYER	DATE	SELLER	DATE

BUYER	DATE	SELLER	DATE

SAMPLE

"STANDARD PROVISIONS"

A. **Additional Principal Payments:** Additional payments (minimum of $100) are allowed unless otherwise stated herein. If Agreement of Sale principal balance is reduced to the principal balance(s) due on Seller's mortgage(s), all further principal payments shall be applied to repay Seller's mortgage(s), thus reducing both principal balances equally. The principal balances under Seller's mortgage(s) shall not exceed the principal balance due under the Agreement of Sale. Buyer and Collection Agency may ascertain from holder(s) of mortgage(s) or prior Agreement(s) of Sale Seller's mortgage balance(s) and status.

B. **Adjustments in Monthly Expense Payments:** If after DROA Reference Date, Monthly Expenses other than Interest [Paragraph 2 (A) on Page 1 of this Addendum] shall increase or decrease, then the required monthly Agreement of Sale payment shall also increase or decrease by a like dollar amount, and such increase or decrease shall be applied toward the same item which shall have so increased or decreased.

C. **Collection Account:** All of Buyer's payments are to be made into a collection account. Payments collected shall be used first to pay mortgage payments owed on Property, then to pay Monthly Expenses referred to in Paragraph 2 (A) on Page 1, and then (subject to Paragraph A, Standard Provisions) to pay any remaining balance to Seller.

D. **Further Mortgaging:** If so indicated in Paragraph 4 on Page 2, Seller may refinance or further encumber Property, and Buyer shall subordinate thereto, except that the principal balance(s) under Seller's total mortgage(s) shall not exceed 85% of the then principal balance due under Agreement of Sale; nor shall the monthly payment(s) under the mortgage(s) exceed the monthly principal and interest payments payable by Buyer under Agreement of Sale. Thereafter, Seller's monthly payment under the mortgage(s) shall continue to be paid through the Collection Account.

E. **Defaults and Late Fees:** Buyer shall be considered in default if Buyer fails to pay monthly or other installments within the required number of calendar days after due date (set forth in Paragraph 5 on Page 2) or fails to perform other obligations within thirty (30) calendar days after written notice of default. Late charges under Agreement of Sale shall be as set forth in Paragraph 5 on Page 2. In addition to late charges, Seller may exercise other customary remedies for Buyer's default including, but not limited to, foreclosure, cancellation of Agreement of Sale, or repossession.

F. **Transferability:** Buyer shall not sell, assign, transfer, or encumber Property or Agreement of Sale or enter into a sub-agreement of sale without Seller's consent, which consent shall not be unreasonably withheld, provided that Seller may condition Seller's consent on the credit worthiness and payment capacity of proposed Buyer. Seller may not change any term of Agreement of Sale nor charge a fee for the consent, except an amount to cover reasonable costs of preparation and processing not to exceed $200.00

G. **Assumption of Existing Mortgage(s):** Subject to Mortgagee's consent, Buyer may assume the mortgage(s) contingent upon the release of Seller from liability under the mortgage(s). Buyer shall pay all costs relating to assumption(s).

H. **Title:** When Agreement of Sale is recorded, title to Property shall be subject only to items set forth in C-35 of DROA, and any mortgage or Agreement of Sale referred to in Paragraph 3 on Page 1.

I. **Insurance:** At closing, Buyer shall furnish fire and extended peril coverage (with inflation guard) at least equal to the full replacement cost of the insurable improvements on Property, comprehensive public liability insurance as customarily provided in Hawaii for homeowner's insurance and flood insurance, if Property is within the Flood Zones eligible for federally subsidized flood insurance. Policies shall name Seller, Buyer and any Lessor and/or Mortgagee as insured's. If Property is a condominium or cooperative apartment, the insurance requirements may be met in part by a blanket insurance policy.

J. **Alterations and Improvements:** Buyer is not permitted to make additions or major improvements to Property without Seller's written consent. Seller may inspect plans and specifications and may condition Seller's consent on Buyer's obtaining required building permit, required consents of Condominium Owners' Association, lenders, or lessors, if any, and evidence of Buyer's adequate financing or bonding to pay for the improvements.

K. **Assessments:** After recordation of the Agreement of Sale, Buyer shall be responsible for payment of any assessments levied against Property.

NOTE: THERE IS NO WARRANTY ON PLAIN LANGUAGE. An effort has been made to put this agreement into plain language. But there is no promise that it is in plain language. In legal terms, THERE IS NO WARRANTY, EXPRESSED OR IMPLIED, THAT THIS AGREEMENT COMPLIES WITH CHAPTER 487A OF THE HAWAII REVISED STATUTES, AS AMENDED. This means that the Hawaii Association of REALTORS® is not liable to any Buyer, Seller, or other person who uses this form for any damages or penalty because of any violation of Chapter 487A. People are cautioned to see their own attorneys about Chapter 487A (and other laws that may apply).

AGREEMENT TO OCCUPY PRIOR TO CLOSE OF ESCROW
Hawaii Association of Realtors® Standard Form
Revised 9/03 (NC)   For Release 11/04

COPYRIGHT AND TRADEMARK NOTICE: This copyrighted Hawaii Association of REALTORS® Standard Form is licensed for use by the entire real estate industry on condition that there shall be no alteration of the printed portions, pagination, or paragraph numbers or breaks. The use of this form is not intended to identify the real estate licensee as a REALTOR®. REALTOR® is a registered collective membership mark which may be used only by real estate licensees who are members of the National Association of REALTORS® and who subscribe to its Code of Ethics.

DROA Reference Date: _____

Property Reference: _____
                                                         Address

Tax Map Key: Div _____ /Zone _____ /Sec. _____ /Plat _____ /Parcel _____ /CPR _____ (if applicable)

Buyer: _____   Seller _____

Buyer and Seller agree to the following

1. **OCCUPANCY DATE.** Buyer may occupy Property on _____
       Time: [   ] A.M. [   ] P.M.

2. **COMPENSATION.** Buyer agrees to pay occupancy fee of $_____ per day from date of occupancy up to but not including the date of closing Estimated number of days until closing is _____

3. **METHOD OF PAYMENT.** (Check applicable)
   [   ] Occupancy fee payable to Seller $_____(U.S. FUNDS) payable in ADVANCE in the form of _____
   _____
   [   ] Entire amount payable in escrow at closing

4. **ACCEPTANCE OF PROPERTY.**
   Buyer will inspect and accept the entire Property prior to occupancy. Exceptions to be noted in paragraph 6(i)

5. **FAILURE TO PERFORM.**
   (a) In addition to those remedies provided for in the DROA, if Buyer fails to perform Buyer's obligations (Seller not being in default), Buyer agrees to
       (1) pay Seller $_____ per day, as compensation for the use of Property, over and above the occupancy fee charged under Paragraph 2;
       (2) vacate Property within_____(   ) days of receipt* of Seller's written demand. Receipt shall be deemed made upon hand delivery to Buyer, posting of the written demand in a conspicuous place on Property or three (3) days from the postmarked date indicating when the written demand was mailed; and
       (3) pay for all fees and costs incurred by Seller, including reasonable attorneys' fees, to enforce the terms of this Agreement To Occupy Prior To Close of Escrow.
   (b) In addition to those remedies provided for in the DROA, if Seller fails to perform Seller's obligations (Buyer not being in default), Seller agrees to
       (1) reduce the occupancy fee charged under Paragraph 2 to _____ per day from the date of Buyer's occupancy until Buyer vacates the Property Buyer shall vacate Property within_____(   ) days of receipt* of Seller's written demand. Receipt shall be deemed made upon hand delivery to Buyer, posting of the written demand in a conspicuous place on Property or three (3) days from the postmarked date indicating when the written demand was mailed; and
       (2) pay for all fees and costs incurred by Buyer, including reasonable attorneys' fees, to enforce the terms of this Agreement To Occupy Prior To Close of Escrow
   (c) Should this purchase be canceled or should escrow fail to close for any reason, Buyer agrees to vacate Property within
       (   ) days of receipt* of Seller's written demand.

   * Receipt shall be deemed made: • upon hand delivery to the Buyer, • posting of the written demand in a conspicuous place on Property or
     • three days from the postmarked date indicating when the written demand was mailed

6. **RESPONSIBILITIES OF SELLER AND BUYER.**
   (a) From date of occupancy, Buyer shall maintain condition of Property as of date of occupancy and further agrees to maintain and to pay for the following utilities and services

[ ] alarm service	[ ] pool service	[ ] telephone (basic)	[ ] tv cable (additional)
[ ] cesspool pumping	[ ] refuse	[ ] telephone (additional)	[ ] water
[ ] electricity	[ ] sewer	[ ] tv cable (basic)	[ ] yard service
[ ] gas			
[ ] other _____			

   (b) Buyer will refrain from making any alterations without prior written consent of Seller until escrow is closed.
   (c) Buyer and Seller will abide by all laws, governmental regulations, lease provisions and home owner's association rules if applicable, with respect to the use or occupancy of Property.
   (d) No pets may occupy without prior written consent of Seller
   (e) Buyer will allow Seller or authorized agent admittance at reasonable times for the purpose of inspecting Property until Escrow is closed
   (f) From date of occupancy RISK OF LOSS PASSES TO BUYER (Per DROA) Buyer agrees to hold Seller and agents harmless from any claims for damages to Property or injury to Buyer or others.

_____   _____
    BUYER'S INITIALS & DATE   Page 1 of 2   SELLER'S INITIALS & DATE

©Hawaii Association of REALTORS®
Agreement to Occupy Prior to Close of Escrow
RR202 Rev 9/03

(g) Seller agrees to hold Buyer and agents harmless from any claim for damages to Property or injury to Buyer or others.

(h) Seller shall provide an insurance policy for fire and extended coverage, and liability on Property until closing. Buyer shall obtain liability insurance in the minimum amount of $_____ and shall name Seller and agent as additional insured. Buyer reserves option to obtain personal property coverage.

(i) Special Conditions and Terms. (Please number).

_____

_____

7.   The following will be occupants on subject property. Any additional parties to the agreement must obtain written consent from Seller

_____

THIS AGREEMENT IS NOT INTENDED TO CREATE A RELATIONSHIP OF LANDLORD AND TENANT, AND THE RIGHT OF BUYERS TO OCCUPY THE PREMISES SHALL BE ON A DAY-TO-DAY (PRORATED) BASIS SUBJECT TO THE ABOVE TERMS. Buyer and Seller acknowledge that Buyer/Seller have read, understand and agree to the terms and conditions of this AGREEMENT TO OCCUPY PRIOR TO CLOSE OF ESCROW ADDENDUM, and have not relied upon any advice from Broker(s) involved in this transaction and further acknowledge receipt of a completed copy hereof

_____   _____   _____   _____
Buyer   Date   Seller   Date

_____   _____   _____   _____
Buyer   Date   Seller   Date

NOTE: THERE IS NO WARRANTY ON PLAIN LANGUAGE. An effort has been made to put this agreement into plain language. But there is no promise that it is in plain language. In legal terms, THERE IS NO WARRANTY, EXPRESSED OR IMPLIED, THAT THIS AGREEMENT COMPLIES WITH CHAPTER 487A OF THE HAWAII REVISED STATUTES, AS AMENDED. This means that the Hawaii Association of REALTORS® is not liable to any Buyer, Seller, or other person who uses this form for any damages or penalty because of any violation of Chapter 487A. People are cautioned to see their own attorneys about Chapter 487A (and other laws that may apply).

BUYER REPRESENTATION AGREEMENT
(Exclusive Right to Represent)
Hawaii Association of Realtors® Standard Form
Revised 10/04   For Release 11/04

COPYRIGHT AND TRADEMARK NOTICE: This copyrighted Hawaii Association of REALTORS® Standard Form is licensed for use by the entire real estate industry on condition that there shall be no alteration of the printed portions, pagination, or paragraph numbers or breaks. The use of this form is not intended to identify the real estate licensee as a REALTOR®. REALTOR® is a registered collective membership mark which may be used only by real estate licensees who are members of the National Association of REALTORS® and who subscribe to its Code of Ethics.

THIS AGREEMENT is between _____ ("Brokerage Firm"),
and _____ ("Buyer").

1. **AGENCY DISCLOSURE:**
The Buyer and/or Seller in a real estate transaction in Hawaii may retain a real estate Brokerage Firm as their agent. In such case, the Buyer and/or Seller is represented by the Brokerage Firm and all of its licensees. Hawaii law requires real estate licensees to disclose orally or in writing to Seller and/or Buyer whom the licensee represents. The form of representation may be one of the following:
    a. **Seller's Agent.** Brokerage Firm represents Seller only unless a disclosed dual agency exists. Seller's Agent owes the highest duties to Seller, including confidentiality, loyalty, and utmost care.
    b. **Buyer's Agent.** Brokerage Firm represents Buyer only unless a disclosed dual agency exists. Buyer's Agent owes the highest duties to Buyer, including confidentiality, loyalty, and utmost care.
    c. **Dual Agent.** Brokerage Firm represents both Buyer and Seller. This commonly occurs when licensees in the Brokerage Firm representing Seller have Buyer clients looking for types of property similar to Seller's property. In such event, the Brokerage Firm and all of its licensees represent both Buyer and Seller and are dual agents. Dual agents must remain neutral in negotiations and must not advance the interest of one party over the other. **A separate Dual Agency Agreement is required under Hawaii law.**

2. **APPOINTMENT OF EXCLUSIVE AGENT:**
Buyer agrees that Brokerage Firm will assist Buyer in negotiating the purchase of Property. Buyer agrees to conduct all negotiations for the Property through Brokerage Firm and to refer all letters and inquiries to Brokerage Firm concerning purchase of the Property received from real estate licensees, prospective sellers, and any other sources during the term of this Agreement. Buyer shall inform Brokerage Firm of any properties that may be of interest to Buyer from all sources, including but not limited to the Internet, newspaper, real estate magazines, etc.

    Type of Property:

    [   ] Residential   [   ] Condo/Co-op   [   ] Land   [   ] Commercial/Industrial   [   ] Business/Income   [   ] Any Real Estate

3. **TERM OF AGREEMENT:**
Buyer grants to Brokerage Firm the exclusive right to represent Buyer as Buyer's Agent from (Date) _____ to midnight on (Date) _____. Either party may end this Agreement with _____ days advance written notice to the other. Neither party may end this Agreement before midnight, (Date) _____, unless we both agree in writing to an earlier date.

4. **DUAL AGENCY:**
Buyer acknowledges that, from time to time, Brokerage Firm may represent both Seller and Buyer in the same transaction. If such a dual agency situation arises, Seller and Buyer will be asked to sign a separate dual agency consent agreement prior to entering into a purchase agreement. Buyer further acknowledges that, in a dual agency situation, there is a limitation on Brokerage Firm's ability to represent either party exclusively and fully, and that Brokerage Firm may not act for one party to the detriment of the other. Buyer hereby gives approval to the concept of disclosed dual agency and limited representation. Buyer further acknowledges and agrees that Brokerage Firm may represent other Buyers, whether such representation arises prior to, during, or after the termination of this Agreement. In such a situation, Brokerage Firm shall not disclose to any Buyer the terms of any other Buyer's offer.

5. **BROKERAGE FIRM OBLIGATIONS:**
Brokerage Firm will exercise reasonable skill and care for Buyer, and make reasonable efforts to locate properties in which Buyer may be interested. Brokerage Firm will promote the interests of Buyer with good faith, loyalty, and fidelity, including but not limited to: (a) Seeking a price and terms that are acceptable to Buyer with the exception that Brokerage Firm shall not be obligated to seek other properties while Buyer is a party to a contract to purchase a Property; (b) Procuring acceptance of any offer to purchase the Property and to assist in the completion of the transaction; (c) Presenting all offers to and from Buyer in a timely manner; (d) Disclosing to Buyer any material facts known to Brokerage Firm which would measurably affect the Property value. Brokerage Firm shall not be obligated to make an independent investigation or evaluation of the Property, independently verify statements of Seller or any expert, or verify any information or statements made by Buyer.

6. **BUYER'S OBLIGATIONS:**
Buyer is obligated to act in good faith to cooperate with Brokerage Firm by furnishing it with all relevant personal, financial, or other information that may be necessary to facilitate the purchase of Property. This includes keeping appointments, attending inspections, returning messages, and advising all other real estate agents that Buyer has executed this exclusive Agreement with Brokerage Firm.

Buyer understands and accepts that neither Brokerage Firm nor Licensee can render tax advice, tax planning, tax-deferred exchange information, and the like, or any other technical or legal advice in connection with this Agreement. Whenever specialized advice is deemed necessary, Buyer is strongly advised to seek the services of an appropriate professional. Buyer acknowledges that the decision to retain any particular specialist is wholly the decision of the Buyer. Buyer shall notify Brokerage Firm in writing of any areas of particular concern.

Buyer agrees to consider properties selected by Brokerage Firm. Buyer further agrees to act in good faith toward the completion of any property contract entered into in furtherance of this Agreement. Buyer has an affirmative duty to protect him/herself, including discovery of the legal, practical

_____   _____
BUYER'S INITIALS & DATE   BROKER'S INITIALS & DATE

©Hawaii Association of REALTORS®   Page 1 of 2
Buyer Representation Agreement
Exclusive Right To Represent
RR104 Rev. 10/04

and technical implications of discovered or disclosed facts, and investigation of information and facts which are known or made known to Buyer or are within the diligent attention and observation of Buyer. **Buyer further agrees that he/she has not entered into a binding "Exclusive Right to Represent" Agreement with any other Brokerage Firm.**

7. **NONDISCRIMINATION:**
Buyer understands that Brokerage Firm cannot discriminate because of race, age, color, sex, marital status, national origin, familial status, HIV infection, handicap/disability, religion or ancestry of such person.

8. **MEGAN'S LAW:**
If the presence of a registered sex offender is a matter of concern to Buyer, Buyer understands that Buyer must contact local law enforcement officials regarding obtaining such information. Brokerage Firm makes no representation that any such information is available for public access.

9. **MEDIATION AND ARBITRATION**: If any dispute or claim in law or equity arises out of this Agreement, and Buyer and Brokerage Firm are unable to resolve the dispute, Buyer agrees to attempt in good faith to settle such dispute or claim by non-binding mediation through the Local Board of REALTORS® or, in the event the Local Board of REALTORS® does not provide mediation services, then through a mutually agreed upon mediator. If the mediation is not successful, then Buyer will consider arbitration and may seek legal counsel to make this determination. It is understood that if the parties are involuntarily named as defendants in a lawsuit by a third party in any matter arising out of this Agreement, this paragraph shall no longer be binding.

10. **COMPENSATION:** Brokerage Firm's compensation shall be paid through escrow at the time of closing as follows:
   a. Buyer agrees to cooperate in Brokerage Firm's efforts to be compensated out of the sales proceeds in the transaction. Brokerage Firm will accept as compensation _____% of the purchase price or $_____, which will be paid by Seller either directly or through an authorized commission agreement with Brokerage Firm representing Seller.
   b. Buyer shall pay the amount stated above, or any portion thereof, not paid by Seller or Brokerage Firm representing Seller. Buyer understands and agrees that compensation payable by Buyer to Brokerage Firm shall be earned by Brokerage Firm and payable upon Buyer's purchase of real estate whether or not Brokerage Firm was involved in the transaction. Should Buyer purchase a property without Brokerage Firm's assistance (such as through an open house or "For Sale By Owner" or Foreclosure), Buyer would owe Brokerage Firm the full compensation.
   c. Entitlement to compensation shall apply to any purchase agreement executed during the term of this Agreement or any extension thereof. Entitlement to compensation will also apply to any purchase agreement executed within _____ days after the expiration or other termination of this Agreement, if the Property acquired was presented to or identified by Buyer during the term of this Agreement.
   d. If the transaction fails to close through no fault of Buyer, the compensation shall be waived. If the transaction fails to close because of Buyer's default, the compensation shall NOT be waived and shall become immediately due and payable by Buyer. Options exercised after the termination of this Agreement shall be considered as purchases for purposes of this Agreement.
   e. Non-Refundable Fee: Buyer has paid and Brokerage Firm acknowledges receipt of a non-refundable fee in the amount of $_____ payable to Brokerage Firm for initial consultation and research. Fee shall be credited against any other compensation owed by Buyer.

11. **OTHER SPECIAL TERMS:** _____
_____
_____

12. **ACCEPTANCE:** Buyer hereby agrees to all of the terms and conditions herein and acknowledges receipt of a copy of this Agreement.

By signing this document, Buyer acknowledges that Brokerage Firm has advised Buyer that this document has important legal consequences and has recommended consultation with legal, tax, or other counsel, before signing this Agreement.

Buyer's Name (Print) _____

Buyer's Signature _____

Buyer's Address _____

_____

Phones _____ Fax _____

E-Mail _____

Buyer's Name (Print) _____

Buyer's Signature _____

Buyer's Address _____

_____

Phones _____ Fax _____

E-Mail _____

Brokerage Firm _____

Brokerage Firm Address _____

_____

Phones _____

Broker's Signature _____

Licensee Name _____

Phones _____ Fax _____

E-Mail _____

NOTE: THERE IS NO WARRANTY ON PLAIN LANGUAGE. An effort has been made to put this agreement into plain language. But there is no promise that it is in plain language. In legal terms, THERE IS NO WARRANTY, EXPRESSED OR IMPLIED, THAT THIS AGREEMENT COMPLIES WITH CHAPTER 487A OF THE HAWAII REVISED STATUTES, AS AMENDED. This means that the Hawaii Association of REALTORS® is not liable to any Buyer, Seller, or other person who uses this form for any damages or penalty because of any violation of Chapter 487A. People are cautioned to see their own attorneys about Chapter 487A (and other laws that may apply).

CONSENSUAL DUAL AGENCY AGREEMENT

DROA Reference Date: _____ TMK: _____
Property Address: _____
Seller: _____
Buyer: _____

Seller and Buyer have previously been informed of the possibility of dual agency should a buyer client become interested in a seller client's property. Buyer and Seller now consent to this dual representation and agree to the type of representation it provides.

I.   Broker's/Agent(s)' role:

Since the Brokerage is acting as an agent for both Seller and Buyer, every effort shall be made to remain impartial between the parties. Seller and Buyer acknowledge that prior to this time, Brokerage has acted as the exclusive agent of the Seller and as the exclusive agent of the Buyer. Since the Brokerage may have obtained information which, if disclosed, could harm the bargaining position of the parties, Seller and Buyer agree that the Brokerage shall not be liable to either party for refusing or failing to disclose information which could harm one party's bargaining position but would benefit the other party.

The Brokerage agrees not to disclose to Buyer information about what price Seller will accept other than the listing price, nor to Seller about what price Buyer will pay other than any written offered price. Nothing contained herein shall prevent the Brokerage from disclosing any known material defect(s) in the property.

II.   Seller's and Buyer's role:

Seller and Buyer understand that, under the dual agency relationship, they have the responsibility of making their own decisions about the terms and conditions of any purchase agreement between them. They also are aware of the implications of working with a broker in a dual agency role and have deemed that the benefits outweigh any detriments.

Seller and Buyer are free to seek legal counsel at any time during the transaction. Seller and Buyer indemnify and hold harmless the Brokerage and its agents against any claims, damages, and losses arising from this dual agency relationship.

III. THE BROKERAGE AND ITS SALES AGENTS CAN PROVIDE THE FOLLOWING SERVICES FOR SELLERS AND BUYERS WHEN ACTING AS A DUAL AGENT:

1. Must disclose all material facts about the property that are known to us.
2. Can explain real estate terms and procedures.
3. Can explain closing costs and closing procedures.
4. Will provide helpful information about the property and the neighborhood to the Buyer.
5. Will disclose financial qualifications of the Buyer to the Seller.
6. Can help the Buyer arrange for property inspections and compare financing alternatives.
7. Will prepare the standard purchase agreement form that will include the standard protections and disclosures for the Seller and Buyer.
8. Will provide information about comparable property to both Seller and Buyer so that they can make an informed decision on what price to accept and/or offer.
9. Will work diligently to facilitate the sale and will advise when experts should be retained to assist.
10. Will treat the Seller and Buyer fairly and honestly.

Page 1 of 2

IV. THE BROKERAGE AND ITS SALES AGENTS *CANNOT* DISCLOSE THE FOLLOWING TO THE SELLERS AND BUYERS:

1. We cannot recommend a price that the Buyer should offer for the property.
2. We cannot recommend a price that the Seller should accept for the property.
3. We cannot disclose the price the Seller will take, other than the listing price, without written permission from the Seller.
4. We cannot disclose the price the Buyer is willing to pay without written permission from the Buyer.
5. We cannot disclose confidential information we may know about the Seller or Buyer without written permission from the Seller and/or Buyer. (This could include motivation to sell or purchase, negotiating strategy, time frame to sell or purchase, etc.)

By signing below, you agree that the brokerage and its agents may act as dual agent in this transaction. If you do not understand this agreement, consult an attorney before signing.

_____   _____
Seller   Date   Buyer   Date

_____   _____
Seller   Date   Buyer   Date

BROKERAGE REPRESENTATIVES:

_____   _____
Listing Agent   Date   Selling Agent   Date

_____
Principal Broker/Broker-In-Charge   Date

COUNTER OFFER
Hawaii Association of Realtors® Standard Form
Revised 3/04 (NC) For Release 11/04

COPYRIGHT AND TRADEMARK NOTICE: This copyrighted Hawaii Association of REALTORS® Standard Form is licensed for use by the entire real estate industry on condition that there shall be no alteration of the printed portions, pagination, or paragraph numbers or breaks. The use of this form is not intended to identify the real estate licensee as a REALTOR®. REALTOR® is a registered collective membership mark which may be used only by real estate licensees who are members of the National Association of REALTORS® and who subscribe to its Code of Ethics.

Counter Offer Reference Date: _____, _____ AM/PM Submitted by: [   ] **Buyer**   [   ] **Seller**

Reviewed by _____   Brokerage Firm: _____
                   Principal Broker/Broker-in-Charge

DROA Reference Date: _____

INSTRUCTIONS:
1. To Accept this Counter Offer: Complete the boxed section entitled "Acceptance of Counter Offer".
2. To Reject this Counter Offer: Draw a diagonal line across the acceptance language. Write "reject" on the line and then sign and date on the diagonal line.
3. If you wish to make a new Counter Offer: Complete a new Counter Offer form.
   a. A NEW COUNTER OFFER CANCELS AND SUPERSEDES ANY AND ALL PRIOR COUNTER OFFERS. DO NOT REFERENCE AN ITEM FROM ANY PRIOR COUNTER OFFER IN THIS COUNTER OFFER. DOING SO MAY JEOPARDIZE THE BINDING NATURE OF THIS REAL ESTATE AGREEMENT.
   b. Do not make changes on this Counter Offer.
   c. Provide a new Counter Offer Reference Date and time.
   d. The DROA Reference Date should be that of the original DROA. No changes are to be made on the referenced original DROA.
   e. Write down those terms from any prior Counter Offer that you agree to, including terms contained in addenda or attach the addenda to this Counter Offer.
   f. Add any new terms and/or modifications you wish to make to the DROA.

Seller's Name: _____

Buyer's Name: _____

Property Reference or Address: _____

Tax Map Key   Div _____ /Zone _____ /Sec _____ /Plat _____ /Parcel _____ /CPR _____ (if applicable)

This Counter Offer cancels and supersedes any and all prior Counter Offers to the referenced DROA.

Fill in all check boxes. Write "NC" if no change and "X" if there is a change. In the blanks provided, indicate the change(s) and/or addition(s) which constitute the terms of this Counter Offer. Reference paragraph number of the DROA. Do not make any changes on the DROA.

[   ] SECTION A: AGENCY DISCLOSURE _____

[   ] SECTION B: DEPOSIT RECEIPT _____

SECTION C: ADDENDA AND OFFER

[   ] ADDENDA (add or delete) _____

[   ] C-1 Purchase price for the Property is $ _____ U.S. Dollars, paid as follows:

   $ _____ Initial deposit from Section B above.

   $ _____ Additional cash deposit, if any, paid into Escrow on or before _____.

   $ _____ Balance of down payment (or balance of purchase price if all cash) paid into Escrow before closing

$ _____ TOTAL CASH FUNDS FROM BUYER (exclusive of closing costs)

$ _____ By way of _____

$ _____ _____

$ _____ TOTAL PURCHASE PRICE

_____   _____
     BUYER'S INITIALS & DATE   SELLER'S INITIALS & DATE

©Hawaii Association of REALTORS®
Counter Offer
RR204 Rev. 3/04

SAMPLE

[   ]   Paragraphs C-2 to C-79 and addenda terms changes, if any. (Please number)

_____
_____
_____
_____
_____
_____
_____
_____
_____
_____
_____
_____
_____
_____
_____
_____
_____
_____
_____
_____
_____
_____
_____
_____
_____
_____
_____
_____

The undersigned agrees to sell/buy the above described Property on the terms and conditions set forth in the DROA as modified by this Counter Offer. If the terms of this Counter Offer are accepted, Seller agrees to pay a commission as per Section D of the DROA. **This Counter Offer can be withdrawn at any time prior to delivery of a written acceptance to the undersigned's Brokerage Firm.**

EXPIRATION: This Counter Offer shall expire at _____ AM/PM on _____

Counter Offer date _____, _____ AM/PM.

_____   _____
Signature of Party **Submitting** Counter Offer   Signature of Party **Submitting** Counter Offer
[   ] Buyer   or   [   ] Seller   [   ] Buyer   or   [   ] Seller

ACCEPTANCE OF COUNTER OFFER I/We accept this Counter Offer and agree to sell/buy the Property on the terms and conditions in the DROA, as modified by this Counter Offer, and acknowledge receipt of a copy of this Counter Offer.

Acceptance date: _____, _____ AM/PM.

_____   _____
Signature of Party **Accepting** Counter Offer   Signature of Party **Accepting** Counter Offer
[   ] Buyer   or   [   ] Seller   [   ] Buyer   or   [   ] Seller

NOTE: THERE IS NO WARRANTY ON PLAIN LANGUAGE. An effort has been made to put this Agreement into plain language. But there is no promise that it is in plain language. In legal terms, THERE IS NO WARRANTY, EXPRESSED OR IMPLIED, THAT THIS AGREEMENT COMPLIES WITH CHAPTER 487A OF THE HAWAII REVISED STATUTES, AS AMENDED. This means that the Hawaii Association of REALTORS® is not liable to any Buyer, Seller, or other person who uses this form for any damages or penalty because of any violation of Chapter 487A. People are cautioned to see their own attorneys about Chapter 487A (and other laws that may apply)

©Hawaii Association of REALTORS®   Page 2 of 2   RR204 Rev. 3/04 (NC) For Release 11/04

Hawaii Association of REALTORS®

DEPOSIT RECEIPT OFFER AND ACCEPTANCE (DROA)
Hawaii Association of Realtors® Standard Form
Revised 3/04 (NC)   For Release 11/04

Reviewed by: _____
  Principal Broker/Broker-in-Charge

Reference Date: _____

Property Reference or Address: _____

CONTRACT: THIS IS MORE THAN A RECEIPT FOR MONEY. IT IS A LEGALLY BINDING CONTRACT. READ IT CAREFULLY. HANDWRITTEN OR TYPED PROVISIONS HEREIN SHALL SUPERSEDE ANY PRINTED PROVISIONS IF THERE IS A CONFLICT. FILL IN ALL BLANKS. WRITE "NA" IF NOT APPLICABLE. SECTIONS AND PARAGRAPHS WITH CHECK-OFF BOXES ARE OPTIONAL, ALL OTHERS ARE STANDARD PROVISIONS.

SECTION A: AGENCY DISCLOSURE

A-1 **AGENCY.** The Buyer and/or Seller in a real estate transaction in Hawaii may retain a real estate Brokerage Firm as their agent. In such case, the Buyer and/or Seller is represented by the Brokerage Firm and all of its licensees. Hawaii law requires real estate licensees to disclose orally or in writing to Seller and/or Buyer whom the licensee represents. The form of representation may be one of the following:

  (a) **Seller's Agent.** Brokerage Firm represents Seller only unless a disclosed dual agency exists. Seller's Agent owes the highest duties to Seller, including confidentiality, loyalty, and utmost care.

  (b) **Buyer's Agent.** Brokerage Firm represents Buyer only unless a disclosed dual agency exists. Buyer's Agent owes the highest duties to Buyer, including confidentiality, loyalty, and utmost care.

  (c) **Dual Agent.** Brokerage Firm represents both Buyer and Seller. This commonly occurs when licensees in the Brokerage Firm representing Seller have Buyer clients looking for types of property similar to Seller's property. In such event, the Brokerage Firm and all of its licensees represent both Buyer and Seller and are dual agents. Dual agents must remain neutral in negotiations and must not advance the interest of one party over the other. **A separate Dual Agency Agreement is required under Hawaii law.**

  (d) **No Agency Representation** (see A-2 below)

A-2 **DISCLOSURE.**

  (a) **Seller Representation:** Seller is represented by the Brokerage Firm _____ and all its licensees. Brokerage Firm is[   ] is not[   ] a member of the National Association of REALTORS®.

  (b) **Buyer Representation:** Buyer is represented by the Brokerage Firm _____ and all its licensees. Brokerage Firm is[   ] is not[   ] a member of the National Association of REALTORS®.

  (c) **Dual Agency Representation:** Seller and Buyer are represented by the Brokerage Firm _____. Brokerage Firm is[   ] is not[   ] a member of the National Association of REALTORS®. **A separate Dual Agency Agreement is required.**

  (d) **No Agency Representation:**
  [   ] **Seller** is a Customer and is not represented by a Brokerage Firm.
  [   ] **Buyer** is a Customer and is not represented by a Brokerage Firm.
  It is recommended that Customers seek legal counsel prior to signing a DROA.

If requested, a licensee may present a Customer's DROA to Seller and report Seller's response. A licensee cannot, however, negotiate for or otherwise advise a Customer in the transaction.

Buyer and Seller acknowledge that oral or written disclosure relative to agency representation was provided to them before the signing of this DROA.

_____ (Buyer's initials)   _____ (Seller's initials)

NAR Code of Ethics: Buyer and Seller are aware that the National Association of REALTORS® holds its members accountable for their actions through a strict Professional Code of Ethics, which includes a grievance system to address complaints. Non-members are not held to the same standards as members, nor are they required to participate in the grievance system.

_____
BUYER'S INITIALS & DATE

_____
SELLER'S INITIALS & DATE

SECTION B: DEPOSIT RECEIPT

Received from _____, the "Buyer," the sum of $_____

in the form of _____ as an initial earnest money deposit.

Acknowledged by _____ Agent's name: _____
             (Signature of Broker or Salesperson)

Bus._____ Fax _____ Cell _____ E-mail _____

Brokerage Firm/Address: _____

[ ]B-1 The initial deposit check shall remain uncashed, shall be retained by the Brokerage Firm assisting Buyer, and shall be deposited with Escrow or in a trust fund account by the next business day after the Acceptance Date.

INTEREST ON DEPOSIT FUNDS

(Choose B-2 OR B-3).

[ ]B-2 Buyer to Earn Interest. The parties instruct Escrow to place Buyer's deposit(s) into an interest-bearing account with all interest to be credited to Buyer at closing. Buyer shall pay any processing fee required by Escrow and all costs of setting up, maintaining and closing the account. Fees/costs may exceed the interest earned.

[ ]B-3 Buyer not to Earn Interest. Buyer hereby waives the right to place Buyer's deposits in an interest-bearing account. Buyer understands any interest earned on such deposits shall belong to Escrow.

SECTION C: ADDENDA AND OFFER

ADDENDA. The following addenda, if checked, are attached to and made a part of this DROA.

[ ] Existing "As Is" Condition	[ ] Lead Based Paint
[ ] Residential Leasehold Property	[ ] Dual Agency
[ ] Standard Oceanfront Property	[ ] VA Financing
[ ] FHA Financing/Real Estate Certification	[ ] 1031 Exchange
[ ] Agreement to Occupy Prior to Close of Escrow	[ ] Rental Agreement
[ ] Plain Language	[ ] Purchase Money Mortgage
[ ] Agreement of Sale	[ ] Short Sale
[ ] Other _____	[ ] Other _____
[ ] Other _____	[ ] Other _____

OFFER TO BUY. Buyer offers to buy the Property described below on the terms and conditions contained herein, acknowledges receipt of a copy, and agrees that this Offer shall be binding if accepted by Seller on or before:

Date _____ Time _____ AM/PM

C-1   Purchase price for the Property is $ _____ U.S. Dollars, paid as follows:

$_____ Initial deposit from Section B above.

$_____ Additional deposit, if any, paid into Escrow on or before _____

$_____ Balance of down payment (or balance of purchase price if all cash) paid into Escrow before closing.

$_____ TOTAL CASH FUNDS FROM BUYER (exclusive of closing costs).

$_____ By way of _____
_____
_____

$_____ _____
_____
_____

$_____ TOTAL PURCHASE PRICE

_____
BUYER'S INITIALS & DATE

Page 2 of 12

_____
SELLER'S INITIALS & DATE

(c)Hawaii Association of REALTORS®   RR201 Rev. 3/04 (NC) For Release 11/04

PROPERTY

C-2 Description: Tax Map Key: Div. _____/Zone_____/Sec. _____/Plat_____/Parcel_____/CPR_____ (if applicable).

All of that _____ Property situated at: _____
 leasehold/fee simple

Described as follows: _____
_____
_____

C-3 Sale Includes: All built-in furniture, attached existing fixtures, built-in appliances, water heater, electrical and/or gas and plumbing fixtures, attached carpeting, and the following indicated items:

[ ] Range	[ ] Microwave	[ ] Refrigerator	[ ] Smoke/Heat Detectors
[ ] Disposal	[ ] Washer	[ ] Dryer	[ ] Existing Window Coverings
[ ] Dishwasher	[ ] Ceiling Fan	[ ] Chandelier	[ ] Solar Heating System
[ ] Air Conditioner	[ ] TV Antenna	[ ] TV Cable Outlet	[ ] Automatic Gate/Door Openers
[ ] Sprinkler System	[ ] Security Alarm	[ ] All Pool Equipment	[ ] Furnishings per Inventory
[ ] Other_____			

C-4 Specifically Excluded: _____

CLOSING

C-5 For purposes of this DROA, closing shall be the date when all appropriate conveyance documents are recorded. Buyer and Seller agree to promptly execute appropriate or customary documents when requested by Escrow.

C-6 The "Scheduled Closing Date" shall be on or before _____.

(Choose C-7 OR C-8) Any Change to the Scheduled Closing Date Shall Be Handled as Follows:

[ ]C-7 Extensions. There is no automatic right to extend. If, for reasons beyond a Buyer's or Seller's control, a party cannot perform the obligation to close by the Scheduled Closing Date, then such party may extend the Scheduled Closing Date up to _____ days by delivery of written notice to the other party prior to the Scheduled Closing Date. Thereafter, time shall be of the essence and if a party fails to perform by the extended Scheduled Closing Date, such party shall be considered in default and the Default Provision shall apply. The extended Scheduled Closing Date may not be further extended unless both Buyer and Seller so agree in writing. This provision relates only to the extension of the Scheduled Closing Date.

[ ]C-8 Time is of the essence and the Scheduled Closing Date may not be extended unless both Buyer and Seller so agree in writing.

C-9 Escrow. This transaction shall be escrowed by: _____ ("Escrow").
_____

The parties shall timely provide to Escrow fully executed copies of all notices, receipts, responses (approvals and disapprovals), acknowledgments and extensions which are part of this transaction.

C-10 Prorations and Closing Adjustments. At closing, Escrow shall prorate the following, if applicable, as of the date of closing: real property tax, lease rents, interest on assumed obligations, mortgage and other insurance premiums, maintenance, private sewer, marina, and/or association fees, tenant rents, and _____
When applicable, Escrow shall charge to Seller and credit to Buyer the amount of any tenant's security deposit.

C-11 Closing Costs. The following are customary closing costs (including Hawaii General Excise Tax where applicable) and **are not intended to be an all-inclusive list**. Escrow may charge the appropriate party other closing costs as directed by the parties.

Charge to Buyer, if applicable	Charge to Seller, if applicable
40% of the premium for standard coverage title insurance and any additional costs relating to the issuance of extended coverage policy (including a lender's policy)	60% of the premium for standard coverage title insurance
	Cost of drafting of conveyance documents and bills of sale
Cost of drafting mortgage and note or agreement of sale	Cost of obtaining Seller's consents
Cost of obtaining Buyer's consents	50% of Escrow fee
Buyer's notary fees	Seller's notary fees
All recording fees except documents to clear Seller's title	Cost of required staking or survey
50% of Escrow fee	Recording fees to clear Seller's title
Condominium and Association ownership transfer fees	FHA or VA mandatory closing fees
FHA or VA discount points and any mortgage fees	Conveyance tax
	FIRPTA (Federal withholding tax)
	HARPTA (State withholding tax)

_____   _____
    BUYER'S INITIALS & DATE   SELLER'S INITIALS & DATE

©Hawaii Association of REALTORS®   **Page 3 of 12**   RR201 Rev. 3/04 (NC) For Release 11/04

ASSESSMENTS

For purposes of Paragraphs C-12, C-13, and C-14, an assessment is defined as any obligation (not including prorations in Paragraph C-10) levied against the Property by a homeowner's association, governmental body, or any other entity with a legal right to assess. Assessments, if any, shall be charged as follows:

C-12   Any lump sum assessments levied against the Property prior to the Acceptance Date shall be paid by Seller [   ] or assumed by Buyer [   ]. Exceptions, if any: _____

C-13   Any assessments levied against the Property prior to the Acceptance Date which are being paid in installments shall be paid in full by Seller [   ] or pro-rated by Escrow as of the date of closing [   ]. Exceptions, if any: _____

C-14   If a new assessment is authorized against the Property between the Acceptance Date and the Scheduled Closing Date, such assessment shall be paid as Buyer and Seller shall agree. If Buyer and Seller cannot reach an agreement within five (5) days of both parties being aware of the new assessment, either party may terminate this DROA and the Termination Provision (C-21) shall apply.

OTHER CLOSING MATTERS

C-15   **Risk of Loss.** Risk of loss passes to Buyer upon closing or possession, whichever occurs sooner.

C-16   **Consents.** Buyer and Seller may be required to obtain consents of lessors, homeowner or condominium associations, co-op boards, existing lenders, vendors or other entities. Buyer or Seller shall cooperate and take all reasonable action to obtain such consents.

C-17   **Possession.** Seller shall give Buyer possession at closing or _____.

C-18   **Keys to the Property.** Seller, at Seller's sole cost and expense, shall provide Buyer at closing with all existing, but at least one set of functioning keys/controls (entry, interior, mail box, pool, security, parking area, and all garage door openers). **Buyer shall pay all deposits which may be required for any of these items.** Unless Buyer and Seller agree otherwise, all keys/controls and garage door openers shall be released to Buyer only after Escrow has verbally notified Seller or Seller's Agent that the closing has occurred.

C-19   **Tenancy and Vesting.** Title shall vest in Buyer(s) as follows: (insert full legal name(s) and marital status)

_____

_____

Tenancy: _____

[   ] Tenancy to be determined. If Buyer has not yet determined the vesting and/or tenancy, Buyer shall provide Escrow in writing with the selected names and tenancy within fifteen (15) days after the Acceptance Date.

CONTINGENCY PROCEDURES AND TERMINATION

C-20   **Contingencies.** Buyer's obligation to buy and Seller's obligation to sell the Property may be subject in this DROA to satisfaction of one or more conditions (each called a "Contingency"). As used in this DROA, the term "Benefited Party" shall mean (a) Buyer, as to each Contingency which must be satisfied before Buyer is required to close on the purchase of the Property from Seller; and (b) Seller, as to each Contingency which must be satisfied before Seller is required to close on the sale of the Property to Buyer. If a Contingency is not satisfied within the time period specified for meeting such Contingency ("Contingency Period"), the Benefited Party may elect (a) to terminate this DROA and the Termination Provision (C-21) shall apply; or (b) to waive the Contingency. **Unless otherwise specified in writing in this DROA contingencies shall expire at 11:59 PM, Hawaiian Standard Time, on the day the Contingency period expires.**

C-21   **Termination.** If the Benefited Party elects to terminate this DROA because a Contingency for that party's benefit has not been satisfied, the Benefited Party must deliver to the other party a written notice terminating this DROA prior to the expiration of the Contingency Period, or such other termination period which may be set forth in a specific Contingency in this DROA. If the Benefited Party fails to deliver the written notice to the other party within such time period, the Contingency shall be deemed to be waived. Each party understands and acknowledges the requirement to act upon each Contingency according to the strict deadlines described herein.

If a Benefited Party so terminates this DROA, Buyer and Seller shall promptly execute all cancellation documents requested by Escrow, and Escrow shall, unless otherwise agreed to in this DROA, return to Buyer all deposits previously made, less the amount of any escrow expenses or fees chargeable to Buyer. Thereafter, neither Buyer nor Seller shall have any further rights or obligations under this DROA. This Section is subject to the special provisions for Financing Contingencies set forth in Paragraphs C-24 to C-27. Any termination under this DROA shall be in writing and delivered to the other party to be effective.

BUYER'S INITIALS & DATE

©Hawaii Association of REALTORS®

SELLER'S INITIALS & DATE

RR201 Rev. 3/04 (NC) For Release 11/04

<u>CONTINGENCY FOR CASH FUNDS</u>
(Choose C-22 <u>OR</u> C-23)

[   ]C-22   **No Contingency for Obtaining "Cash Funds".** Buyer represents that there are no contingencies to Buyer's obtaining the cash portions of the purchase price and closing costs to buy the Property (collectively the "Cash Funds"). Buyer shall neither delay nor extend the Scheduled Closing Date to obtain the Cash Funds.

[   ]C-23   **Contingency on Obtaining "Cash Funds".** Buyer's obligation to buy the Property is subject to the following contingencies to Buyer obtaining the Cash Funds:_____

_____

_____

<u>FINANCING CONTINGENCIES</u>

[   ]C-24   **Financing Contingency.** Buyer's obligation to buy the Property is contingent upon Buyer obtaining the loan described in this DROA ("Mortgage Loan"). If Buyer does not obtain a conditional loan commitment letter, or is unable to satisfy all conditions of the loan commitment letter within the time periods specified in Paragraph C-25, then Buyer may terminate this DROA and the Termination Provision (C-21) shall apply. Buyer may waive this Financing Contingency and purchase the Property on an all cash basis or increase the amount of CASH FUNDS to thereby satisfy all of Lender's requirements for funding the loan. If Buyer elects either of these two options, Buyer shall promptly provide written notice of such election to Seller, together with evidence of Buyer's ability to perform PRIOR to expiration of the time periods stated in Paragraph C-25.

[   ]C-25   **Buyer's Obligations.** Buyer shall act in good faith to obtain the loan as described in this DROA. Buyer is obligated to submit an application for a Mortgage Loan with required fees, and to deliver to Seller a pre-qualification letter within _____ days after the Acceptance Date. The pre-qualification letter shall state that Buyer is credit worthy and qualified for the loan subject to Lender's requirements. Buyer is obligated to deliver to Seller by _____ (Date) a conditional loan commitment letter which shall state that Buyer has been approved and Lender will make the loan under specified conditions. Buyer shall deliver to Seller written evidence that Buyer has satisfied all conditions specified by Lender except conditions which cannot be satisfied by Buyer until closing, such as payoff of Buyer's debt or receipt by Buyer of proceeds from the sale of Buyer's property, not later than _____days after issuance of such commitment letter. Buyer authorizes Seller and Seller's Agent to contact Buyer's Lender and Escrow regarding the status of Buyer's loan, including commitment letter and satisfaction of conditions.

C-26   **Seller's Right to Cancel.** Should Buyer fail to satisfy any obligation under C-25 within the time period specified, Seller shall have the right to terminate this DROA by providing written notice to Buyer. In the event of notice of termination by the Seller, Buyer and Seller shall promptly execute all cancellation documents requested by Escrow, and Escrow shall, unless otherwise agreed to in this DROA, return to Buyer all deposits previously made, less the amount of any escrow expenses or fees chargeable to Buyer. Thereafter, neither Buyer nor Seller shall have any further rights or obligations under this DROA.

[   ]C-27   **Contingency on Assumption of Seller's Existing Mortgage(s).** Buyer's obligation to buy the Property is subject to Buyer's assumption of Seller's existing loan(s) ("Seller's Mortgage") on the terms described in Paragraph C-1. Buyer shall make application to assume Seller's Mortgage within _____ days after the Acceptance Date and shall provide evidence of approval for the assumption no later than _____ days after the Acceptance Date. Buyer understands Seller does not warrant the assumability, the terms and conditions of Seller's Mortgage or the assumption terms. If the terms to assume Seller's Mortgage materially differ from those set forth in this DROA, then Buyer may either elect to terminate this DROA or to assume Seller's Mortgage on such terms. Buyer shall reimburse Seller at closing for Seller's existing reserve account balances. If a Lender does not release Seller from liability under Seller's Mortgage, Seller may elect to terminate this DROA and the Termination Provision (C-21) shall apply.

<u>DEFAULT PROVISIONS</u>

C-28   In the event Buyer fails to perform Buyer's obligations under this DROA (Seller not being in default), Seller may (a) bring an action for damages for breach of contract, or (b) retain the initial deposit and all additional deposits provided for herein as liquidated damages, and Buyer shall be responsible for any costs incurred in accordance with this DROA.

C-29   In the event Seller fails to perform Seller's obligations under this DROA (Buyer not being in default), Buyer may (a) bring an action for damages for breach of contract, (b) seek specific performance of this DROA, and (c) Seller shall be responsible for any costs incurred in accordance with this DROA.

C-30   The foregoing shall not exclude any other remedies available under this DROA to either Seller or Buyer on account of the 0other party's default.

C-31   In the event of default by a party and/or a legal action or arbitration (including a claim by a Broker for commission), the prevailing party shall be entitled to recover all costs incurred including reasonable attorneys' fees.

MEDIATION AND ARBITRATION

C-32   **Mediation.** If any dispute or claim arises out of this DROA during this transaction or at any time after closing between Buyer and Seller, or between Buyer and/or Seller and a Brokerage Firm and all its licensees assisting in this transaction, and the parties to such dispute or claim are unable to resolve the dispute, Buyer and Seller agree in good faith to attempt to settle such dispute or claim by non-binding mediation. This paragraph shall not apply to any complaint of unethical conduct against a Brokerage Firm and all its licensees who are obligated to comply with the Code of Ethics of the National Association of REALTORS®. Such complaints must be brought before the Local Board of REALTORS® of which the Brokerage Firm and all its licensees are members.

C-33   **Arbitration.** If any dispute or claim arises out of this DROA during this transaction or at any time after closing, between Buyer and Seller, or between Buyer and/or Seller and a Brokerage Firm and all its licensees assisting in this transaction and if such dispute cannot be resolved through mediation, then the parties are encouraged to consider arbitration. It is recommended that the parties seek legal counsel to make this determination.

C-34   **Third Party Claims.** It is understood that if such dispute or claim is made by or against a third party who is not obligated or willing to mediate or arbitrate such dispute or claim, then Buyer and Seller shall not be required to mediate or arbitrate such dispute or claim.

TITLE

Preliminary Title Report. Escrow is instructed to promptly order a Preliminary Title Report on the Property for delivery to Seller, Buyer and their agents.

C-35   **Title.** Seller agrees, subject to Paragraph C-36 if selected, to convey the Property with warranties vesting marketable title in Buyer, free and clear of all liens and encumbrances EXCEPT: (a) easements, covenants, conditions, reservations or restrictions now of record **WHICH DO NOT MATERIALLY AFFECT THE VALUE OF THE PROPERTY** and (b) _____

(Choose C-36 OR C-37)

[   ]C-36   If the Preliminary Title Report, or any other report reveals that title cannot be delivered by Seller in accordance with Paragraph C-35, Seller shall use Seller's best efforts to cure any defects. If, within _____ days following receipt of any reported discrepancies Seller is unable to cure such defects in title, Buyer may elect to purchase the Property with such defect(s) in title and Seller shall not be liable if Seller had acted in good faith. If Buyer elects not to accept the Property with such defects, either Buyer or Seller may terminate this DROA and the Termination Provision (C-21) shall apply.

[   ]C-37   If Buyer is not satisfied with the Preliminary Title Report, Buyer may elect, within _____ days of Buyer's receipt of the Preliminary Title Report, to terminate this DROA and the Termination Provision (C-21) shall apply.

TRANSACTIONS INVOLVING FOREIGN OR NON-RESIDENT BUYER AND SELLER

C-38   **HARPTA Withholding Required if Seller is a Non-Resident of the State of Hawaii.** Under Hawaii law, if Seller is a non-resident person or entity (corporation, partnership, trust, or estate) of the State of Hawaii, Buyer must withhold a specified percentage of the "amount realized" by Seller on the sale of the Property and forward the amount with the appropriate form to the State Department of Taxation. Such withholding may not be required if Seller obtains and provides Buyer with an authorized exemption or waiver from withholding. If Seller does not provide Buyer with a certificate of exemption or waiver from HARPTA within fourteen (14) days of the Acceptance Date, Escrow is hereby authorized and instructed to withhold/collect from Seller the required amount at closing and forward it to the State Department of Taxation.

C-39   **FIRPTA Withholding Required if Seller is a Foreign Person.** Under the Internal Revenue Code, if Seller is a foreign person or entity (non-resident alien, corporation, partnership, trust, or estate), Buyer must generally withhold a specified percentage of the "amount realized" by Seller on the sale of the Property and forward this amount with the appropriate Internal Revenue Service ("IRS") form. Such withholding may not be required if Seller obtains and provides Buyer with an authorized exemption or waiver from withholding. If Seller does not provide Buyer with a certificate of exemption or waiver from FIRPTA within fourteen (14) days of Acceptance Date, Escrow is hereby authorized and instructed to withhold/collect from Seller the required amount at closing and forward it to the IRS.

C-40   **Additional Disclosures Required by Foreign Buyers and Sellers.** Buyer and Seller understand that under statutes and ordinances such as the Agricultural Foreign Investment Disclosure Act of 1978, the International Investment and Trade in Services Survey Act, and the revised Ordinances of the City and County of Honolulu, among others, disclosures are required by foreign Buyers and/or Sellers under certain conditions.

STAKING & SURVEY This may/may not apply to condominiums or cooperatives.
(Choose C-41 OR C-42)

[   ]C-41   **Staking (Boundary Markers).** Prior to the Scheduled Closing Date, Seller shall, at Seller's sole cost and expense, have a registered land surveyor stake the Property. Buyer may have a registered land surveyor verify the accuracy of the location of the stakes prior to closing. Seller shall reimburse Buyer for the cost of this verification at closing ONLY if the location of the original stakes proves to be inaccurate. Buyer understands that staking is not the same type of survey as described in Paragraph C-42, and does not confirm the accuracy of the description or the land area of Property, or the existence or absence of encroachments onto the Property or onto a neighboring property.

[   ]C-42   **Survey.** Prior to the Scheduled Closing Date, Seller shall, at Seller's sole cost and expense, have a registered land surveyor (a) stake the Property even if the stakes are visible and, (b) if improvements exist along the Property line, provide Buyer with a map (with surveyor's stamp) and accompanying report to show the perimeters of the Property and the location of any improvements in the vicinity of the perimeter Property lines. This survey and map may not address whether improvements on the Property are in compliance with State and/or County requirements, and/or subdivision covenants, conditions, and restrictions.

C-43   **Boundary Encroachment.** If an encroachment onto an adjoining property or onto the Property by an adjoining owner is revealed or discovered, such encroachment either shall be removed or Seller shall obtain encroachment agreement(s) with the affected adjoining owner(s) which is acceptable to Buyer. If neither occurs within _____ days of discovery or by the Scheduled Closing Date, whichever occurs earlier, Buyer may accept the encroachment(s) terminate this DROA and the Termination Provision (C-21) shall apply. Buyer should be aware that, under certain circumstances, Hawaii law allows acceptable tolerances for discrepancies involving improvements built in the vicinity of the perimeter of the Property lines.

SELLER'S DISCLOSURES (Required by Hawaii Statute for residential real property)

C-44   **Seller's Obligation to Disclose.** Under Hawaii law, Seller is obligated to fully and accurately disclose in writing to Buyer any fact, defect, or condition, past or present, that would be expected to measurably affect the value of the Property to a reasonable person. Within _____ days from the Acceptance Date, Seller shall provide Buyer with a written disclosure statement signed and dated by Seller within six (6) months before or ten (10) days after the Acceptance Date. Such Disclosure shall be prepared in good faith and with due care and shall disclose all material facts relating to the Property that: (i) are within the knowledge or control of Seller; (ii) can be observed from visible, accessible areas; or, (iii) which are required by Section 508D-15 of the Hawaii Revised Statutes.

Section 508D-15 of the Hawaii Revised Statutes covers property which lies: (i) within the boundaries of a special flood hazard area as officially designated on Flood Insurance Administration maps promulgated by the appropriate Federal agencies for the purposes of determining eligibility for emergency flood insurance programs; (ii) within the boundaries of the noise exposure area shown on maps prepared by the Department of Transportation in accordance with Federal Aviation Regulation Part 150-Airport Noise Compatibility Planning (14 Code of Federal Regulations Part 150) for any public airport; (iii) within the boundaries of the Air Installation Compatibility Use Zone of any Air Force, Army, Navy or Marine Corps airport as officially designated by military authorities; or (iv) within the anticipated inundation areas designated on the Department of Defense's Civil Defense Tsunami Inundation Maps. Subject to the availability of maps that designate the four areas by tax map key (zone, section, plat, parcel), the Seller shall include such material fact information in the Disclosure Statement provided to the Buyer. If such information is not available, no information will be provided to Buyer.

C-44A   **Later Discovered Information.** Under Hawaii law, if after Seller delivers a disclosure statement to Buyer and prior to closing, Seller becomes aware of information which was not previously disclosed or which makes any statement in the disclosure statement inaccurate, and said information directly, substantially, and adversely affects the value of the Property, then Seller shall provide an amended disclosure statement (a written statement prepared by Seller or at Seller's direction) to Buyer within ten (10) days after the discovery of the inaccuracy, and in any event, no later than twelve noon of the last business day prior to the recorded sale of the Property. Buyer's rights upon receipt of the amended disclosure statement are found in Paragraph C-46.

C-45   **Seller's Disclosure is Not a Warranty.** This disclosure statement is NOT a warranty of any kind. Under Hawaii law, the disclosure statement shall not be construed as a substitute for any expert inspection, professional advice, or warranty that Buyer may wish to obtain.

C-46 **Buyer's Rights Upon Receipt of Disclosure Statement.** Seller is required by law to obtain from Buyer an acknowledgment of receipt of the disclosure statement in writing. Buyer shall acknowledge receipt of the disclosure statement in writing. Upon receipt of the disclosure statement, Buyer shall have _____ days to examine the statement and to rescind the DROA. Should Buyer elect to rescind the DROA, Buyer must give Seller directly or Seller's Agent written notice of such rescission within the stated time period. Upon receipt by Buyer of an amended disclosure statement, or upon discovery by Buyer of a failure by Seller to disclose material facts, or upon discovery by Buyer that the disclosure statement contains an inaccurate assertion that directly, substantially, and adversely affects the value of the Property, Buyer may elect to rescind the DROA. Buyer shall have _____ days from discovery thereof or from receipt of the amended disclosure statement, whichever is earlier, to indicate in writing an election to rescind the DROA. Buyer may elect, in writing, to accept the amended disclosure statement prior to the end of the rescission period.

C-47 **Buyer's Remedies If Seller Fails to Comply with Paragraphs C-44 or C-44A.** Buyer may elect to complete the purchase of the Property even if Seller fails to comply with Paragraphs C-44 or C-44A. When Buyer is provided a disclosure statement or amended disclosure statement and Buyer decides to rescind the DROA, Buyer is limited in damages to the return of all deposits; and in such case, Buyer's deposits shall be immediately returned. If Seller negligently fails to provide the required disclosure statement or amended disclosure statement, Seller shall be liable to Buyer for the amount of actual damages suffered as a result of the negligence. In addition to the above remedies, a court may also award the prevailing party's attorneys' fees, court costs, and administrative fees.

C-48 **Mediation.** Under Hawaii law, any dispute pertaining to the Mandatory Seller's Disclosure Statute shall be handled pursuant to Paragraphs C-32 and C-33.

C-49 **Asbestos Disclosure.** Buyer is aware that asbestos materials are hazardous to one's health, particularly if asbestos fibers are released into the air and inhaled. In the past (before 1979, but possibly since) asbestos was a commonly used insulation material in heating facilities and in certain types of floor and ceiling materials, shingles, plaster products, cement and other building materials. Buyer is aware that Buyer should make appropriate inquiry into the possible existence of asbestos on the Property. Structures having "popcorn" or "cottage cheese" type ceilings may contain asbestos fibers or asbestos-containing material. Such ceilings should not be disturbed since it could release asbestos fibers in the air. Any disturbance should be done only by licensed abatement contractors.

C-49A **Hazardous Waste and Toxic Substances Disclosure.** Buyer is aware that federal and state laws place strict liability on property owners for dangers caused by hazardous waste management and may require that such owner pay for the cost of the cleanup of hazardous substances and other toxic substances. Buyer is aware that Buyer should make appropriate inquiries into the past use of the Property and should seek an environmental assessment to ascertain the possible existence of such hazardous substances or materials on or under the Property. Buyer is aware Buyer may have liability for hazardous substances located on or under the Property even if Buyer did not cause such substances to be on or under the Property.

C-49B **Mold Disclosure.** Buyer is aware that mold and/or other microscopic organisms may exist on the Property. Molds are simple, microscopic organisms, present everywhere. Mold spores may cause health problems. Mold will grow and multiply whenever sufficient moisture, temperature and organic material are present. Real estate Brokerage Firms, brokers, and agents are not qualified to inspect the Property or to make recommendations or determinations concerning possible health or safety issues.

C-50 **Sex Offender Registration ("Megan's Law").** Hawaii has enacted a law requiring sex offenders to register with the Attorney General's office. Seller makes no representation as to whether or not the public will have access to this information. Neither Seller nor any real estate agent is required to obtain information regarding sex offenders.

INSPECTIONS, MAINTENANCE AND WARRANTIES

C-51 **Inspection of Property.** At Buyer's sole cost and expense Buyer may (personally or by any expert, professional, or other representative of Buyer's choice): (a) inspect the Property or any portion thereof; (b) inspect all major appliances and fixtures (plumbing, electric, and gas) included in the sale; (c) inspect all public records relating to the Property; and (d) inspect all applicable laws and regulations which may affect the Property. Seller shall provide Buyer and Buyer's representatives access to the Property for this purpose, during reasonable hours with reasonable prior notice to Seller. The obligation of Buyer to purchase the Property is contingent upon Buyer's approval of inspection results and acceptance of the condition of the Property within _____ days after the Acceptance Date. All inspections must be completed within this time period.

If Buyer disapproves of the inspection results within such time period, Buyer may elect to terminate the DROA pursuant to the Termination Provision (C-21).

If Buyer requests that Seller make certain corrections to the Property, and the parties cannot reach agreement, Buyer may, within the specified time period, accept the Property or terminate the DROA and the Termination Provision (C-21) shall apply.

IF BUYER FAILS TO MAKE AN ELECTION IN WRITING WITHIN THE SPECIFIED TIME PERIOD, BUYER WILL HAVE WAIVED THIS CONTINGENCY.

[ ]C-52 **Property Condition Maintenance.** Seller shall maintain the interior and exterior of the Property in the same condition and repair as when Buyer inspected the Property pursuant to Paragraph C-51, or as otherwise agreed between Buyer and Seller. If the Property has not been maintained, then the provisions of Paragraph C-53A shall apply.

[ ]C-53 **Final Walk Through.** Buyer and/or Buyer's representative shall have the right to conduct a final walk through of the Property no later than _____ days prior to closing: (a) to confirm that the Property is in the same condition and repair that it was on the date that Buyer inspected the Property pursuant to Paragraph C-51; and/or (b) to inspect the repairs and/or replacements made by Seller, as agreed between Buyer and Seller. Seller understands that the final walk through requires that the utilities be on, including propane, if applicable, at Seller's expense. If Buyer and/or Buyer's representative fails to conduct the final walk through within the time period, Buyer will have waived this right.

C-53A **Withheld/Collected Funds.** If required repairs and maintenance have not been completed by closing, an amount equal to 150% of the estimated cost shall be withheld/collected from Seller and retained in Escrow until completion. All repairs and maintenance bills will be paid through Escrow. Any balance remaining after completion of all repairs and maintenance shall be returned to Seller; provided, however, that if repairs and maintenance are not completed within _____ days after closing, said funds will be disbursed to Buyer.

C-54 **No Continuing Warranty.** Buyer understands that no continuing warranty after closing regarding the interior or exterior of the Property is expressed or implied.

C-55 **Home Warranty Programs.** Buyer understands that Buyer may obtain from a third party for a fee, home warranties covering appliances, electrical and plumbing equipment and other items included with the Property. If such a home warranty is available, it may be obtained at Buyer's expense from any provider of Buyer's choice.

[ ]C-56 **Existing Warranties, Plans, etc.** Seller shall provide to Buyer at closing all existing warranty documents in Seller's possession covering the improvements and personal property being sold to Buyer such as instruction booklets in Seller's possession covering the appliances being sold, all originals and copies in Seller's possession of blueprints, specifications, and copies of architectural or engineering drawings relating to the Property. Buyer understands: (a) any warranties delivered by Seller to Buyer represent obligations of other persons, not Seller; (b) the warranties and other documents are provided for informational purposes only; (c) may not reflect improvements as built; and (d) Seller does not promise that any such warranties are transferable to Buyer, and that Buyer must contact the providers of such warranties to determine whether the warranties are transferable to Buyer.

[ ]C-57 **Removal of Items from Property.** Seller shall dispose of all personal belongings, trash and junk, both inside and outside any improvements.

(Choose C-57A OR C-57B OR NEITHER)

[ ]C-57A **Cleaning.** Prior to closing, Seller shall, at Seller's expense, have the interior of the improvements on the Property cleaned. Cleaning shall include all appliances, carpets, cupboards, drawers, floors, jalousies, screens and windows.

[ ]C-57B **Cleaning Credit.** Seller shall credit Buyer at closing $_____ for cleaning, as described in Paragraph C-57A.

[ ]C-58 **Pet Related Treatment.** Seller shall, at Seller's expense, remove any pets from the Property, have the carpets within the improvements on the Property professionally cleaned, and the interior of the Property treated for fleas/ticks by a professional. If Seller does not have the Property treated for fleas/ticks by a professional as stated, and provide satisfactory evidence of same to Buyer and Escrow not later than _____ days prior to the scheduled Closing Date, then Seller agrees that an amount equal to 150% of the estimated cost of professionally treating the Property for fleas/ticks shall be held in Escrow until completed; provided however, that any remaining funds held shall be automatically disbursed to Buyer by Escrow if the Property is not professionally treated for fleas/ticks within _____ days after closing. All professional treatment bills shall be paid through Escrow and any balance remaining after completion of professional treatment shall be returned to Seller.

TERMITE PROVISIONS

Buyer is aware that the State-approved Termite Inspection Report (TIR) addresses only visible evidence of active (i.e. live) termite infestation and visible damage in accessible areas. It does not address infestation or damage occurring in inaccessible areas of the improvements described in this DROA. Seller agrees to disclose, in Seller's disclosures, any prior and/or current infestation and damage of which Seller is aware.

C-59   **Termite Inspection Contingency.** Within _____ days of the Acceptance Date _____ shall select a
Buyer or Seller

licensed pest control company ("Company"), to conduct an inspection and issue a TIR on the improvements which are part of the Property. Should such party fail to select a Company and notify the other party in writing of the name of a Company within the time stated, the other party shall select a Company within five (5) days thereafter. Seller shall promptly order the inspection and TIR from the selected Company. The TIR shall be delivered to Buyer by _____, shall pay for the inspection and

_____   _____
Time period/date   Buyer or Seller

the issuance of the TIR at a cost not to exceed _____. If Buyer's Lender requires an updated TIR prior to funding Buyer's loan, Buyer shall pay for the updated report.

If the TIR indicates visible evidence of active (i.e. live) termite infestation, Seller shall order and pay for recommended treatment for that condition (not to include preventive maintenance). Buyer and Seller understand such treatment may cause damage to plants. The obligation of the Buyer to purchase the Property is contingent upon the delivery to Buyer within the time specified above of a TIR stating that there is no visible evidence of active (i.e. live) termite infestation, or the treatment of such improvements by no later than five (5) days prior to the Scheduled Closing Date. If the Contingency is not fulfilled within the time period(s) specified, Buyer may terminate this DROA and the Termination Provision (C-21) shall apply.

C-60   **Termite Damage.** In the event the TIR indicates there is visible damage to the improvements caused by termite infestation, and said damage directly, substantially and adversely affects the value of the Property, then Seller shall make appropriate disclosures under Paragraph C-44A.

RENTAL PROPERTY MATTERS

(Choose C-61 OR C-62)

[   ]C-61   **Existing Leases.** Buyer shall accept title to the Property subject to the existing: *(Choose all that apply)*

[   ] Leases   [   ] Short Term Vacation Rental Reservation(s)
[   ] Property Condition Form   [   ] Other _____
[   ] Rental Management Contract(s)   [   ] Other _____

Any security deposits or vacation deposits will be transferred to Buyer at closing. Copies of such documents shall be delivered to Buyer within _____ days of the Acceptance Date. If within _____ days of receipt of these item(s), Buyer does not accept the Property based upon information in these documents, Buyer may terminate this DROA and the Termination Provision (C-21) shall apply.

[   ]C-62   **Delivery of Property at Closing.** Seller shall deliver possession of the Property at closing vacant and free of tenants, leases, rental management contracts, short term rental reservations, or any other rental or service commitments.

C-63   **Lease Changes During Escrow.** During the escrow period, Seller shall not, without the written consent of Buyer, make any changes to existing leases or enter into any new leases which extend beyond the Scheduled Closing Date.

CONDOMINIUM/SUBDIVISION/HOMEOWNER ORGANIZATIONS *(Choose all that apply)*

[   ]C-64   **Contingency on Homeowner Organization Documentation Approval.** Buyer's obligation to purchase the Property is contingent upon Seller providing the following documentation to the Buyer for review and approval:

[   ] Approved Minutes of the last three (3) Board of   [   ] Current and/or Proposed Budget
       Directors Meeting   [   ] Current Financial Statement
[   ] Articles of Incorporation/Association and   [   ] Current House Rules
       Amendments, if any   [   ] Declaration and Amendments
[   ] Board of Directors and Association Minutes issued   [   ] Insurance Summary
       during the escrow period, if applicable   [   ] Minutes of the last Annual Meeting
[   ] By-laws and Amendments   [   ] Property Information Form RR105c, if obtainable
[   ] Copy of any and all pending litigation complaints   [   ] Reserve Study or Summary, if obtainable
       filed by or against the Owner's Association and/or   [   ] Other _____
       its directors that are currently unresolved, if any   [   ] Other _____

Seller, at Seller's expense, shall furnish the specified documents to the Buyer within _____ days of Acceptance Date. If within _____ days of receipt of these documents Buyer does not accept the Property based on information contained in these documents, Buyer may terminate this DROA and the Termination Provision (C-21) shall apply. In the event that this DROA is canceled, Buyer agrees to promptly return all documents specified here to Seller or Seller's Agent, including any other documents provided to Buyer during the escrow period or, Seller not being in default, Buyer shall reimburse the Seller for the cost of such documentation.

_____
BUYER'S INITIALS & DATE

_____
SELLER'S INITIALS & DATE

RR201 Rev 3/04 (NC) For Release 11/04

C-65   **Common Element Discrepancies.** Seller is not responsible for repair of condominium common and limited common elements or cooperative common areas. Seller is only responsible for reporting such defects or damage to the Association of Apartment Owners or other governing body insofar as Seller's unit is affected.

[   ]C-66   **Contingency on Subdivision Documentation Approval.** Buyer's obligation to purchase the Property is contingent upon Seller providing the CC&R's (Covenants, Conditions, and Restrictions) Design Standards and/or Guidelines and any other applicable subdivision and/or title documents to the Buyer for review and approval. Seller, at Seller's expense, shall deliver the documents to the Buyer within _____ days of Acceptance Date. If within _____ days of receipt of the documents, Buyer does not accept the Property based on information contained in the documents, Buyer may terminate this DROA and the Termination Provision (C-21) shall apply. In the event that this DROA is canceled, Buyer agrees to promptly return all documents to Seller or Seller's Agent, including other documents provided to Buyer during the escrow period or, Seller not being in default, Buyer shall reimburse the Seller for the cost of such documentation.

[   ]C-67   <u>**OTHER SPECIAL TERMS**</u> (Please number)_____

_____

_____

_____

_____

_____

_____

_____

<u>**BROKERAGE FIRMS SERVICES AND DISCLAIMERS**</u>

C-68   **Scope of Services.** The Brokerage Firms assisting in this transaction, including their owners, licensees, salespersons, and employees, recommend that Buyer and Seller each consult their own attorney, accountant, appraiser, architect, pest control expert, home inspector, insurance advisor, contractor, land surveyor, civil engineer, structural engineer, soils engineer, land use professional, zoning expert, environmental expert, designer, estate planner, title insurer, other professionals and/or subject matter experts should they have any questions within those fields about this transaction. Buyer and Seller understand and acknowledge that neither party is relying upon the Brokerage Firms for any of the foregoing services or advice.

C-69   **Disclaimers by Brokerage Firms.** Buyer and Seller understand that the Brokerage Firms have not made any representations or warranties, and have not rendered any opinions about: (a) the legal or tax consequences of this transaction; (b) the legality, validity, correctness, status or lack of any building permits which may have been required for the Property; or (c) the land area of the Property, the location of the boundaries, or the size of any improvements on the Property.

C-70   **Rental Property.** Buyer understands that Seller and the Brokerage Firms are not offering to sell or selling the Property together with any existing or future rental pool or other rental arrangement. Seller and the Brokerage Firms make no representations or guarantees about future rents or future resale value. Buyer understands that should Buyer rent the Property after closing, Buyer is assuming all risks relative to all of the foregoing. This sale includes real property only, and the intent is not to convey a security or investment security as defined by the U.S. Securities and Exchange Commission or other governmental agency.

C-71   **Obligations.** Brokerage Firms shall not be held liable to either Buyer or Seller for the failure of either Buyer or Seller to perform their obligations pursuant to this DROA.

C-72   **Permission.** The parties grant the Brokerage Firms permission to supply data to the Multiple Listing Service regarding the sales price, terms, and listing status of this transaction for use by other brokers and real estate professionals in making market studies, providing service to the public and advising their clients.

[   ]C-73   **Disclosure of Real Estate Licensing Status.** Hawaii law requires that licensees disclose that they hold a real estate license in any transaction in which they are purchasing or selling real property as a principal, or in which they are buying for themselves, immediate relatives, or an entity in which they have an interest. If applicable, the licensee(s) in this transaction disclose the following: _____

<u>**FACSIMILE (FAX) SIGNATURES AND COUNTERPARTS**</u>

C-74   Fax executed copies of this DROA and any related documents shall be fully binding and effective for all purposes, whether or not originally executed documents are transmitted to Escrow. Fax signatures on documents will be treated the same as original signatures; however, each party agrees to promptly forward original executed documents to Escrow. The parties understand conveyance, mortgage and other recordable documents must be delivered in original form and will not be acceptable if signed only on facsimile.

C-75   This DROA and any addenda and related documents may be executed in any number of counterparts and by different parties in separate counterparts, each of which when so signed shall be deemed to be an original, and all of which taken together shall constitute one and the same document, which shall be binding upon all of the parties, notwithstanding that all of the parties do not sign the original or the same counterpart.

ACCEPTANCE DATE AND OTHER DEFINITIONS

C-76 As used in this DROA, the term "Acceptance Date" means the date on which this DROA becomes binding upon the parties (i.e. when Buyer's Offer is accepted by Seller or Seller's Counter Offer is accepted by Buyer).

C-77 As used in this DROA, the term "day" means a calendar day. All dates and times are based on Hawaiian Standard Time.

C-78 **Time is of the Essence.** Except as otherwise provided in this DROA, time is of the essence in the performance by all parties in their respective obligations under this DROA.

C-79 **Complete Agreement.** This DROA constitutes the entire agreement between Buyer and Seller and supersedes and cancels any and all prior negotiations, representations, warranties, understandings or agreements (both written and oral) of Buyer and Seller. No variation or amendment of this DROA shall be valid or enforceable without written approval by Buyer and Seller. All agreements and representations about the Property must be set forth in writing, and the parties agree that to be effective, any representation made by a Brokerage Firm or any party hereto must be set forth in writing in this DROA, or an amendment hereto or in any required Disclosure Statement. Buyer and Seller shall each hold harmless and release the Brokerage Firms from any claims based upon any alleged representation which is not set forth in writing as stated in this paragraph.

Offer Date _____, _____ AM/PM   Buyer's Name _____

Buyer's Address _____   Signature _____

_____   Buyer's Name _____

Phones _____   Signature _____

Fax _____   E-Mail _____

SECTION D: ACCEPTANCE OR COUNTER OFFER

[ ] **ACCEPTANCE OF OFFER.** Seller agrees to sell the Property at the price and terms offered above and acknowledges receipt of a copy of this Offer and acceptance.

[ ] **COUNTER OFFER.** Seller agrees to sell the Property at the price and terms offered above as amended by the attached Counter Offer and acknowledges receipt of a copy of the Offer.

IN EITHER EVENT:

Seller agrees to pay to_____ (Brokerage Firm) a commission for the sale of the Property in the amount of _____ per the terms of the Listing Contract, or if there is no listing contract, then per other agreement between Seller and Brokerage Firm. Seller instructs Escrow to pay the commission directly to Brokerage Firm at closing in U.S. Dollars. These instructions cannot be changed without the written agreement of the Brokerage Firm and Seller. Seller further consents to Brokerage Firm sharing of the commission with another Brokerage Firm which may have provided services to Buyer. In the event Buyer defaults and Seller retains any of Buyer's deposit or obtains other monetary damages against the Buyer, Seller shall pay one-half thereof to Brokerage Firm as a commission, provided, however, that this amount so paid to Brokerage Firm shall not exceed what would have been the full commission to the Brokerage Firm.

Date _____, _____ AM/PM   Seller's Name _____

Seller's Address _____   Signature _____

_____   Seller's Name _____

Phones _____   Signature _____

Fax _____   E-Mail _____

Seller is a Foreign Person [ ]   Non-Hawaii Resident [ ]   Owner/Occupant [ ]   Other [ ] _____

NOTE: THERE IS NO WARRANTY ON PLAIN LANGUAGE. An effort has been made to put this agreement into plain language. But there is no promise that it is in plain language. In legal terms, THERE IS NO WARRANTY, EXPRESSED OR IMPLIED, THAT THIS AGREEMENT COMPLIES WITH CHAPTER 487A OF THE HAWAII REVISED STATUTES, AS AMENDED. This means that the Hawaii Association of REALTORS® is not liable to any Buyer, Seller, or other person who uses this form for any damages or penalty because of any violation of Chapter 487A. People are cautioned to see their own attorneys about Chapter 487A (and other laws that may apply).

EXCLUSIVE RIGHT-TO-SELL LISTING AGREEMENT
Hawaii Association of Realtors® Standard Form
Revised 9/03 (NC) For Release 11/04

COPYRIGHT AND TRADEMARK NOTICE: This copyrighted Hawaii Association of REALTORS® Standard Form is licensed for use by the entire real estate industry on condition that there shall be no alteration of the printed portions, pagination, or paragraph numbers or breaks. The use of this form is not intended to identify the real estate licensee as a REALTOR®. REALTOR® is a registered collective membership mark which may be used only by real estate licensees who are members of the National Association of REALTORS® and who subscribe to its Code of Ethics.

Listing Broker is[   ] is not[   ] a REALTOR® and member of the National Association of REALTORS®. Seller is aware that the National Association of REALTORS® holds its members accountable for their actions through a strict Professional Code of Ethics, which includes a grievance system to address complaints. Non-members are not required to participate in the grievance system.

TO_____

Name of Real Estate Firm and Address

_____

_____

Name of Real Estate Agent and Phone

TYPE OF PROPERTY

[   ] Residential   [   ] Condo/Co-op   [   ] Land
[   ] Commercial/Indus   [   ] Business/Income

PROPERTY TMK:_____

ADDRESS:_____

_____

I own the property described on the ATTACHED EXHIBIT A or I have the right to sign this listing agreement. I want to hire you to market the property. I offer you a listing on this property from_____ to _____. Either you or I may end the listing with _____ days advance written notice to the other. However, neither of us may end this listing before midnight, _____, unless we both agree to an earlier date. I will list the property at a sales price of $ _____.

I will pay you a commission of _____ of the sales price or exchange value of the real and personal property sold or exchanged (refer to Standard Listing Term regarding Commission). The PROTECTION PERIOD for paragraph 4 and 14 shall be _____ days.

Agency: State law requires real estate licensees in Hawaii, prior to preparing any contract, to disclose orally or in writing to Seller and/or Buyer whom it is that they represent. The licensee could be:

(a) **Seller's Agent.** Represents Seller only, unless a disclosed dual agency exist. Seller's agent owes highest duties to Seller, including confidentiality, loyalty, and utmost care.

(b) **Buyer's Agent.** Represents Buyer only, unless a disclosed dual agency exist. Buyer's agent owes the highest duties to Buyer, including confidentiality, loyalty, and utmost care.

(c) **Seller's Subagent.** Represents Seller only. Seller's subagent owes the same duties to you as does your agent. The subagency arises if Seller offers subagency in the Multiple Listing Service ("MLS") and the cooperating broker accepts your offer. There will be no subagency unless it is specifically agreed to as a special term or as an addendum to this listing agreement and made a part of the DROA.

(d) **Dual Agent.** Represents both Seller and Buyer as clients. To lessen the conflict, the dual agent plays a neutral role in negotiations and must not advance the interest of one party ahead of the other. It commonly arises when other licensees in the listing company have Buyer clients looking for similar types of property. Both Seller and Buyer need to sign a written agreement describing the role of the dual agent. The dual agent acts as a facilitator to bring Seller and Buyer to a common ground of understanding in the negotiations.

Customer. Seller's Agent can also assist Buyer, as a customer. As a customer Buyer is not represented by Seller's Agent. Seller's Agent can assist Buyer in writing the DROA, can present the DROA to Seller, and can report back any acceptance or request for changes to the DROA.

THIS OFFER TO LIST INCLUDES ALL THE STANDARD LISTING TERMS. This offer also includes the following special terms:

_____

_____

By executing this offer to list, I affirmatively state that I own the property and/or hold a power of attorney to execute this document on behalf of the other owners of property.

_____	_____	_____
Date	Signature	Name (print or type)
	_____	_____
	Address	Phone
_____	_____	_____
Date	Signature	Name (print or type)
	_____	_____
	Address	Phone

We accept your offer to list and agree to comply with the terms of this agreement.

_____   _____   By: _____   _____
Name of Real Estate Firm   Phone   Principal Broker or Broker-in-Charge   Date

I have received a filled-in and fully signed copy of this listing agreement and the attached Exhibit A (MLS Data Sheet). _____

Initials of Seller

©Hawaii Association of REALTORS®
Exclusive Right-To-Sell Listing Agreement
RR101 Rev. 9/03

Page 1 of 3

STANDARD LISTING TERMS

DEFINITIONS: The word "I" refers to the person or to all persons (if more than one) signing this listing as property owners. Each person who signs this listing as a property owner is fully responsible, either alone or with the others, for this agreement. The word "you" refers to the real estate firm that accepts the listing. The word "Buyer" refers to any person who has bought or may buy in the future. The word "days" refers to calendar days. "Exclusive Right To Sell" means that I shall list this property only with you and you are entitled to a commission if the property is sold by you, by me, or by anyone else. "Option" is an agreement to keep open, over a set period, an offer to sell or buy property.

1. **ADVERTISING:** You may advertise the property by newspaper, radio, TV, internet, MLS or by placing signs on the property, or by way of any other medium which is in compliance with County, State, or Federal law or any subdivision/CPR covenants.

2. **AGENT'S OBLIGATIONS:** I expect you to try to find a Buyer for the property and to keep me informed of your efforts. You are not responsible for the care or control of the property.

3. **BUYER'S DEPOSIT:** You may accept deposits from any person. If any deposit is forfeited, we shall each get one-half of the deposit. But you shall not get more than what would have been your full commission.

4. **COMMISSION:** I will pay you the commission and any agreed upon general excise tax under this agreement: (a) if a Buyer and I sign a binding sales or exchange contract at any price and terms during the listing period no matter who finds Buyer (even if I find one); (b) if you find a Buyer who is ready, willing and able to pay the asking price and meet the other terms of this listing even if I refuse to sign a written sales contract; (c) if I sign a written sale or exchange contract with any of your prospects within the PROTECTION PERIOD (your prospects include only those persons to whom the property was presented during this listing and who are named on a written list which you must give me within ten days of the end of this listing); or (d) if I withdraw the property from sale before the end of this listing without your consent. I will pay you commission in U.S. dollars.

5. **CONFLICT IN TERMS:** Any handwritten word in this listing prevails over any typed or printed word. Any typed word prevails over any printed. Any special term prevails over any standard term.

6. **COSTS:** I will pay for the following items if required: (a) customary closing costs; (b) my own legal fees (if any); (c) fees for a termite inspection report; (d) costs related to providing documents for homeowner associations; and (e) any other costs agreed to by me.

7. **DISCLOSURE OF MATERIAL FACTS:** I understand that under Hawaii law I am obligated and hereby agree to give a written disclosure statement to a Buyer containing any fact, defect, or condition, past or present, that would be expected to measurably affect the value of the Property to a reasonable person. Such disclosure statement shall be prepared in good faith and with due care and shall disclose all material facts relating to the Property that: (i) are within my knowledge or control; (ii) can be observed from visible, accessible areas; or, (iii) which are required by Section 508D-15 of the Hawaii Revised Statutes.

    Section 508D-15 of the Hawaii Revised Statutes provides that when the Property lies: (i) within the boundaries of a special flood hazard area as officially designated on Flood Insurance Administration maps promulgated by the appropriate Federal agencies for the purposes of determining eligibility for emergency flood insurance programs; (ii) within the boundaries of the noise exposure area shown on maps prepared by the Department of Transportation in accordance with Federal Aviation Regulation Part 150-Airport Noise Compatibility Planning (14 Code of Federal Regulations Part 150) for any public airport; (iii) within the boundaries of the Air Installation Compatibility Use Zone of any Air Force, Army, Navy or Marine Corps airport as officially designated by military authorities; or (iv) within the anticipated inundation areas designated on the Department of Defense's Civil Defense Tsunami Inundation Maps; subject to the availability of maps that designate the four areas by tax map key, I must include this information in the disclosure statement.

    I understand that I may be liable for damages if I purposely or negligently fail to comply with this disclosure law. I further understand that if I fail to provide a written disclosure statement or if your inspection of the Property reveals facts inconsistent with or contradictory to my disclosure statement or the inspection of a third party, Hawaii law requires that you disclose those facts to me, to Buyer and to Buyer's agent. This obligation of disclosure limits your agency duty of confidentiality. It is also my understanding that at any time prior to closing I am required to provide an amended disclosure statement if that information is incomplete or inaccurate and it directly, substantially, and adversely affects the value of the Property. This amended disclosure statement shall be delivered to Buyer within ten (10) days of my discovery and in no event later than twelve noon on the last business day prior to the recorded sale of the Property.

8. **ESCROW:** I agree to use a bonded company to help with the conveyance of this property. I hereby instruct Escrow to pay your commission and any agreed upon general excise tax directly to you at closing. I agree that I cannot change this instruction without your written consent.

9. **FAIR HOUSING LAWS:** You and I will both comply with state and federal antidiscrimination laws. I understand that it is illegal to discriminate against prospective Buyers on the basis of sex, race, religion, color, national origin, handicap, and familial status.

10. **FIRPTA: Withholding Required If Seller Is A Foreign Person.** Under the Internal Revenue Code, if Seller is a foreign person or entity (non-resident alien, corporation, partnership, trust or estate), then Buyer is, generally, required to withhold a specified percentage of the "amount realized" by Seller on the sale of the property and forward the amount to the Internal Revenue Service ("IRS"). Such withholding may not be required if Seller obtains and provides Buyer with an authorized exemption or waiver from withholding. **Seller must complete the authorized exemption or waiver form, or Escrow will withhold/collect from Seller the required amount at closing and forward it to the IRS.**

SELLER'S INITIALS & DATE

BROKER'S INITIALS & DATE

©Hawaii Association of REALTORS®   Page 2 of 3   RR101 Rev. 9/03 (NC) For Release 11/04

11.   **HARPTA: Withholding Required If Seller Is A Non-Resident Of The State Of Hawaii.** Under Hawaii law, if Seller is a non-resident person or entity (corporation, partnership, trust or estate) of the State of Hawaii, Buyer must withhold a specified percentage of the "amount realized" by Seller on the sale of the property and forward the amount with the appropriate form to the State Department of Taxation. Such withholding may not be required if Seller obtains and provides Buyer with an authorized exemption of waiver from withholding. **Seller must complete the authorized exemption or waiver form, or Escrow will withhold/collect from Seller the required amount at closing and forward it to the State Department of Taxation.**

12.   **LEASEHOLD DISCLOSURE:** If the property is leasehold, I agree to provide at my expense a leasehold disclosure as required by Hawaii State law. I authorize the listing agent to order such a disclosure from a qualified professional, if such professional service is available.

13.   **MEDIATION AND ARBITRATION:** If any dispute or claim in law or equity arises out of this agreement, and you and I are unable to resolve the dispute ourselves, I agree to attempt in good faith to settle such dispute or claim by non-binding mediation through the Local Board of REALTORS® or, in the event the Local Board of REALTORS® does not provide mediation services, then through a mutually agreed upon mediator. If the mediation is not successful, then I will consider arbitration and may seek legal counsel to make this determination. It is understood that if both of us are involuntarily named as defendants in a lawsuit by a third party in any matter arising out of this agreement, this paragraph shall no longer be binding on either of us.

14.   **OPTIONS:** I will pay you one-half of the option premium, if I give any person an option during the listing period. If I give an option to any of your prospects within the PROTECTION PERIOD, I will likewise pay you one-half of the option premium. But I will not pay you more than what would have been your full commission. I will pay the balance, if any, of my commission and any agreed upon general excise tax whenever the option is exercised, even after the listing period. I will not owe you any more commission and any agreed upon general excise tax if an option expires.

15.   **OTHER BROKERS:** You may put the listing and other data in the MLS. You and other MLS members may use this information to make market studies, give service to the public and advise clients or customers. You may work with and share your commission with other brokers to market the property.

16.   **PROPERTY INFORMATION:** I have read the information on the attached Exhibit A, which is the MLS Data Sheet. As far as I know the facts on Exhibit A are correct. If any facts on the MLS Data Sheet are known to me to be incorrect or incomplete, I will be fully responsible for any actions and costs which may result.

17.   **PROSPECTS FROM PRIOR LISTINGS:** When I sign this listing, I will give you a copy of any prospect lists given to me from any earlier listing with any broker. If the other broker earns a commission because of a sale to any prospect on such a list, I will not pay you any commission.

18.   **RELEASE OF INFORMATION:** You and Escrow may get any information regarding mortgage balances, lease rents, maintenance fees, property management, collection accounts, property taxes or like items. I hereby authorize any person having such information to give it to you and Escrow. You may give such information to any prospective Buyer.

19.   **SELLER'S OBLIGATIONS:** (a) Assistance. I will help you sell the property. I will prepare the property for showings and "open houses". I will give you any information, documents, access, and keys you need. I will let any specialist (termite inspectors, appraisers, surveyors, etc.) inspect the property. You may place a lock box or electronic key device on the property to allow access for showings and inspections. (b) Securing Valuables. I agree to secure all of those items which I consider valuable. If I have a tenant residing on the property, I will notify the tenant to secure their valuables. I further understand that you will not be responsible for securing or protecting any of my tenant's valuables. (c) I understand that you recommend that I consult my attorney, accountant, or any professional expert within those fields of question about the sale of this property. I acknowledge that I am not relying upon you for any of the foregoing services or advice.

20.   **SEX OFFENDER REGISTRATION ("Megan's Law"):** I understand that Hawaii has enacted a law requiring sex offenders to register with the State Attorney General's office. I also understand that you are not making any representations as to whether or not the public has access to this information. You are not required by law to obtain information regarding sex offenders for me.

NOTE: THERE IS NO WARRANTY ON PLAIN LANGUAGE. An effort has been made to put this agreement into plain language. But there is no promise that it is in plain language. In legal terms, THERE IS NO WARRANTY, EXPRESSED OR IMPLIED, THAT THIS AGREEMENT COMPLIES WITH CHAPTER 487A OF THE HAWAII REVISED STATUTES, AS AMENDED. This means that the Hawaii Association of REALTORS® is not liable to any Seller, or other person who uses this form for any damages or penalty because of any violation of Chapter 487A. People are cautioned to see their own attorneys about Chapter 487A (and other laws that may apply).

SELLER'S INITIALS & DATE   BROKER'S INITIALS & DATE

©Hawaii Association of REALTORS®   Page 3 of 3   RR101 Rev. 9/03 (NC) For Release 11/04

EXISTING "AS IS" CONDITION ADDENDUM
Hawaii Association of Realtors® Standard Form
Revised 9/03 (NC) For Release 11/04

COPYRIGHT AND TRADEMARK NOTICE: This copyrighted Hawaii Association of REALTORS® Standard Form is licensed for use by the entire real estate industry on condition that there shall be no alteration of the printed portions, pagination, or paragraph numbers or breaks. The use of this form is not intended to identify the real estate licensee as a REALTOR®. REALTOR® is a registered collective membership mark which may be used only by real estate licensees who are members of the National Association of REALTORS® and who subscribe to its Code of Ethics.

EXISTING "AS IS" CONDITION ADDENDUM is made a part of DROA.

DROA Reference Date: _____

Property Reference _____
_____
Address

Tax Map Key: Div _____ /Zone _____ /Sec _____ /Plat _____ /Parcel _____ /CPR _____ (if applicable).

Purpose of "AS IS" Addendum: Property is being sold in its existing condition. Except as may be agreed to elsewhere in DROA, Seller will make no repairs and will convey Property without any representations or warranties, either expressed or implied.

Seller's Responsibilities: By selling Property in **Existing "AS IS" Condition**, Seller remains obligated to disclose in writing any known defects or material facts of Property or improvements. However, there may be material facts of which Seller is not aware which qualified experts may be able to discover or latent or hidden defects which time may reveal. Seller is not responsible for latent defects, hidden defects, or defects which time may reveal.

Buyer's Rights and Responsibilities: Buyer is advised to obtain professional property inspection(s) and to inspect all public records relating to Property within the time frames of the DROA as agreed to by Buyer and Seller. Should Buyer find Property unacceptable, Buyer has the right to cancel DROA prior to the expiration of Term C-51 **"Inspection of Property"** time frame as stated in DROA. Buyer will be provided the opportunity to conduct a final walk through of Property prior to recordation <u>only</u> to assess that Property is in no worse condition and repair than it was in upon removal of "Inspection of Property" Contingency.

Unless otherwise agreed to by Buyer and Seller, **Existing "AS IS" Condition Addendum** does not eliminate the termite inspection report, staking and/or survey.

The improvements on Property may not conform to current building codes and/or may not have all required building permits. Buyer is strongly advised to inspect all public records, have a professional home inspection to ascertain the exact condition of Property, and make reasonable inquiry regarding individual concerns before Term C-51 **"Inspection of Property"** contingency deadline as stated in DROA.

Buyer acknowledges that Property is being sold "AS IS", with knowledge of the conditions disclosed by Seller and/or discovered during inspection(s) of Property. Buyer understands and agrees that all land and improvements, (including but not limited to the roof, walls, foundations, soils, plumbing, electrical and mechanical systems, etc.) real property, and personal property (if any) will be sold in **Existing "AS IS" Condition, WITHOUT WARRANTY OR REPRESENTATIONS, EXPRESSED OR IMPLIED** except as may be otherwise stated in DROA.

Buyer must approve or disapprove of Property condition by the contingency deadline. If said deadline expires, non-response is considered approval and acceptance of Property condition.

Buyer understands and agrees to give up, waive and relinquish all rights to assert any claim, demand, proceeding or lawsuit of any kind against Seller and/or real estate agents involved with respect to the condition of the land, improvements and any personal property, except for claims which are based upon Seller's and/or real estate agent's concealment of material facts and defects, which those parties are required to disclose by law.

Additional Comments: _____
_____
_____
_____
_____

BUYER SHOULD NOT SIGN ADDENDUM UNLESS BUYER HAS FIRST READ AND UNDERSTOOD IT. BUYER IS ADVISED TO CONSULT WITH AN ATTORNEY REGARDING EXISTING "AS IS" CONDITION ADDENDUM.

_____ _____   _____ _____
Buyer   Date   Seller   Date

_____ _____   _____ _____
Buyer   Date   Seller   Date

NOTE: THERE IS NO WARRANTY ON PLAIN LANGUAGE. An effort has been made to put this agreement into plain language. But there is no promise that it is in plain language. In legal terms, THERE IS NO WARRANTY, EXPRESSED OR IMPLIED, THAT THIS AGREEMENT COMPLIES WITH CHAPTER 487A OF THE HAWAII REVISED STATUTES, AS AMENDED. This means that the Hawaii Association of REALTORS® is not liable to any Buyer, Seller, or other person who uses this form for any damages or penalty because of any violation of Chapter 487A. People are cautioned to see their own attorneys about Chapter 487A (and other laws that may apply)

©Hawaii Association of REALTORS®
Existing "AS IS" Condition Addendum
RR213 Rev. 9/03

OPTION AGREEMENT INPUT FORM
Hawaii Association of Realtors® Standard Form
Revised 9/03 (NC)   For Release 11/04

COPYRIGHT AND TRADEMARK NOTICE: This copyrighted Hawaii Association of REALTORS® Standard Form is licensed for use by the entire real estate industry on condition that there shall be no alteration of the printed portions, pagination, or paragraph numbers or breaks. The use of this form is not intended to identify the real estate licensee as a REALTOR®. REALTOR® is a registered collective membership mark which may be used only by real estate licensees who are members of the National Association of REALTORS® and who subscribe to its Code of Ethics.

This information is to be supplied to an attorney for the drafting of an Option Agreement between Buyer/Optionee and Seller/Optionor. The Option Agreement prepared by the attorney, is subject to review and approval of Buyer/Optionee, Seller/Optionor and their attorneys, if any.

Buyer/Optionee: _____

Address _____

Seller/Optionor: _____

Address: _____

1. Effective date of Option: _____

2. Option Consideration $_____ (must be stated)   Option consideration to be applied towards the purchase price if the Option is exercised [   ] No   [   ] Yes, and amount $_____

3. Property Description: Tax Map Key Div. _____ /Zone _____ /Sec. _____ /Plat _____ /Parcel _____ /CPR _____ (if applicable)
Location: _____ Square footage. _____

[   ] Fee Simple   [   ] Leasehold, Improvements _____
_____

4. Purchase Price: $ _____

5. Terms and Condition of Purchase, if Option is exercised: attach a Deposit Receipt Offer & Acceptance form (DROA) to spell out details of purchase. Include language that "this contract is effective only in the event the option to purchase, incorporated herein by reference, is exercised". Address "due on sale" clause, if applicable in DROA

6. Deadline to exercise Option (Date & Time) _____. Written notice to exercise Option shall be delivered or mailed to: _____ [   ] Additional deposit required at time of notice to open escrow $ _____

7. Escrowed by: _____

[   ] Conveyance document   [   ] Holding Escrow to be established   [   ] Option to be recorded   [   ] Release of Option

8. Expiration of Option Terms _____ Upon expiration of Option, Buyer/Optionee to vacate the Property if this is an Option with Lease. (Date & Time) _____ In the event Option is not exercised by expiration date, Seller/Optionor shall retain the Option Consideration and Buyer/Optionee shall have no further interest in Property.

9. If this is a Lease with Option to Purchase, attach a rental agreement which spells out the terms of Lease - date of occupancy, length of Lease, responsibility for utilities, etc. The Landlord-Tenant Code will apply. Rent paid to be applied to the purchase price, if the Option to Purchase is exercised: [   ] No   [   ] Yes, and amount $ _____

10. Transferable Option [   ] can   [   ] cannot be sold, assigned or conveyed. If transferable, allowed [   ] with   [   ] without written consent of Seller/Optionor. Lease, if applicable, [   ] can   [   ] cannot be assigned without the Option.

11. Commissions/Brokers' Fees [   ] Seller/Optionor   [   ] Buyer/Optionee herein agrees to pay commissions/brokers' fees in the amount of $ _____ directly to _____
_____ upon execution of an Option Agreement and the balance of the commission stated in the DROA shall be paid at closing of escrow if the Option is exercised

12. Preparation of Option Agreement. Option Agreement shall be prepared by [   ] Seller/Optionor's attorney   [   ] Buyer/Optionee's attorney. Each party will pay their own attorneys fees.

We, the undersigned, approve the above stated terms and conditions and request that the terms be incorporated into an Option Agreement which we will review and, if approved by us and our attorneys, execute on _____, _____.

DATED at _____, _____ this _____ day of _____, _____.

_____   _____
Buyer/Optionee   Seller/Optionor

NOTE: THERE IS NO WARRANTY ON PLAIN LANGUAGE. An effort has been made to put this agreement into plain language. But there is no promise that it is in plain language. In legal terms, THERE IS NO WARRANTY, EXPRESSED OR IMPLIED, THAT THIS AGREEMENT COMPLIES WITH CHAPTER 487A OF THE HAWAII REVISED STATUTES, AS AMENDED. This means that the Hawaii Association of REALTORS® is not liable to any Buyer, Seller, or other person who uses this form for any damages or penalty because of any violation of Chapter 487A. People are cautioned to see their own attorneys about Chapter 487A (and other laws that may apply).

©Hawaii Association of REALTORS®
Option Agreement Input Form
RR303 Rev 9/03

PURCHASE MONEY MORTGAGE ADDENDUM
Hawaii Association of Realtors® Standard Form
Revised 9/03 (NC) For Release 11/04

Purchase Money Mortgage Addendum is made a part of DROA

DROA Reference Date: _____

Property Reference. _____
                                                    Address

Tax Map Key: Div _____/Zone _____/Sec. _____/Plat _____/Parcel _____/CPR _____ (if applicable).

BUYER (BORROWER). SELLER (LENDER).

LOAN AGREEMENT: Seller and Buyer hereby agree to all terms and conditions herein set forth unless otherwise indicated.
  1. **Loan.** Seller will make a loan to Buyer to buy Property.
    [ ] First Mortgage
    [ ] Second Mortgage
    [ ] Other _____
  2. **Note and Mortgage.** Seller will convey title to Buyer and Buyer will give Seller a Note and Mortgage to secure payment of the Loan
  3. **Credit Check and Information.** Seller requires the following information from Buyer within _____ days from acceptance of DROA.
    [ ] Credit Report   [ ] Tax return(s)_____ year(s)
    [ ] Current financial statement   [ ] Other _____

    • If Buyer fails to provide Seller the Credit Report and/or other information within the time required, Seller may elect to terminate DROA, pursuant to Paragraphs C-20 and C-21.
    • Within _____ days after receipt and after reasonable review of all financial information provided, Seller may deem the credit worthiness of Buyer unacceptable and may terminate the DROA pursuant to Paragraphs C-20 and C-21 of DROA.
    • In the event DROA is terminated, Seller agrees to return all documents to Buyer.

SPECIFIC TERMS OF LOAN:
  1. **Loan Amount.** The Principal of Loan is $ _____
  2. **Interest.** Annual simple interest rate will be _____ % percent
    [ ] Other _____
    _____

  3. **Payment:**
    [ ] Monthly interest only $_____   [ ] Annually interest only $_____
    [ ] Quarterly interest only $_____   [ ] Monthly principal and interest $_____
    [ ] Other: _____

  4. **Term of Loan.** Loan must be paid in full by _____.
PREPAYMENT: Prepayment means payment of the entire or any portion of Loan before it is due.
Prepayment penalty [ ] No [ ] Yes (describe)._____
BUYER TO MAKE PAYMENTS TO:
[ ] Seller directly (and Seller to provide Buyer with annual accounting within 30 days of year end.)
[ ] a licensed collection agency/financial institution designated by Seller
COSTS FOR THE COLLECTION AGENCY OR FINANCIAL INSTITUTION (IF APPLICABLE) WILL BE:
[ ] shared equally between Buyer and Seller
[ ] (describe) _____

LATE PAYMENT AND FEES: Any payment not received within _____ days after it is due will be a "Late Payment". For each Late Payment, Buyer shall promptly pay Seller a late fee of $_____ or _____ % of payment then due.
DEFAULT: Default means any Late Payment or other failure by Buyer to keep Buyer's promises made in Note and Mortgage. For each default, Seller may exercise customary remedies, including foreclosure.

_____
BUYER'S INITIALS & DATE

Page 1 of 2

_____
SELLER'S INITIALS & DATE

TRANSFER OF MORTGAGED PROPERTY/DUE ON SALE:
[   ] Option 1: If Buyer transfers the Property to someone else (a "transferee"), Seller may require immediate payment in full of the Note and Mortgage ("due on sale" clause).
[   ] Option 2: Buyer may transfer the Property without Seller's consent. There will be no "due on sale" clause in the Mortgage.
[   ] Option 3: Buyer may transfer the Property with the consent of Seller. Seller may not unreasonably withhold consent. However, Seller may condition the consent on the credit worthiness and payment capacity of the proposed transferee. Seller may not change any terms of Note or Mortgage or charge for the consent, except for $_____

OTHER MORTGAGES: Buyer may:
[   ] further mortgage Property subject to the following conditions: _____
[   ] not further mortgage Property

PERSONAL PROPERTY: Items of personal property are included in the sale to Buyer. Items are part of Seller's security.
[   ] Yes   [   ] No

DOCUMENT PREPARATION: The Note and Mortgage will be drafted by an attorney:
[   ] selected by escrow
[   ] (name Attorney): _____

ADDITIONAL PROVISIONS: _____
_____

INSURANCE: By the time of recording, Buyer will obtain and maintain insurance for the duration of the mortgage as follows (check those that apply):
[   ] Fire and extended peril coverage (with inflation guard) in an amount at least equal to the full replacement costs of the insurable improvements on Property;
[   ] Comprehensive public liability insurance as customarily provided in Hawaii for homeowners insurance;
[   ] Hurricane Property Insurance Policy;
[   ] Flood insurance, if Property is within the Flood zone eligible for federally subsidized flood insurance.
Insurance Policies must name Seller and Buyer and any lessor and/or other mortgagee as insureds
If Property is a condominium or cooperative apartment, these insurance requirements may be met in part by the master insurance policy riders for the condominium or cooperative.

ALTERATIONS AND IMPROVEMENTS: Buyer may not make additions or major improvements to Property without Seller's written consent. Seller has the right to inspect plans and specifications and may condition Seller's consent on Buyer's obtaining required building permits, consents of Condominium Owner's and/or Homeowner's Association, lenders, or lessors, if any, plus evidence of Buyer's adequate financing and/or bonding to pay for the improvements.

RELEASE: When the loan is paid in full, Seller shall, at Seller's expense, promptly provide Buyer with a Release of Mortgage in recordable form

PLEASE NOTE: No representation is made as to the legal validity of any provision in Addendum or the adequacy of any provisions in any specific transaction. Addendum should not be used in complex transactions

Buyer and Seller acknowledge that they have read, understand and agree to the terms and conditions of this PURCHASE MONEY MORTGAGE ADDENDUM

SAMPLE

Buyer	Date	Seller	Date

Buyer	Date	Seller	Date

NOTE: THERE IS NO WARRANTY ON PLAIN LANGUAGE. An effort has been made to put this agreement into plain language. But there is no promise that it is in plain language. In legal terms, THERE IS NO WARRANTY, EXPRESSED OR IMPLIED, THAT THIS AGREEMENT COMPLIES WITH CHAPTER 487A OF THE HAWAII REVISED STATUTES, AS AMENDED. This means that the Hawaii Association of REALTORS® is not liable to any Buyer, Seller, or other person who uses this form for any damages or penalty because of any violation of Chapter 487A. People are cautioned to see their own attorneys about Chapter 487A (and other laws that may apply)

SELLER'S REAL PROPERTY DISCLOSURE STATEMENT
SINGLE FAMILY RESIDENCE
Hawaii Association of Realtors® Standard Form
Revised 6/04 (NC)   For Release 11/04

COPYRIGHT AND TRADEMARK NOTICE: This copyrighted Hawaii Association of REALTORS® Standard Form is licensed for use by the entire real estate industry on condition that there shall be no alteration of the printed portions, pagination, or paragraph numbers or breaks. The use of this form is not intended to identify the real estate licensee as a REALTOR®. REALTOR® is a registered collective membership mark which may be used only by real estate licensees who are members of the National Association of REALTORS® and who subscribe to its Code of Ethics.

Information Obtained from Public Records
(May Be Completed by Listing Broker)

Seller(s) Name(s) (All on Title):_____

Property Reference: _____

Tax Map Key: Div. _____/Zone _____/Sec. _____/Plat _____/Parcel _____/CPR _____ (if applicable).

Land: Area _____ Zone _____ [   ] FS [   ] LH (Disclosure to be provided) Flood Zone _____

Broker/Salesperson: _____ Company: _____

Purpose of Disclosure Statement: Under Hawaii law, a Seller is obligated to fully and accurately disclose in writing to a Buyer any fact, defect or condition, past or present, that would be expected to measurably affect the value of the Property to a reasonable person. This statement is intended to assist Seller in organizing the facts to be presented to Buyer and to provide Buyer with notice concerning the condition of Property and to assist Buyer in evaluating Property. Seller's agent, Buyer and Buyer's agent may rely on Seller's answers. It is important that Seller exercise due care in preparing responses and that responses are made in good faith, are truthful and complete to the best of Seller's knowledge. **THIS DISCLOSURE STATEMENT IS NOT A WARRANTY OF ANY KIND BY SELLER OR BY ANY AGENT REPRESENTING SELLER OF PROPERTY. THIS STATEMENT IS NOT A SUBSTITUTE FOR ANY EXPERT INSPECTION, PROFESSIONAL ADVICE, OR WARRANTY THAT BUYER MAY WISH TO OBTAIN.**

BUYERS ARE ADVISED TO OBTAIN BUYER'S OWN PUBLIC RECORDS, PROFESSIONAL ADVICE AND/OR HAVE AN EXPERT INSPECT PROPERTY. SELLER MAY WISH TO OBTAIN PROFESSIONAL ADVICE AND/OR HAVE AN EXPERT INSPECT PROPERTY.

MUST be completed by Seller <u>Only</u>

Seller's Statement: This is a statement concerning information relating to the condition of Property that: (i) are within the knowledge or control of Seller; (ii) can be observed from visible, accessible areas; or (iii) which are required by Section 508D-15 of the Hawaii Revised Statutes. Seller may be ignorant of problems affecting Property, and Buyer should take care to protect Buyer's own interests by conducting thorough inspections and obtaining expert help in evaluating Property. Unless Buyer has been otherwise advised, Seller has not conducted any inspection of generally inaccessible areas of Property. There may be material facts of which Seller is not aware which qualified experts may be able to discover or time may reveal. The representations made below are made by Seller and are not the representations of Seller's agent. This form and the disclosures made by Seller are provided exclusively to Buyers involved in this transaction only and do not apply to any subsequent sales *not* involving this Seller. Seller has [   ] has not [   ] seen Property. Period of ownership from _____ to _____.

Instructions to Seller: (1) Answer <u>ALL</u> questions. (2) Identify and clearly explain any material facts concerning Property that are known to you. (3) Attach additional pages with your signature if additional space is needed. (4) Complete this form yourself. (5) Complete a separate form for each separate structure. (6) NTMK means NOT TO MY KNOWLEDGE. (7) If the item does not apply to Property, line it out.

A. Are you aware of any current or past defects/malfunctions/major repairs with respect to:
If answer is "yes", using the SAME number below, describe in the space provided.

	YES	NTMK			YES	NTMK			YES	NTMK	
(1)	[ ]	[ ]	Appliances	(10)	[ ]	[ ]	Fans or Air Movers	(20)	[ ]	[ ]	Slabs
(2)	[ ]	[ ]	Bathtubs/Showers and	(11)	[ ]	[ ]	Fireplace/Chimney	(21)	[ ]	[ ]	Smoke Detectors
			Basins	(12)	[ ]	[ ]	Floors/Floor Coverings	(22)	[ ]	[ ]	Solar Water Heating
(3)	[ ]	[ ]	Ceilings	(13)	[ ]	[ ]	Foundation	(23)	[ ]	[ ]	Spa
(4)	[ ]	[ ]	Cooling/Heating	(14)	[ ]	[ ]	Gutters	(24)	[ ]	[ ]	Swimming Pool
(5)	[ ]	[ ]	Decking	(15)	[ ]	[ ]	Interior Walls	(25)	[ ]	[ ]	Walkways
(6)	[ ]	[ ]	Doors/Door Bell	(16)	[ ]	[ ]	Other Water Features	(26)	[ ]	[ ]	Walls/Fences
(7)	[ ]	[ ]	Driveways	(17)	[ ]	[ ]	Plumbing	(27)	[ ]	[ ]	Windows/Skylight
(8)	[ ]	[ ]	Electrical Systems	(18)	[ ]	[ ]	Roofs	(28)	[ ]	[ ]	Other _____
(9)	[ ]	[ ]	Exterior Walls	(19)	[ ]	[ ]	Security Systems				

_____   _____
    BUYER'S INITIALS & DATE   SELLER'S INITIALS & DATE

Property Reference:_____

Number of Question answered "Yes" and Explain: _____

_____
_____
_____
_____
_____
_____
_____
_____
_____

Have you given any release or waiver of liability, or release from a warranty to any government agency, contractor, engineer, architect, land surveyor, or landscape architect, for any defect, mistake, or omission in the design or construction of the Property?

If the answer is "Yes," describe below:

_____
_____
_____
_____
_____

B. Do any of the following conditions exist on Property?
If answer is "yes", using the SAME number below, describe in the space provided.

	YES	NO	NTMK	
29)	[ ]	[ ]	[ ]	Does any other party have an unrecorded interest in this Property and/or a say in its disposition?
30)	[ ]	[ ]	[ ]	Are there any lawsuits or foreclosure actions affecting this Property?
31)	[ ]	[ ]	[ ]	Are there any easements affecting this Property?
32)	[ ]	[ ]	[ ]	Are there any roadways, driveways, walls, fences, and/or other improvements which are shared with adjoining land owners?
32a)	[ ]	[ ]	[ ]	(a) Are there any known encroachments?
32b)	[ ]	[ ]	[ ]	(b) Are there any written agreements concerning these items?
33)	[ ]	[ ]	[ ]	Are there substances, materials, or products which may be an environmental hazard such as, but not limited to, asbestos, formaldehyde, radon gas, lead-based paint, fuel or chemical storage tanks, contaminated soil or water on this subject Property?
34)	[ ]	[ ]	[ ]	Is there filled land on this Property?
35)	[ ]	[ ]	[ ]	Is there any settling or slippage, sliding, subsidence, or other soil problems?
36)	[ ]	[ ]	[ ]	Are there any drainage, water infiltration, seepage, flooding, or grading problems?
37)	[ ]	[ ]	[ ]	Are there, or have there been, any visible signs of mold, mildew and/or fungus in or about this Property?
38)	[ ]	[ ]	[ ]	Were the original improvements built without building permits?
38a)	[ ]	[ ]	[ ]	(a) Were any additions, structural modifications, or alternations made without building permits?
38b)	[ ]	[ ]	[ ]	(b) If any improvements were built within the last 12 months, did you fail to file the Notice of Completion?
38c)	[ ]	[ ]	[ ]	(c) If you have not obtained all necessary permits for additions and/or structural changes or remodeling, are you willing to obtain them prior to closing?
39)	[ ]	[ ]	[ ]	Were any of the improvements to this Property built under an owner-builder permit?
39a)	[ ]	[ ]	[ ]	(a) Is the Seller/Builder a licensed contractor who is providing warranties?
39b)	⟶			(b) Date of Completion of the improvements covered under the owner-builder permit: _____
40)	[ ]	[ ]	[ ]	Has the roof ever been repaired?
40a)	⟶			(a) If so, when was it repaired and by whom? _____
40b)	⟶			(b) What is the age of the roof? _____
40c)	[ ]	[ ]	[ ]	(c) Are there any transferable warranties? If yes, date of expiration: _____
41)	[ ]	[ ]	[ ]	Are there any violations of government regulations/ordinances related to this Property?
41a)	[ ]	[ ]	[ ]	(a) Are there any zoning or setback violations and/or citations?
41b)	[ ]	[ ]	[ ]	(b) Are there any nonconforming uses or restrictions on rebuilding?
42)	[ ]	[ ]	[ ]	Are there any violations of existing land leases?
43)	[ ]	[ ]	[ ]	Is this Property subject to Covenants, Conditions and Restrictions (CC&Rs)?
43a)	[ ]	[ ]	[ ]	(a) Are there any violations of the Covenants, Conditions and Restrictions covering this Property?
44)	[ ]	[ ]	[ ]	Are there any rental agreements affecting this Property?
44a)	[ ]	[ ]	[ ]	(a) Are there any violations of the rental agreements?
45)	[ ]	[ ]	[ ]	Is there any presence of wood boring insects/termites in the improvements?
45a)	[ ]	[ ]	[ ]	(a) Is there any known termite damage in the improvements?
45b)	[ ]	[ ]	[ ]	(b) Are there any past repairs made due to wood boring insect/termite damage?
46)	[ ]	[ ]	[ ]	Has there been any termite treatment?
46a)	⟶			(a) type and date of treatment _____

_____
BUYER'S INITIALS & DATE   SELLER'S INITIALS & DATE

Property Reference:_____

46b)	[ ]	[ ]	[ ]	(b) Are there any warranties? _____ Expiration Date(s):_____
47)	[ ]	[ ]	[ ]	Is there any existing dry rot or other structural damage?
48)	[ ]	[ ]	[ ]	Is the location of this Property in a tsunami (tidal wave) inundation area and/or flood zone?
49)	[ ]	[ ]	[ ]	Is this Property located in volcanic hazard Zone 1 or 2? (Only applicable to Island of Hawaii)
50)	[ ]	[ ]	[ ]	Is there any existing or past damage to this Property or any of the structures from earthquake, fire, floods, landslides, tsunami, volcanic activity, or winds?
51)	[ ]	[ ]	[ ]	Is this Property subject to air pollution?
52)	[ ]	[ ]	[ ]	Is this Property located in an aircraft path and/or does it experience regular excessive aircraft noise?
52a)	[ ]	[ ]	[ ]	(a) Is this Property exposed to other types of recurring excessive noise (ie. night club, school, etc.)?
53)	[ ]	[ ]	[ ]	Is this Property part of a Condominium Property Regime (CPR)?
53a)	[ ]	[ ]	[ ]	(a) Has a Final Public Report been issued?
53b)	[ ]	[ ]	[ ]	(b) Are there any "common area" facilities (such as pools, tennis courts, walkways, or other areas) co-owned in undivided interest with others?
54)	[ ]	[ ]	[ ]	Is this Property subject to a Homeowners' and/or Community Association?
54a)	⎯⎯⎯⎯⎯⎯⟶			(a) If yes, what are the fees and payments? _____
54b)	[ ]	[ ]	[ ]	(b) Is membership mandatory?
55)	[ ]	[ ]	[ ]	Do you have hazard insurance on this Property?
56)	[ ]	[ ]	[ ]	Are you aware of any adverse conditions existing in this general neighborhood/area (such as pesticides, soil problems, irrigation, etc.)?
57)	[ ]	[ ]	[ ]	Is there any additional information you should disclose (examples: history of homicide, felony, or suicide occurring on this Property, pending development in the area, road widening projects; zoning changes; etc.)?
58)	[ ]	[ ]	[ ]	Is this Property located within the boundaries of the Air Installation Compatibility Use Zone of any Air Force, Army, Navy, or Marine Corps airport as officially designated by military authorities?

Number of question answered "Yes" and Explain: _____

SAMPLE

_____
BUYER'S INITIALS & DATE

_____
SELLER'S INITIALS & DATE

Property Reference:_____

Page 3 of 4

RR102 Rev. 6/04 (NC) For Release 11/04

C. Utilities:
If answer is "yes", using the SAME number below, describe in the space provided.

59)   Source of Water Supply:
      [   ] Public   [   ] Private   [   ] Well   [   ] Other_____
      [   ] Catchment: Type _____ Capacity _____ Age_____ Condition_____
      Any problems regarding filters, pumps, covers, liners, etc.? _____

60)   Does this Property have water conserving fixtures?   [   ] No   [   ] Yes If applicable, check box and note location below.

      [   ] Ultra low flush toilets   [   ] Low-flow showerheads
      [   ] Low-flow bathroom aerator   [   ] Low-flow kitchen aerator

61)   Waste Water/Sewage System:
      [   ] Public: Connected   [   ] Yes   [   ] No   If no, is connection required upon transfer?   [   ] Yes   [   ] No
      [   ] Private
      [   ] Cesspool or Septic System: Type _____ Last Pumped _____ How Often?_____
      Location: _____
      Any problems? If so, describe below.
62)   Source of Electrical Power:
      [   ] Public   [   ] Other:_____

63)   Source of Gas Power: [   ] Piped   [   ] Propane Tank
64)   Telephone Service: [   ] Yes   [   ] No   [   ] Only party line
65)   Television Cable Service: [   ] Yes   [   ] No   [   ] Not available

Number of Question answered "Yes" and Explain: _____

_____
_____
_____
_____
_____
_____
_____
_____
_____
_____
_____
_____
_____
_____
_____

Under Hawaii law, unless otherwise agreed in the DROA, Buyer shall have fifteen (15) calendar days from the date of receiving the Disclosure Statement to examine the Disclosure Statement or to rescind the DROA. Such rescission must be made in writing and provided to Seller directly or Seller's agent. If timely written notice is provided, then all deposits made by Buyer shall be immediately returned to Buyer.

Seller gives permission to any Broker to provide this statement to any Buyer whose identity has been made known to Seller, a lending institution, or the escrow company involved in the transaction between the parties.

_____   _____
SELLER   DATE   SELLER   DATE

NOTE: THERE IS NO WARRANTY ON PLAIN LANGUAGE. An effort has been made to put this agreement into plain language. But there is no promise that it is in plain language. In legal terms, THERE IS NO WARRANTY, EXPRESSED OR IMPLIED, THAT THIS AGREEMENT COMPLIES WITH CHAPTER 487A OF THE HAWAII REVISED STATUTES, AS AMENDED. This means that the Hawaii Association of REALTORS® is not liable to any Buyer, Seller, or other person who uses this form for any damages or penalty because of any violation of Chapter 487A. People are cautioned to see their own attorneys about Chapter 487A (and other laws that may apply).

_____   _____
      BUYER'S INITIALS & DATE   SELLER'S INITIALS & DATE

Property Reference:_____

©Hawaii Association of REALTORS®   Page 4 of 4   RR102 Rev. 6/04 (NC) For Release 11/04

SELLER'S REAL PROPERTY DISCLOSURE STATEMENT
Condominium/Co-op/PUD and other Homeowner Organizations
Hawaii Association of Realtors® Standard Form
Revised 6/04 (NC) For Release 11/04

COPYRIGHT AND TRADEMARK NOTICE: This copyrighted Hawaii Association of REALTORS® Standard Form is licensed for use by the entire real estate industry on condition that there shall be no alteration of the printed portions, pagination, or paragraph numbers or breaks. The use of this form is not intended to identify the real estate licensee as a REALTOR®. REALTOR® is a registered collective membership mark which may be used only by real estate licensees who are members of the National Association of REALTORS® and who subscribe to its Code of Ethics.

Information Obtained from Public Records
(May Be Completed by Listing Broker)

Seller(s) Name(s) (All on Title): _____

Property Reference _____

Tax Map Key: Div _____ /Zone _____ /Sec _____ /Plat _____ /Parcel _____ /CPR _____ (if applicable).

Public Report # _____ Final Report Date _____ [   ] FS   [   ] LH (Disclosure to be Provided)

Current Legal Name of Project: _____

Land Area: _____ # of Units in Complex _____

Floors in Your Building _____ # of Elevators in Your Building _____

Construction: Interior Walls _____ Exterior Walls _____

Name & Address of Management Company _____

_____

Managing Agent: _____ Telephone # _____

Broker/Salesperson: _____ Company: _____

Purpose of Disclosure Statement: Under Hawaii law, a Seller is obligated to fully and accurately disclose in writing to a Buyer any fact, defect or condition, past or present, that would be expected to measurably affect the value of the Property to a reasonable person. This statement is intended to assist Seller in organizing the facts to be presented to Buyer and to provide Buyer with notice concerning the condition of Property and to assist Buyer in evaluating Property. Seller's agent, Buyer and Buyer's agent may rely on Seller's answers. It is important that Seller exercise due care in preparing responses and that responses are made in good faith, are truthful and complete to the best of Seller's knowledge. **THIS DISCLOSURE STATEMENT IS NOT A WARRANTY OF ANY KIND BY SELLER OR BY ANY AGENT REPRESENTING SELLER OF PROPERTY. THIS STATEMENT IS NOT A SUBSTITUTE FOR ANY EXPERT INSPECTION, PROFESSIONAL ADVICE, OR WARRANTY THAT BUYER MAY WISH TO OBTAIN.**

BUYERS ARE ADVISED TO OBTAIN BUYER'S OWN PUBLIC RECORDS, PROFESSIONAL ADVICE AND/OR HAVE AN EXPERT INSPECT PROPERTY. SELLER MAY WISH TO OBTAIN PROFESSIONAL ADVICE AND/OR HAVE AN EXPERT INSPECT PROPERTY.

MUST be Completed by Seller Only

Seller's Statement: This is a statement concerning information relating to the condition of Property that: (i) are within the knowledge or control of Seller; (ii) can be observed from visible, accessible areas; or (iii) which are required by Section 508D-15 of the Hawaii Revised Statutes. Seller may be ignorant of problems affecting Property, and Buyer should take care to protect Buyer's own interests by conducting thorough inspections and obtaining expert help in evaluating Property. Unless Buyer has been otherwise advised, Seller has not conducted any inspection of generally inaccessible areas of Property. There may be material facts of which Seller is not aware which qualified experts may be able to discover or time may reveal. The representations made below are made by Seller and are not the representations of Seller's agent. This form and the disclosures made by Seller are provided exclusively to Buyers involved in this transaction only and do not apply to any subsequent sales *not* involving this Seller.
Seller has [   ] has not [   ] seen Property. Period of ownership from _____ to _____

Instruction to Seller: (1) Answer _ALL_ questions. (2) Identify and clearly explain any material facts concerning Property that are known to you. (3) Attach additional pages with your signature if additional space is needed. (4) Complete this form yourself. (5) Complete a separate form for each separate structure. (6) NTMK means NOT TO MY KNOWLEDGE. (7) If the item does not apply to Property, line it out.

Seller has [   ] has not [   ] held a position in the Association of Owners Board of Directors or standing committees.
[   ] Attachment – Property Information Form, (RR105c).

_____   _____
  BUYER'S INITIALS & DATE   SELLER'S INITIALS & DATE

Property Reference _____

©Hawaii Association of REALTORS®
Seller's Real Property Disclosure Statement
Condominium/Co-op/PUD and other Homeowner
Organizations
RR105a Rev. 6/04

MUST BE COMPLETED BY SELLER <u>ONLY</u>

A.   GENERAL PROPERTY INFORMATION

Current Monthly Maintenance Fee $ _____ (precise amount)

Maintenance Fee includes. _____

How many parking stalls are included in the sale of this apartment? _____

Stall Designation Numbers: _____

| [ ] Tandem | [ ] Covered | [ ] Open | [ ] Unassigned |

Stall Designation Numbers: _____

| [ ] Tandem | [ ] Covered | [ ] Open | [ ] Unassigned |

Stall Designation Numbers: _____

| [ ] Tandem | [ ] Covered | [ ] Open | [ ] Unassigned |

If answer is "yes", using the SAME number below, describe in the space provided.

Yes	No	NTMK		
[ ]	[ ]	[ ]	(1)	Does any other party have an unrecorded interest in this apartment and/or say in its disposition?
[ ]	[ ]	[ ]	(2)	Are there any lawsuits or foreclosure actions affecting your apartment?
[ ]	[ ]	[ ]	(3)	Do you have assigned and/or deeded storage space outside of your apartment?
[ ]	[ ]	[ ]	(4)	Were additions, modifications, and/or alterations made to your apartment without obtaining association approval?
[ ]	[ ]	[ ]	(5)	Were additions, modifications, and/or alterations made to your apartment without building permits?
[ ]	[ ]	[ ]	(6)	Were additions, modifications, and/or alterations made to your apartment without a licensed contractor?
[ ]	[ ]	[ ]	(7)	Is your apartment currently rented?
[ ]	[ ]	[ ]	(8)	Has a homicide, felony, or suicide occurred at the project or in the apartment?
[ ]	[ ]	[ ]	(9)	Are pets allowed? Note. This does not apply to certified guide, signal, or service dogs or other animals allowed under HUD regulations.
[ ]	[ ]	[ ]	(10)	Has your Association notified you of future maintenance fee increases, special assessments, and/or association loans?
[ ]	[ ]	[ ]	(11)	Are there substances, materials or products which may be an environmental hazard such as, but not limited to, asbestos, formaldehyde, radon gas, or lead based paint within your apartment?
[ ]	[ ]	[ ]	(12)	Is your apartment exposed to recurring excessive noise?
[ ]	[ ]	[ ]	(13)	Is the project located in an aircraft path and/or experiences regular aircraft noise?
[ ]	[ ]	[ ]	(14)	Is the project subject to excessive air pollution? (For example, such things as "VOG")
[ ]	[ ]	[ ]	(15)	Do you have a functioning smoke alarm?
[ ]	[ ]	[ ]	(16)	Is your apartment sprinklered for fire protection?
[ ]	[ ]	[ ]	(17)	Do you have, or have you had, any live active termite infestation in your apartment?
[ ]	[ ]	[ ]	(18)	Do you have any leaks or water damage in your apartment?
[ ]	[ ]	[ ]	(19)	Has there been any leakage or water penetration from apartments above or adjacent to your apartment?
[ ]	[ ]	[ ]	(20)	Are there, or have there been, any visible signs of mold, mildew and/or fungus in or about this Property?
[ ]	[ ]	[ ]	(21)	Is the project serviced by a private sewer system?
[ ]	[ ]	[ ]	(22)	Do any of the sinks, tubs or basins have rubber stoppers?
[ ]	[ ]	[ ]	(23)	Have you had any pest problems within the last 12 months (i e roaches, fleas/ticks, ants, rats, etc.)?
[ ]	[ ]	[ ]	(24)	Are there any nonconforming uses or restrictions on rebuilding?
[ ]	[ ]	[ ]	(25)	Is your apartment located within the boundaries of the Air Installation Compatibility Use Zone of any Air Force, Army, Navy, or Marine Corps airport as officially designated by military authorities?
[ ]	[ ]	[ ]	(26)	Is your apartment located in a Flood Hazard Zone and/or in a tsunami inundation area?

Number of Question answered "YES" and Explain: _____

_____

_____

_____

_____

_____

_____

_____

_____

_____

_____

_____   BUYER'S INITIALS & DATE   _____   SELLER'S INITIALS & DATE

Property Reference: _____

©Hawaii Association of REALTORS®   Page 2 of 4   RR105a Rev. 6/04 (NC) For Release 11/04

_____

Have you given any release or waiver of liability, or release from a warranty to any government agency, contractor, engineer, architect, land surveyor, or landscape architect, for any defect, mistake, or omission in the design or construction of the Property?

If the answer is "Yes," describe below:

_____

Have there been any substantial defects, malfunctions, or major repairs with respect to this apartment within the past 5 years?

	Yes	NTMK			Yes	NTMK	
(27)	[ ]	[ ]	Appliances	(35)	[ ]	[ ]	Floors & Floor Coverings
(28)	[ ]	[ ]	Bathtubs/Showers/Basins	(36)	[ ]	[ ]	Interior Walls
(29)	[ ]	[ ]	Ceilings	(37)	[ ]	[ ]	Plumbing System
(30)	[ ]	[ ]	Counters, Cabinets	(38)	[ ]	[ ]	Security Systems
(31)	[ ]	[ ]	Decking, Railings & Lanai	(39)	[ ]	[ ]	Water Heater
(32)	[ ]	[ ]	Doors	(40)	[ ]	[ ]	Window/Jalousie Sinks or Faucets
(33)	[ ]	[ ]	Electric Outlets/Switches/Lights	(41)	[ ]	[ ]	Other____
(34)	[ ]	[ ]	Fans/AC Systems	(42)	[ ]	[ ]	Other____

Number of Question answered "YES" and Explain: _____

SAMPLE

_____ BUYER'S INITIALS & DATE   _____ SELLER'S INITIALS & DATE

Property Reference: _____

_____
_____
_____
_____
_____

GENERAL DISCLOSURE

UNIT MODIFICATIONS & LANAI ENCLOSURES: If Buyer is contemplating enclosing a lanai or making other modifications to Property, an attorney, architect or other professionals knowledgeable in such matters should be consulted first. Obtaining permission to make enclosures or other modifications may involve more than approval by the Association's Board of Directors. Approval may be complex and may require approval from the City & County Building Department.

_____   _____
Buyer's Initials & Date

RESERVE STUDY: State law requires certain common interest properties to perform a study and make projections of upcoming maintenance expenses for the common elements. The Association must set aside appropriate reserves for those needs. Currently, there is no standardized reserve study. Some studies are very short and simple, while others are long and complex. Some properties may have a summary of the reserve study. It is recommended that Buyer obtain a copy of the summary of the reserve study or if unavailable, the reserve study. Buyer should read the information and seek the guidance of an attorney, accountant and/or other competent professionals to analyze its contents.

_____   _____
Buyer's Initials & Date

Under Hawaii law, unless otherwise agreed to in the DROA, Buyer shall have fifteen (15) calendar days from the date of receiving the disclosure statement to examine the Disclosure Statement and to rescind the DROA. Such rescission must be made in writing and provided to Seller directly or Seller's agent. If timely written notice is provided, then all deposits made by Buyer shall be immediately returned to Buyer.

Seller gives permission to any Broker to provide this statement to any Buyer whose identity has been made known to Seller, a lending institution, or the escrow company involved in the transaction between the parties.

_____   _____   _____   _____
Seller   Date   Seller   Date

NOTE: THERE IS NO WARRANTY ON PLAIN LANGUAGE. An effort has been made to put this agreement into plain language. But there is no promise that it is in plain language. In legal terms, THERE IS NO WARRANTY, EXPRESSED OR IMPLIED, THAT THIS AGREEMENT COMPLIES WITH CHAPTER 487A OF THE HAWAII REVISED STATUTES, AS AMENDED. This means that the Hawaii Association of REALTORS® is not liable to any Buyer, Seller, or other person who uses this form for any damages or penalty because of any violation of Chapter 487A. People are cautioned to see their own attorneys about Chapter 487A (and other laws that may apply).

_____   _____
BUYER'S INITIALS & DATE   SELLER'S INITIALS & DATE
Property Reference: _____

©Hawaii Association of REALTORS®   Page 4 of 4   RR105a Rev. 6/04 (NC) For Release 11/04

Standard Addendum

DROA Reference Date: _____

Property: _____

Seller: _____

Buyer: _____

1. **Termite Report.** Standard DROA paragraphs C-59 and C-60 are amended as follows: Seller understands that this offer is contingent on Buyer's sole approval of the Termite Inspection Report within five (5) calendar days of receipt of said report. If Buyer does not approve said report, Buyer may cancel the DROA pursuant to paragraph C-20 and C-21 of the DROA.

   Buyer acknowledges that there may be hidden termite damage, which Seller and Seller's agent do not know about for which Seller and Seller's agent will not be held liable. Seller, Seller's agent and Buyer's agent make no representations or warranty that the property is free from hidden infestation or damage, about which they are now unaware; and Buyer and Seller release Agents from any and all liability with regard to termites. Once Buyer has (a) exercised his/her inspection right and approved the current TIR or (b) waived his/her inspection right, Buyer agrees to take the property "AS IS" with respect to such damage, if any.

2. **Building Permits Disclosure.** Buyer is aware that many residential properties do not have all building permits as required by county ordinances and/or may not be built according to the plans or building permits issued. **During the C-51 Inspection Period, Buyer or Buyer's contractor, architect or other expert(s) are advised to review, among other things, the Property's building permit file, which may indicate whether structural modifications, additions and/or other items modified and/or changed were done with properly issued permits and if these building permits were inspected and signed by the appropriate county officials.** Buyer understands that Real Estate Brokers are not qualified to give opinions on these matters including but not limited to proper examination and analysis of the permit file contents.

3. **Professional Home/Property Inspection/Home Warranty Programs.** Buyer and Seller understand that the Inspections referred to in paragraph C-51 encompass a wide range of professional fields and expertise. Buyer and Seller understand that Real Estate Brokers are not qualified to give opinions on these matters and acknowledge that neither party is relying on the Brokers for these services. **HOMEQUEST, REALTORS STRONGLY RECOMMENDS THAT BUYER OBTAIN A PROFESSIONAL GENERAL HOME INSPECTION AS WELL AS SURVEYS AND INSPECTIONS IN SPECIALIZED AREAS BEYOND THE SCOPE OF GENERAL HOME INSPECTION.** Buyer further acknowledges that Buyer's Broker at Buyer's request may provide Buyer a list of at least three home inspectors.

   Check One: (Buyer to check the appropriate choice at submission or acceptance of DROA).
   ☐ Buyer elects to obtain a professional home inspection at Buyer's Expense.
   ☐ Buyer declines to obtain a professional home inspection.

   Check One: (Buyer to check to appropriate choice at submission or acceptance of DROA).
   ☐ Buyer elects to obtain a Home Warranty at _____ expense.
   ☐ Buyer declines to obtain a Home Warranty.

   _____   _____   _____   _____
   Buyer   Date   Seller   Date

   _____   _____   _____   _____
   Buyer   Date   Seller   Date

   1/1/04

Index